A BREED APART

by
Charles H. Weems
Retired Special Agent,
U.S. Treasury Department

with
W. Horace Carter
Pultizer Prize-winning Journalist

Copyright © 1992
by Charles H. Weems

Library of Congress Card Catalog Number 92-090110

Published by
SSI Publications

Printed in the United States of America
by Rose Printing Company Inc.
Tallahassee, Florida 32314

ISBN 0 - 9634357 - 0 - 1

Photographs by various Treasury Agents

Cover Design by Joe C. Weems

Cover Art by Robbie Walker

Second Edition

ABOUT THE AUTHOR

Charles Harvey Weems is a retired Special Agent with the U.S. Treasury Department Bureau of Alcohol, Tobacco and Firearms (ATF). He was raised in Clayton County, Georgia, and attended grammar and high school in Jonesboro, graduating in 1944 at the age of 16. He could not wait to serve in the military. The war was about to pass him by. His mother refused to sign the necessary papers for him to join the Army or Navy, but finally did sign for the U.S. Maritime Service, not knowing that a greater percentage of merchant seamen had lost their lives than regular Navy. Between submarines and mines, merchant shipping had suffered devastating losses. On October 7, 1944, just two weeks after his 17th birthday, he was on a train to Brooklyn, New York—the first time he had been over 50 miles from home. In January 1945, he was on a liberty ship in convoy in the North Atlantic. In Salerno and Naples, Italy, he saw the devastation of war and the look of starving people as they fought over scraps of food.

On the return trip the ship stopped in North Africa, and at the age of 17 he was wandering alone through the back alleys of Casablanca. Subsequent trips as a merchant seaman took him to Leghorn and Genoa where he saw more hunger and devastation; yet the spectacular beauty of the Mediterranean and the coastal cities of Italy made a lasting impression.

In January, 1946, he joined the U.S. Army and volunteered for the paratroopers. On June 8, he graduated from airborne training at Fort Benning, Georgia, and qualified as a parachutist and gliderman. He got his paratrooper wings one day and was married the following day to Dot McKibben of Riverdale, Georgia. After a ten-day honeymoon, he was on a troop ship headed to Germany. In Frankfurt he served with the 508th Parachute Infantry Regiment as Honor Guard at USFET Headquarters. Later that year, the 508th was returned to the U.S. and deactivated. He spent the remainder of his military service with the 82nd Airborne Division at Fort Bragg, North Carolina.

After receiving an honorable discharge, he went to work for Southern Railway Company in Atlanta. By going to law school at night for three years on the G.I. Bill, he was able to receive an education he says he never would have been able to afford otherwise. He graduated with a Masters Degree in law.

In the summer of 1954, he heard through a stroke of Providence that the U.S. Treasury Department was hiring agents in the Southeast. He jumped at the chance.

By age 27 he had crossed the North Atlantic four times, made more than 20 parachute jumps, seen some of the devastation of war, been married nine years and was the father of two sons. Now his life was really going to get exciting. He went to work as a Treasury Agent on August 16, 1954.

Charles H. Weems

ACKNOWLEDGEMENTS

The following people have been instrumental in the writing of this book: Vicki Herrmann, ATF Librarian, who furnished statistics and advice; Milton Walton, retired ATF agent; Bill Griffin, retired ATF Regional Director; Elsie Tipton, a friend and advisor; Joe Carter, retired ATF agent; my sons, Joe and Charles, for their support and advice; and certainly M.L., my wife, who worked for hours at the computer deciphering my handwriting.

There are others, too many to mention, who encouraged me and made this dream come true. I thank them all.

DEDICATED

to
The Men and Women of ATF
Past and Present

FOREWORD

This is a story of federal law enforcement officers and the war they waged, not on the small-time bootlegger making ten gallons of moonshine a week, but on the organizations operated as big businesses which produced 1,000 gallons of whiskey per day, seven days a week; who not only made large amounts of moonshine but also corrupted law enforcement officers.

Their work involved raiding illegal distilleries, working undercover, chasing moonshine whiskey vehicles, investigating assaults on federal officers and numerous other aspects of law enforcement. It covered a wide variety of activities including the Montgomery, Alabama, race riots.

The story is a factual look at the many facets of large-scale illegal production and distribution of moonshine whiskey. It begins in 1954 and includes extensive undercover work involving car thieves and murderers through 1964.

During this period, ATF agents in the Southeast Region (North Carolina, South Carolina, Georgia, Florida, Alabama, Mississippi and Tennessee) seized and destroyed 72,159 stills and 1,712,438 gallons of moonshine and arrested 71,266 violators. The whiskey alone constituted a tax fraud on the United States of over 18 million dollars, not including taxes lost to local and state governments. Twelve ATF agents were killed in the line of duty during this period. Almost every agent who worked in the Southeast was injured, either by direct confrontation with liquor law violators or in their pursuit. These injuries ranged from being shot, stabbed and beaten to running through barbed wire fences and falling into ravines at night. It was a dangerous occupation.

Moonshining was at its peak in the southeastern United States during these years. In the 1970's the efforts to control it began to pay off. It is now part of a bygone era.

Every incident in this book actually took place and is told as it happened, using copies of statements, daily reports and other reference data. There are many humorous incidents included.

For obvious reasons, the names of most of the violators have been changed. The real names of all ATF special agents have been used, with the exception of "Spade", "Cutter", "Horace", "Hank" and "Albert."

The real names of most state and local officers have been used except where noted. Spade's real name is never mentioned in any context.

Improvisation has been a unique and distinctive trait of the ATF agent for the past 60 years. It sets him apart, especially from FBI agents, in that he has had the latitude to make on-the-spot decisions and use his own initiative in apprehending criminals. The days of "hitting the ground" to do surveillance work are almost a thing of the past. Computers and all types of modern surveillance equipment are now being used by ATF agents. I'm afraid that before long the "paper trail" agent may become dominant in ATF as it is in the FBI; nevertheless, from the 1930's through the 1980's, ATF agents were definitely "a breed apart."

Chapter I

Trial By Fire

"Jim, I don't know how much longer I can hold this trunk lid closed without locking us both inside," I said.

"It's not much further—damn, I wish he'd slow down, though," Jim grumbled.

I barely heard him. I was lost in thought, looking back on the past week. When I reported for duty at the U.S. Treasury Department's ATF office (Alcohol, Tobacco and Firearms Division) on Monday, I had no idea that on Friday night I would be squeezed into a hot car trunk with Georgia State Revenue Agent Jim Robinson. I wondered, What have I gotten myself into?

The car bounced down the rural road with dust and exhaust fumes curling back into the trunk. I held on to the trunk lid and anything else I could reach. My imagination was working overtime, trying to anticipate what might happen when we arrived at James Mathis' house. We had met the informer and Regional Special Investigator McQuon at a small church about two miles from Sunnyside, Georgia.

"The informer will drive the car. You and Jim stay in the trunk. He'll try to buy some liquor and if Mathis takes the bait, you and Jim arrest him on the spot," McQuon said.

By the time the car pulled into the yard, my heart was pounding. I had no previous law-enforcement experience. The only training I had was two days in the field with Investigator Ted Cone, and my firearms qualification consisted of firing 12 rounds at a target leaning against a tree.

The informer parked the car about 75 feet from the back porch and turned off the engine. It was a hot, still, quiet Georgia night. The only sound was from Mathis' television tuned to the "Gillette Friday Night Fights." The blue light of the TV flickered in the darkness. Forever etched in my memory is the commercial jingle, "Look sharp, feel sharp, be sharp—use Gillette Blue Blades." About two minutes later, the informer came back to the rear of the car and whispered, "He's gone after it."

1

Jim and I eased the trunk lid up, slipped out and crouched down on the ground behind the car. The informer moved back toward the house. A big, red-headed barefoot farmer wearing a pair of overalls walked toward the car with a gallon of moonshine in each hand.

I was so keyed up that I was ready to do anything.

"Let's get him," Robinson whispered.

I ran across the yard, catching Mathis by one arm. He swung around and tried to get away. Robinson grabbed his other arm.

"You're under arrest," I grunted.

The huge moonshiner struggled and I was lifted completely off the ground. The informer took off. Mathis was perturbed at being caught by a black informer and began to curse profusely. He kicked one of the gallon glass jugs of moonshine whiskey with his bare foot about ten feet into the air. It hit the bumper of the government car and rolled to a stop, miraculously not breaking.

"Goddam nigger, I'll kill him," Mathis fumed.

After subduing Mathis, we signaled Cone and McQuon with a flashlight. They wheeled into the yard and took custody of Mathis while Robinson and I went into the house. Someone was pouring something into the bathroom commode.

Jim pounded on the door. "Open the goddam door," he shouted.

A woman screamed back, "Don't come in here!" This was followed by flushing sounds. After several minutes of door-pounding and general confusion, Mathis' wife opened the door and calmly walked past us into the living room. In the bathroom were eight empty one-gallon glass jugs. It was a violator's tactic I would see many times throughout my career.

This was the first of hundreds of arrests I made during the next 24 years, working in most areas of the continental U.S., first as criminal investigator, then special agent, then regional special agent, area supervisor, air operations program leader and chief of air operations for ATF.

* * *

Someone once said that you never forget your first love and the same is true of your first training officer. Ted Cone was my training officer and I came to love him as a partner and a friend. He was about 55 years old, a big Swede who had been with ATF for many years, most of the time in Georgia. Ted always wore a homburg hat. In the winter, he wore corduroy pants and a different colored corduroy shirt. Most of the time he sported a flowered tie

2

and paratrooper boots. This was his work outfit. Of course, when he appeared in court he was always dressed in a nice suit and tie. He had a large bald head, droopy eyelids and no teeth. He had false teeth, but never used them. He was an imposing figure, always standing straight and tall at over six feet, and weighing 220 pounds. His partner was State Revenue Agent Jim Robinson. Jim was about the same age as Ted, and he dressed in work clothes most of the time. He was also an old-time "revenuer" and knew almost all the liquor law violators in the seven counties south of Atlanta that comprised their assigned territory.

This area was mostly farmland and open woods. Ted, Jim and I would walk for miles in the hot Georgia sun checking sign or cutting sign (walking through areas of reported suspicious activity checking for foot paths or vehicle tracks around known violators' homes or areas of operation). Luckily I had kept myself in pretty good physical condition since being discharged from the paratroopers. I had played on the Southern Railway basketball team and continued to work out and swim a great deal. On these long, hot walks I found that grazing rights went with the territory. Any time we came upon a strawberry or watermelon patch, it was fair game. Few farmers objected to anyone stealing a few melons. We also grazed on such things as pears, apples, wild plums and muscadines.

One especially hot day, as I followed Ted through dense undergrowth, I noticed that he had stuck his old .38-caliber revolver in his front pocket—butt first. This left the business end of the barrel pointing upward and to the rear at a 45-degree angle. As he walked, the muzzle of the pistol would swing from side to side, and I found myself looking down the barrel with every step he took. Ted never wore a holster and had worn out his hip pocket with the barrel of the pistol, so now he carried it butt first in his front pocket. I decided to swap places with him. It was safer!

Jim looked around and exclaimed, "Damn, Charley hasn't even broke a sweat." They didn't know I was about to break a sweat, but not because of the heat!

From the first week, the work was exciting and there was something new every day. I had been reared in the country and being in the woods almost all the time was great. I took to it like a duck to water.

When I applied for a position as Investigator, I had a vague idea what the job would be like. It turned out to be *really* vague. Instead of wearing a shirt and tie all the time like a movie detective, I was dressed in work clothes and boots and carrying a World War II .38 Colt military revolver. This was my beginning.

3

* * *

My first illicit distillery (still) raid came on September 4, 1954, about three weeks after I started work. ATF Investigator Jimmy Causey and State Agent Roy Gordon worked the territory east of Atlanta, including Newton County. Causey asked me to help them raid a still. We had met on the previous afternoon and dropped out in a rural area. As we walked through the dense woods, I could feel the excitement building.

Causey stopped. "You and Roy wait here while I check the still."

After about 30 minutes, he returned. "The still hands have just left. It's hot and there's freshly run liquor stacked on the ground," Causey said. We decided to leave the area and come back before daylight the next morning.

After supper at a local restaurant in Covington, we went to the county jail, an old-fashioned building with flat steel bars on the small unlit cells. This was my first, but certainly not my last visit inside a penal institution.

"You can spend the night in the jail," Sheriff Berry offered. He knew ATF was operating on limited funds. Our *per diem* (funds for meals and lodging) was $6.00 for a 24-hour period.

The sheriff said, "I'll put some new mattresses on the cots. You can each take a cell. We don't have many customers tonight."

I didn't get much sleep my first night in jail, even though the cell door was left open. Later in my career I interviewed prisoners at the Georgia State Prison at Reidsville, several old chain-gang camps and the Atlanta Federal Penitentiary. Each time I came away with a sigh of relief that I was not a criminal, nor locked up. I think every child aged 12 should be taken on a tour of a penal institution. In my opinion this would do more to deter crime than any other thing. Being behind bars is no fun, even for a short time.

I wondered what the next day would bring. Could I measure up to what was expected of me, or would I "freeze in the door" as they say in the paratroopers? This was what every paratrooper feared more than anything else. I had gotten through all my jumps with no problems and I hoped I could do as well today.

"Okay, let's go!" someone yelled through the door of my cell. I looked at my watch. It was four o'clock. We had a jailhouse breakfast of fried bologna, eggs and coffee and left for the still area. I was apprehensive, but at the same time excited at the prospect of raiding my first distillery. We arrived just before daylight, hid our cars and started walking just as the sun was coming up. It was a beautiful day. As we got close to the still area we could hear the sound of activity.

4

"You stay here, Charley," Causey whispered. "Roy and I'll go around the still and run the violators back toward you and Junior." Sheriff Berry's deputy, Junior Odom, was with us that morning.

We separated, with Causey and Gordon going around the still and Odom and me spreading out on our side. I was alone. All my life I had heard stories of moonshiners carrying rifles and shotguns to their stills and officers being killed or having to kill. I just hoped I was ready for whatever would happen in the next few minutes. I was wound up pretty tight.

After about 30 minutes—it seemed like hours—someone shouted from the still, "He's coming to you!" All of a sudden, I was going in three directions at once. I didn't know whether to run toward the still or not. Remembering that Causey had said the moonshiners would run toward me, I waited nervously. About this time I heard limbs breaking and the sound of someone running through the woods. Talk about excitement!

I started toward the sound and almost immediately saw a black man running to my right. When he saw me, he veered away. I hadn't been instructed as to the proper procedure to make an arrest except that I was supposed to catch him. All this was running through my mind as I gave chase and as I put my hands on the suspect, Causey appeared. Together he and I got this wild man stopped. I was relieved and disappointed at the same time because I was looking forward to making the arrest alone, even though I was still a little unsure of myself.

We walked the prisoner back to the still. I felt great! Gordon had two other men under arrest at the still site.

I was amazed at the ingenuity of the operation. It was comprised of a homemade steam boiler (two 55-gallon steel drums welded together, surrounded by a homemade shell of bricks held together with mortar). The violators were using coke to fire the still. Coke is similar to charcoal, the difference being that charcoal is wood that has been burned without the use of oxygen while coke is coal prepared in the same way. Both coke and charcoal burn at extremely high temperatures, producing heat without smoke. The moonshiners in some areas used coke, in other areas fuel oil, gasoline or propane gas. Only the very small stills used the old wood-burning stone box furnaces.

When using coke for fuel, the moonshiners would come in before daylight and get the coke started. By daylight all the smoke would have dissipated and the coke would burn as long as needed without producing any smoke to be seen or reported.

There were two 220-gallon wood barrel stills, ten 300-gallon wood box fermenters (used to ferment the mash before distillation), and a 220-gallon wood barrel preheater. An old automobile radiator was the condenser. Illicit distilleries come in all sizes and configurations, usually depending upon the state and even the area of the state in which they were located.

In north Georgia the major producers were usually in Dawson, Lumpkin, and Gilmer counties. They normally constructed large "steamer" distilleries. A big steam boiler, made for use in large buildings or cleaning establishments, was used to produce steam that was pumped into a steel still. The alcohol steam ran through an elaborate set of pipes from the still through a preheater and a doubler into a condenser, usually one, two or three automobile radiators connected in series. These would be kept cool by a continuous flow of water pumped or gravity-fed from a nearby stream or well (see pictures and diagram on page 7). This type of distillery could produce as much as 1,000 gallons of moonshine a day, seven days a week. There were no shutdowns for mash refermentation. Steamers were also used in some sections of North Carolina in areas where large producers like Perry Bloom operated.

In the Tallapoosa area large producers used ground-hog type distilleries. These were 800 to 1,500-gallon galvanized "pots" which were placed in a large hole dug into the bank of a creek or large stream of water. Some violators would have as many as ten or twelve 1,000-gallon pots in one location and produce in excess of 600 gallons of moonshine per day. These stills were heated by gasoline or fuel-oil burners. The alcohol steam was piped to radiator condensers, which were usually immersed in a small holding drum of cool water constantly pumped in from the nearby creek.

The packaging of moonshine also varied greatly from area to area, even in the same state. Whiskey from the Tallapoosa area of west Georgia would be packaged in one-gallon tin cans, while most of the north Georgia whiskey would arrive in the Atlanta area in half-gallon fruit jars. Moonshine from east of Atlanta was usually in one-gallon cola jugs; from south of Atlanta, in a mixture of one-gallon glass jugs and half-gallon fruit jars.

Investigators who worked these areas could guess who the major violator was by the type of distillery, its location, how the finished product was packaged and persons who serviced and operated the stills.

Moonshining, as it was commonly called, was run like any other business except that it was illegal. The large operators had an organization controlled by a money man who had connections with

Diagram of Upright Steam Boiler-Type Still

220 Gallon Wood Fermenter Barrels

Wood Fermenter Boxes

Catch Bucket for Moonshire

Flakestand or "Cooler Box"— Two Auto Radiator Condensers Inside

Alcohol Steam

Alcohol Steam

Alcohol Steam

500 Gallon Steel Still Doubler

800 Gallon Steel Still

Path of Steam

Hose used to pump mash into still

Fire Box

Bags of Coke for Fuel in Boiler

suppliers of raw materials and sometimes with local law enforcement officials. In some areas they were looked upon by the local citizens as an asset to the community because they could always be counted on to contribute generously to local projects, churches and charities. This was considered good business and you seldom received information from the locals as to their illegal activities.

On the organizational chart, under the top man were one or two lieutenants who supervised the daily operation of the distillery, the acquisition of raw materials and the disposition of the finished product. Under the lieutenants were the still hands, who were paid a commission on the amount of whiskey they made. The men who hauled the ingredients to make moonshine were paid by the trip or kept on a regular salary. A large distillery would require five tons of sugar a day plus the other ingredients, and over 160 cases of half-gallon jars, 12 to the case. This would require a large truck to deliver at least a load a day into the distillery. The same truck would be reloaded with the moonshine and in that way only one trip in and one trip out was made daily. The still hands lived at the distillery and seldom left it.

The whiskey was moved to a stash location, usually a farmhouse or barn, where it was stored. All the large distillers had regular customers who bought whiskey by the car and truck loads in amounts varying from 150 to 1,000 gallons per load.

In Atlanta, the capital of moonshine consumption, there were other businesses which made large profits trading in moonshine—the wholesale and retail outlets. There were at least 20 wholesalers in the Atlanta area distributing moonshine to hundreds of retailers. The wholesalers bought the whiskey in large quantities from the distiller and then resold it at a profit to the retailer, who in turn resold it at a profit to the consumer. The wholesalers had their own organizations consisting of one or more set-off boys who would deliver the whiskey to retailers in the city, usually one or two cases to each retailer. In some instances payment was not made until the whiskey was sold.

Although we worked all facets of this illegal operation, we were most concerned with obtaining direct or circumstantial evidence against the backer and money man of the operation. Very few records were kept and these usually were in a crude code. All money transactions were in cash—not an easy paper trail to follow. As an old black man once told an ATF agent in the strictest confidence, "Boss, I'll tell you how to catch old Snuffy. All you gotta do is be there when he's there and be sly like a fox and you'll catch him every time." Very true, but being there when he was there could become involved and difficult at times.

Organizational Chart of Typical Major Violator Organization

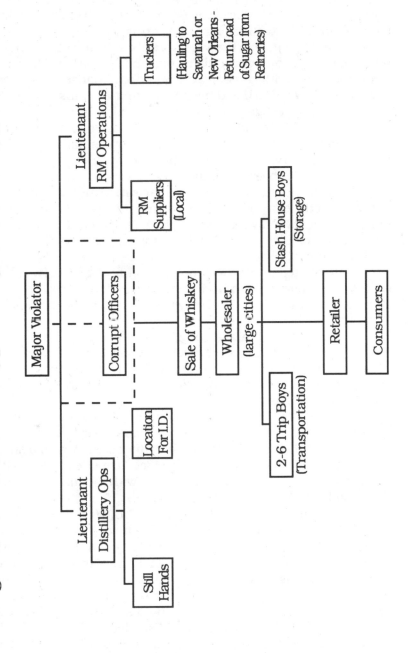

Major Violator

Lieutenant — Distillery Ops
- Still Hands
- Location For I.D.

Corrupt Officers

Lieutenant — RM Operations
- RM Suppliers (Local)
- Truckers (Hauling to Savannah or New Orleans - Return Load of Sugar from Refineries)

Sale of Whiskey

Wholesaler (large cities)
- Stash House Boys (Storage)
- 2-6 Trip Boys (Transportation)

Retailer

Consumers

* * *

After three weeks on the job, I was called into the office by my supervisor. Frank Clark was 66 years old and still full of fire. A slender man, 6'2", with red hair, long arms and fingers, he showed the years he had spent in the woods on all-night and sometimes all-week vigils of moonshine stills in inclement weather. He was an awesome figure, with craggy features and a no-nonsense approach to every problem. Clark had been through it all; thus he had little sympathy for investigators who complained of brutal weather or hazardous working conditions. He was like a sergeant I had in the Army who always said, "If you're looking for sympathy, you'll find it in the dictionary. It's between 'shit' and 'syphilis'."

Clark had been in gunfights and was wounded on several occasions. He was still as dedicated to arresting moonshiners as he had been in the early 1920's. He was a hard man in a lot of ways, but a dedicated family man and federal employee. I was immediately in awe of him and throughout my career heard numerous stories of his exploits.

He worked until he was forced to retire at age 70. I was lucky to have the opportunity to work for a man of his caliber. He got me started in the right direction and with the proper attitude to make it through 24 years with ATF.

Clark said, "I'm assigning you to work in the city with Special Deputy Sheriff Lyle Lateer, making buys of moonshine whiskey from various retailers around town. Since you're the new man and unknown to the violators, we want to use you on undercover work as soon as possible."

So despite the fact that I had little training in law enforcement and only three weeks on the job, I was assigned an old Ford panel truck and started buying moonshine whiskey with a special deputy. The Fulton County sheriff's office furnished Lateer with a list of retail suspects. Atlanta was awash with moonshine in those days and bootleggers weren't hard to find.

This turned out to be an education. Here I was, buying moonshine in some of the worst areas of the city from people who wouldn't hesitate to kill me for $50. Over a period of three months, we bought moonshine whiskey at least twice from 37 different individuals. It was not my idea of what a federal officer should be doing, but now I can see that it was another part of my training and testing period—probably to see if I would stick to unpleasant and distasteful work. Believe me, it was distasteful.

On numerous occasions, in order not to appear suspicious, I was required to "test" the whiskey in the presence of the violator.

10

This meant taking a drink, sometimes in filthy surroundings, from some pretty dirty people. I had never tasted moonshine. I had seen my father drink whiskey and even though he stopped drinking when I was about four or five years old, I could still remember the heartache and worry his drinking had caused my mother. That was during the Great Depression and times were hard for us as well as for a lot of other people. I grew up fast, but even during my time in the U.S. Merchant Marine and Army Paratroopers, I didn't drink liquor. "Testing" whiskey was not a pleasant duty for me and on most occasions I placed the bottle to my lips and pretended to swallow.

THUNDER ROAD

When not working undercover, I helped Ted and Jim on still work in the counties surrounding Atlanta. At night I would ride with Investigator Jack Berry or Vic Bernhardt working transportation, intercepting and chasing trippers bringing moonshine into the city of Atlanta. This was exciting because both these agents had a lot of experience chasing liquor transporters. A number of these trippers later became famous as stock car racers and several are still in the racing business. Vic and Jack both drove Fords with late model Cadillac engines which had been seized while transporting moonshine.

During these episodes we would usually set up observation on one of the Thunder Roads, known routes of liquor cars coming into the Atlanta area. Sometimes we "banked" them—we would park on a rise or bank near the highway and wait in the dark. When a vehicle approached we would use a hand-held spotlight and in the instant the suspect was passing, light up the back seat area of the car. It was so quick that the drivers never knew and the only time it was noticed was when someone was in the back seat. If the car was loaded with whiskey, the rear area would be covered by a blanket or quilt. Then we would ease out of our hiding place and, usually without lights, catch up to the suspect vehicle. It was pretty exciting running 60 miles per hour without lights! When we were close enough, we would turn on our headlights, spotlight and siren at about the same time. The trippers would react to this in different ways. Some would be so surprised they would stop. Others would floorboard it, leading to a high speed chase which sometimes ended in a violent wreck.

About six months before I started work at ATF, two of our special investigators were chasing "Crash" Waller, a known transporter in Haralson County, west of Atlanta. As both cars topped a hill at 95 miles an hour, they discovered they were approaching a

"T" intersection and would have to turn right or left. Waller, driving a souped-up '50 Oldsmobile, hit a ditch almost head on and was severely injured when the load of moonshine whiskey shifted and crushed him. Special Investigator Roy Shields almost made the turn, but hit the ditch sliding sideways and turned over. Shields was killed in the accident and Special Investigator Jesse Thrasher, his partner, was seriously injured. After a long stay in the hospital, Waller had an even longer stay in the Atlanta Federal Penitentiary. I met Thrasher when he returned to duty later that year.

To avoid this type of situation, we would try other tactics. When we had information about a delivery of whiskey, we would put someone on the ground with a radio and park our car in a location from which we could observe the most likely route of the whiskey car. The ground man would drop out and walk as quietly and secretly as possible to a place where he could observe the reported delivery location. If we were lucky, we would have two vehicles and four men to work with, but on most occasions there would be only two or three officers. We took turns working as the observation ground man, catch man and driver.

Sometimes the tripper would drive through the delivery area without stopping to check things out. On other occasions, a convoy car would drive through before the whiskey came in. If everything looked okay, the load of whiskey would be set off. There would be several set-off boys working for the wholesaler who was buying the whiskey, moving the whiskey quickly into a house, garage or "stash" location. If it were to be transferred to another vehicle, there would be only the two drivers and a helper to move the whiskey.

These were busy times and night and holiday work were essential to doing the job. After three months, I had made 44 arrests.

RED MARTIN

Learning came at a fast pace. One morning Frank Clark called me into his office. "Report to Henry Gastley in Regional Headquarters in the Peachtree-Seventh Building. You'll be working for him on an assignment."

I remembered my first trip there for my job interview and was apprehensive as I drove across town. On the fifth floor I found a door marked "Raw Materials Section." There was a tall, red-headed man of about 30 sitting in the waiting room. From his appearance I thought that he must be an informer or a moonshiner. He had on an old suit coat which had a well-worn look—the elbows were ragged on both sleeves. I sat down beside him.

A short time later, a tall, nice-looking man in his early 50's came out and said, "Both of you come on in." Henry Gastley introduced himself.

"Charley, this is Red Martin, one of our agents." Henry indicated the man with the worn-out coat.

This was my first meeting with Gastley, one of the many outstanding agents of ATF. He had worked with many of the old-time prohibition agents and had a vast amount of field work experience, as did all ATF supervisors.

"You and Red are going to be working in north Georgia making buys of raw materials," Henry said. Raw materials were sugar, rye meal, wheat bran, yeast, 1/2 gallon fruit jars and other materials used in the manufacture of illicit whiskey.

"Go with Red and pose as his helper. Just follow his lead. Now this is confidential. I'll be the only one that knows what you're doing."

This was exciting stuff! As we left Gastley's office, Red said, "Leave your credentials, badge and gun in the office and meet me back here at six o'clock."

I made a quick call home. "Just look for me when you see me," I told Dot. "I don't know when I'll be home or when I'll get to call again." Most of the time I didn't have time to call or a telephone wasn't available.

"Okay," she said. I could hear the disappointment in her voice. She was understanding, though, and supported me in every way. She seldom showed any resentment of my working long hours with no overtime pay.

Red and I climbed into a green Dodge pickup truck. I soon realized why Martin was known all over the Southeast as one of the fastest and wildest drivers in ATF. Leaving the city was a little hair-raising, but when we hit the twisting, hilly roads north of Atlanta around Cumming, I had to hang on to keep from being thrown all over the inside of the truck. We were skidding around one sharp curve after another and Red was enjoying every minute. He was looking at me, the scenery, everywhere but at the road, and talking a mile a minute.

Red explained that in order to make a good raw materials case, we had to prove either intent or noncompliance with the demand letter. The government could place a business under a formal letter of demand from the Regional Commissioner of Internal Revenue, requiring them to make reports of all sales of sugar or other materials, as named in the letter, to the Alcohol Tax Unit on a monthly basis. These reports would have to show the date, amount of materials and the license number of the vehicle on which the materials were placed. If the materials were delivered to a store, they had to show the store name and location. This required additional bookkeeping and most wholesalers would refuse suspicious sales rather than make reports.

Some, in order to make an additional profit, would sell to individuals in large quantities. These were the ones we concentrated on and in order to stop these sales we would go undercover to buy raw materials. We would also stake out these outlets and trail vehicles away, attempting to locate the illicit distilleries. Sometimes it worked, sometimes it didn't. On undercover buy cases, without being too obvious, we would let the store owner know that we were going to make whiskey with these materials in order to establish intent on his part.

When we arrived at the home of Frank Baron in Cumming, a woman answered the door.

She said, "Mr. Baron's not at home. Just wait here on the porch."

She made a telephone call and then told Red to go to the store. "Someone is still there," she said. We drove about 12 miles north of Cumming through a rural area of farmland and woods, with only an occasional residence along the road, and stopped at Baron's Store. When Martin and I started toward the front of the store, Charles Bart called from the rear, "Come on in this way."

I was about to learn a valuable lesson about working undercover. Martin was one of the best undercover agents I ever worked with. He was casual and unhurried. Before even mentioning the sugar purchase, he bought two Cokes, six flashlight batteries, three cans of pork & beans, two cans of Vienna sausages and a loaf of bread. This was typical still rations—something else to put the seller at ease. By this time, Bart was ready and anxious to sell us everything we needed.

"I'll ride with you in your truck to get the sugar," Bart said, getting into the cab of the Dodge. We drove a short distance to a house where he said, "Pull around to the back yard."

A Ford truck was parked there. Bart hopped out and removed a tarpaulin from the truck. As we loaded 2,400 pounds of sugar onto the government truck, I made mental notes of the time and location. We drove on to a warehouse building some distance away where we loaded a bag of malt and a bag of rye meal.

After paying Bart for these materials, Martin asked him, "Can you supply jars for our liquor?"

Bart replied, "Sure, you'll need about 40 cases of jars for this much sugar." (100 pounds of sugar would usually make about 12 gallons of moonshine.)

"I would have hated for the law to stop me the last time I got sugar here...I had sugar, meal and a burner[1] on the truck," Red said, peering into the darkness.

"Damn, the law wouldn't have just locked you up, they would have took your truck, too. Hey, put that other license tag on your truck so I can report it instead of the tag issued to the truck," said Bart. This conversation, plus the combination of materials and the method of operation, would later convict both Bart and Baron.

Red and I made buys of raw materials from several other large wholesale grocers and distributors who were under demand to make reports. Although I learned a great deal about working undercover from Red, I never got close to his ability and talent in this line of work. He was one of the masters.

About two years later, while in pursuit of a suspected moonshiner at a high rate of speed, Red was involved in a terrible automobile accident which left him badly crippled. After several months of recovery time, Red was able to come back to work on limited duty, although he had to walk with a cane due to his injuries. Sometime later, his government car was struck by a train and Martin was killed. He was one of several good friends who died in the line of duty during my career with ATF.

---

[1] Homemade galvanized pipe shaped in the form of a rectangle about 28 inches wide and 8 inches deep and connected to another section of 1/2" galvanized pipe about five feet long with a cut-off valve, and threaded on the end to be attached to a homemade pressure tank filled with gasoline. The rectangular section was drilled wih very fine holes about three to six inches apart, through which the vaporized gasoline could escape and be lighted to furnish a hot flame to heat the still.

Upright steam boiler distillery in open woods southwest of Dahlonega, Georgia

Chapter II

No Pain – No Gain

In the summer of 1954, an Atlanta newspaper ran an announcement that the U.S. Treasury was accepting applications for Alcohol, Tobacco and Firearms (ATF) agents. This job promised the excitement I had visualized from reading accounts of fast car chases, blowing up stills and running down bootleggers. A dangerous life style had always appealed to me. Even though I was aware that my chances were slim, I applied, hoping that my law degree would help me meet the qualifications.

To qualify as a special agent with the U.S. Treasury Department, you need a college degree or three years' investigative experience. You must also pass a four-hour written test, an oral interview and an extensive background investigation. I had never been interviewed for a job in my life.

I had worked for Southern Railroad in the summer between my junior and senior years of high school and for about three months after graduation in 1944. I was under age and pleaded with my parents to sign enlistment papers so I could join the Army or Navy. I didn't care which one, I just wanted to get in the service before the war passed me by. My mother finally agreed to sign for me to go into the U.S. Merchant Marine because she thought it would be safer. I was 16 years old.

I sailed as a merchant seaman until shortly after my 18th birthday when I joined the U.S. Army and volunteered for the paratroopers. After serving 18 months in Germany and with the 82nd Airborne Division at Fort Bragg, North Carolina, I was discharged and returned to a comfortable job at Southern Railway in Atlanta. It seemed that the excitement in my life was over— but it was just beginning.

Everyone knew that the railroad was a good place to work. You had job security, good retirement, indoor work and many other benefits. Yet office work was not for me. There had to be something else. I attended law school at night on the G.I. Bill and finally obtained a law degree. Then I began looking for an occupation in law enforcement. I had personal obligations to my family so I turned

17

down a job as a Georgia state trooper, but when I found that the Treasury Department needed agents, I jumped at the opportunity. This was the chance I had dreamed of.

I sweated out the four-hour written examination and in about three weeks received my score. It was nothing to brag about, but I made a passing grade of 76. A date was set for the oral interview. I waited with anticipation and dread. The day of the interview I took leave from my railroad job and tried to prepare myself. I was to be at the Peachtree-Seventh Building in Atlanta at one o'clock.

While working in the payroll department of Southern Railway, operating a check writing machine, I dressed informally, usually in slacks and sport shirt. I did have one suit that my brother-in-law had outgrown which fit me fairly well and two or three white dress shirts that I wore to church. My wife Dot usually washed and ironed the shirts herself, but knowing the importance of making a good impression, she decided to send them to the laundry so they would be just right.

I had backed my 1949 Oldsmobile coupe into the garage. It was a hot day in August. I delayed as long as possible in taking my shower. I didn't want to sweat through my Sunday clothes before I got to Atlanta.

It was about a 45-minute trip from where I lived in rural Clayton County, south of Atlanta, to the Peachtree-Seventh Building on the north side. I had made a dry run to the building and figured my time. At about eleven-thirty, I took a shower and decided to pull the car out of the garage and double check everything before getting dressed.

When I started the car, I sensed something was wrong. I had a flat tire on the right rear. Having allowed some extra time, I took out the bumper jack and started jacking up the right rear of the car. I left the trunk lid up. The dirt garage floor was uneven and as the back end of the car came off the ground, the car began to lean to one side. I tried to hold the car on the jack by pushing on the side of the car, but it fell anyway. The trunk lid fell, striking me a solid blow on the side of the head just above my right ear.

I was stunned for a moment. My hand immediately went to my head and came away covered with blood. I thought, Oh, shit, now I've got to get this tire changed and take another shower. Since I was now wet with sweat, bloody and nervous, I decided to change the tire first.

I was running late, but could still make it on time if I had no more bad luck. I went back into the house, got some sympathy from my wife and took another shower. I still hadn't been able to stop the slow but steady ooze of blood from the cut above my ear. A band-aid wouldn't stick since the cut was in the edge of my hair, and I didn't want to be wearing one to the interview anyway. I thought, What else can go wrong?

Something else did.

"What's the matter with this shirt?" I asked Dot.

"What do you mean? Let me see."

"It's too little—dammit, they've sent me the wrong shirts!" Apparently the owner of the shirts was a very small man. The shirts would barely button across the chest and didn't come close to buttoning at the collar. There was no way I could wear any of them and they were all I had. By now I had just about run out of time and patience. Things were going from bad to worse.

"Why don't you just call and explain that you can't make the interview?" Dot suggested.

Now my hard-headed streak took over and I was determined to make this interview. I had a gnawing feeling that I wasn't going to be accepted anyway, so what difference did it make? I had to try!

Earlier that summer, Rich's Department Store in Atlanta had a sale and I had found a real bargain. It was a pair of light brown slacks with darker brown checks. They were probably on sale because no one else would wear such gaudy trousers in public. But this was the newest, and I thought the nicest, pair of slacks I had. That part was decided! Now, about the shirt. I had a nice two-tone brown polo shirt with short sleeves, so I decided to wear that. On a hot August day I needed something cool. I was already burning up inside and out!

Somehow I made it to the federal office on time and reported to the secretary.

"Wait in here, please." She showed me into an office where three other men were already waiting. My nervousness and despair were multiplied when I saw that they were all wearing dark blue business suits and ties. They looked like bankers. I thought, Well, I have no chance competing with these guys. I'm out of my class.

I had to keep pressing my handkerchief to the cut over my ear. Finally, I went into the rest room and used toilet paper soaked in cold water to stop the bleeding—I hoped. In the process I dripped water on my shirt. Desperate now, I could only hope it would dry before I was called in. What a mess!

At last, the secretary came in and escorted us to a large conference room with office tables in the form of a "T." We were seated on the long part of the "T," with the interviewing officers at the top. I thought, I might yet get through this without too much embarrassment by being here with the other three. No such luck! The interviewing team singled us out and asked us to give a brief history of our background and qualifications. I struggled through this fairly well, although I kept thinking, What am I doing here with these people? I don't know anything about law enforcement. Two of the prospective agents were DeKalb County detectives with extensive experience. The other was an insurance adjuster with years of investigative experience writing reports and testifying in court. I knew I was a goner.

Next, they gave us a set of circumstances and hypothetical questions to discuss among ourselves. I did poorly because I was entirely out of my element. I bluffed my way through it, still self-conscious about my clothing, but being careful to use the best English I could.

Finally, we were sent from the room and called back for individual questioning. I was last and as I waited my turn, I tried to think of what I would tell my wife, my friends at work and others who knew of my big chance to get away from office work. I figured everything was against me that day and there was nothing I could do to salvage the situation. I would soon be back on the check-writing machine at the railroad office.

After all three of the other applicants had been interviewed individually and departed, I was called back in. The interview board was composed of four top executive people from the Southeast Region of the Internal Revenue Service. One of these was Chief of Personnel Shelton Taylor, another was Chief of Criminal Enforcement Bob Miller. I don't recall the others, but I was immediately impressed by the kind approach of Mr. Taylor.

"Mr. Weems, we are not being critical of your tastes or trying to make you feel bad, but we would like to know why, knowing that you were going to be interviewed and having two weeks' notice to prepare for the interview, you wore the type of clothing you have on today?" he said.

I thought, Well, this is it. "I'll have to go back several days to explain," I said.

"That's fine, take all the time you need," said Mr. Miller.

I explained about the flat tire, the trunk lid falling on my head, the wrong shirts and my not having any more, the fact that these were the best clothes I had and that I was determined to make the interview. They grinned and thanked me for the explanation. After several other questions about working long hours and nights in all types of weather, they told me the interview was over. "We'll be in touch with you by mail soon," Miller said.

I left in a stupor. Frustrated, I knew there was no way I could meet the requirements of a U.S. Treasury agent. I was 27 years old, had no previous law enforcement experience and was just a country boy with a burning desire to be in some type of police work. Looking back, I realize that God must have been on my side.

Two weeks later Dot called me at work. "You got your notification letter from the Treasury Department," she said.

"Hold on to it and I'll open it when I get home," I replied, not wanting anyone at work to see my disappointment in case I had not been accepted.

Five o'clock finally came and I rushed home. I ripped the letter open. The first thing to catch my eye was the fact that I had been accepted and my post of duty was to be Atlanta, Georgia. It was a miracle! If I had been offered any other post of duty in the United States I would have had to turn it down.

Someone apparently saw something in me that led him to believe I would be a good federal officer. Something I had said or done, or maybe just plain sympathy, prompted these men to give me a chance.

I've never forgotten their confidence in me, and through 24 years of service I always tried to live up to their expectations.

* * *

In January 1955, I was assigned to work transportation (moonshine whiskey vehicles). It was my job to catch the liquor runners bringing moonshine into Atlanta. These were some of the best cases I ever made. My partner was Carl Koppe, an ex-City of Atlanta policeman who was now a Fulton County deputy. Carl and I worked in a 1946 Ford with a souped-up Olds engine. He taught me a lot, not only about working moonshine in the city, but also about the city itself. Carl knew every street and back alley. His work hours were from about four in the afternoon until two in the morning, and after a nap in the car he would begin working the early morning traffic before daylight. In the summer this meant about five o'clock until nine o'clock. He would go home to sleep until early afternoon and be ready to go again at four o'clock. It took a lot of energy to keep up with this workaholic.

Carl was not required to prepare any reports other than oral to his supervisor. Not only did I have to prepare a daily report showing times, places, arrests and seizures, I also had to type out case reports for use by the U.S. Attorney or State Solicitor depending on whether it was a federal or state case; and with these reports, detailed statements of the circumstances of the arrests and seizures for both Koppe and myself. We averaged seizing two liquor cars a week. After working from four in the afternoon until nine the next morning, I would go to the office and prepare reports. These 16 to 18-hour days were some of the hardest of my career, although I enjoyed being exposed to something new and different every day. It was a great learning experience that made me a better officer, but on reflection I would have been happier without so much paperwork.

In January we made an arrest that impressed upon me the importance of seemingly minor details in the conviction of a criminal.

Koppe and I were working on the west side of Atlanta in the Bankhead Highway area. He had previously shown me a used car lot on Bankhead that belonged to John Elmer, a suspected wholesaler of moonshine. The information was that John had several trip boys working for him, hauling whiskey from outlying rural areas into the city.

At about ten-thirty that night, we turned off Bankhead into Law Street, a half block from Elmer's used car lot on Bankhead. This was a sparsely-populated residential area. We came over a hill to an apparent dead end. There was a dirt alley to the right, and as we turned in, our headlights focused on two automobiles parked side by side blocking the alley. Three men were standing at the rear of the cars. They froze as the lights hit them. The Olds engine roared as Koppe floorboarded it.

"They're running!"

Koppe skidded up to the two cars, throwing gravel 40 feet in all directions, and I hit the ground running. Luckily, it was a moonlight night and I could see very well. The alley ran across two sets of railroad tracks and on through an industrial area with large metal buildings. The three men were crossing the tracks at full speed. One man split off to the right and ran down the tracks. In that split second, I decided to continue after the other two. I was gaining with every step! When I was only about seven yards behind them, they split, one continuing straight ahead and the other turning left. I decided to go straight.

By now I was close enough to identify their clothing. I had never seen their faces. The white man who had split to the left, fell with his hands in front of him in an area of packed gravel. He was wearing dark grey slacks and a brown suede jacket. He was a small man in his late 20's or early 30's. I thought, I can catch the other man, then come back and get this one, too. I caught the other man, who was wearing overalls, by grabbing his galluses. At the same time, I swung him around to look for the one who had fallen. He had disappeared, but I had a firm grip on Bob Ross.

22

"You're under arrest," I told him.

I took Ross back to the automobiles. There were 15 gallons of moonshine whiskey in a '39 DeSoto and 40 gallons sitting on the ground behind a hot-rod '37 Ford. Koppe was with the whiskey and vehicles, knowing that on a previous occasion, a suspect had returned to the liquor car and driven it and the evidence away.

I explained to Koppe what had happened in the chase, describing the individual who had fallen just before I caught Ross. Koppe headed toward the railroad tracks and returned in about ten minutes with John Elmer. Koppe asked, "Is this the man?"

"Show me your hands," I told Elmer. He showed me both hands, which had deep abrasions in the palms. Elmer was the same physical size as the man who had fallen, and he was wearing dark grey slacks and a brown suede jacket.

Koppe said, "I found him hiding in a hole."

"That's the man," I said.

"What were you doing up there, John, hiding in a hole—and why are you breathing hard?" I asked Elmer.

"It's not because I've been running. I could be doing a lot of things," Elmer replied.

I raised the hood on the Ford and saw that it was equipped with a full racing engine with three carburetors. "Look at this, Koppe, this'll make a good car for us to work in." I advised Elmer and Ross that they were under arrest and would be prosecuted in Federal Court.

Elmer pleaded, "Can't you make this a state case? If you want the cars, you can just take 'em—I won't make any claim for 'em."

I had only been on the job four months, but I knew Elmer was treading on dangerous ground. "You've already said too much—you'd better stop while you're ahead." Elmer got the message.

We lodged Elmer and Ross in the Fulton County Jail as federal prisoners. The next morning, we fingerprinted and photographed them and proceeded to the U.S. Commissioner's office at the Federal Court House.

When making a federal case, the arresting officer appears before a U.S. Commissioner to relate the facts of the arrest. Usually it isn't necessary to submit a written or detailed account of all the evidence in order for the commissioner to find probable cause to place the defendant under bond to await a Grand Jury hearing. The Grand Jury returns a True Bill or a No Bill of indictment. If a True Bill is returned, then the defendant's case is remanded to the U.S. Attorney's office for trial.

In this case, the commissioner said there was not enough evidence to put Elmer under bond. I had explained, in detail, the description of the man I chased, his clothes, the condition of his hands, the fact that I saw him fall on his hands, his hiding in the bushes and in the hole and the way he was breathing. The commissioner in effect turned Elmer loose, which I am sure gave him a great deal of satisfaction. I was astounded. The evidence was sufficient I thought, since I had told the truth in detail. Although I hadn't seen the defendant's face until Koppe returned him to the car, I was convinced this was the same man I chased from the liquor cars.

"Did you see his face?" the commissioner asked.

"No, sir," I said quietly.

I made up my mind that I would prepare a case report on Elmer anyway and try to get it approved by my supervisor.

This I did, and the case was approved by Mr. Clark. After a case is approved, it is sent to the U.S. Attorney's office for his approval and submission to a U.S. Grand Jury for action.

To almost everyone's surprise and to my delight, the Grand Jury indicted Elmer for possession of the illicit whiskey. He was placed under bond and a trial date was set.

Prior to the trial it is customary for the prosecuting attorney, whether he be state or federal, to discuss your testimony with you. He has your completed case report and statements of the arresting officers to study, but a review of the evidence is usually made before the trial. I explained to Assistant U.S. Attorney John Stokes the facts as they were related in my statement and that I could not swear that the man I chased was John Elmer. I could swear that he had the same physical appearance as Elmer, that he was wearing the same type clothing, that he had fallen a short distance from me, that I saw his hands slide in the gravel and that Elmer's hands had abrasions which appeared to have been caused by this fall. Koppe would testify as to where Elmer was found and his condition and the statements made by Elmer.

When the case was called for trial, Stokes requested that I be allowed to sit at the prosecutor's table to assist in the case. Elmer hired one of the best criminal lawyers in Atlanta, Wesley Asterbilt, to defend him. After Koppe and I testified, Asterbilt moved for a directed verdict of acquittal for Elmer. The federal judge ruled that the case would go to the jury because he felt that enough evidence had been presented to make the case a jury decision. As the jury left the courtroom to deliberate, Asterbilt whispered something to Elmer. They both smiled.

After about an hour's deliberation, the jury came back with a decision of guilty. Stokes had done a masterful job in prosecuting the case. I was elated. I felt as though we had just won a world championship. From then on throughout my career, Elmer and other law violators would understand that I would not stretch the truth in any way to get a conviction, but I would do everything I could legally to prove my case.

Elmer's lawyer appealed the case all the way to the Supreme Court, but the conviction held. Years later, our paths crossed again as I arrested someone who used the law illegally against Elmer.

BIG GAME HUNTING

Since the beginning of time man has hunted for game to survive. With modern man this survival instinct has been repressed to the point that it has caused a great deal of frustration in our society. By instinct man is a natural hunter. Working as an ATF agent, I found that this instinct consumed you once you got on the trail of a moonshiner.

Among the numerous exciting things I've done, raiding a moonshine still remains the most thrilling. Anyone who has ever hunted deer can appreciate the feeling of stalking and long hours of waiting, sometimes in bitter cold, for the tell-tale crack of a twig signalling the approach of your quarry. Multiply that by 100 and you come close to the feeling of excitement, anticipation and apprehension involved in following on the heels of quarry as intelligent and vicious as man. It is an indescribable feeling.

The chase, whether on foot or in an automobile, is always exhilarating and when you finally get a good grip on your man, it's similar to bagging a 12-point buck or landing a 10-pound bass for the first time. It is big game hunting in its highest form.

In November, I was working with Ted Cone, Jim Robinson and Sheriff Hugh Stinchcomb in Fayette County, south of Atlanta. Hugh was a tall, handsome man who had served as a deputy before being elected sheriff. He seldom carried a pistol. Due to his size and strength, he probably figured he didn't need one. The sheriff had information on an illegal distillery about 12 miles southwest of Fayetteville. After Ted dropped us off about a mile from the still, Stinchcomb, Robinson and I walked in.

We found the distillery, which had operated the previous night. As we were examining the area, we noticed a trail leading from the still through the woods and across an open sage field. Sage is a tall grass which grows about three feet high. It dries in the winter months and turns a brown color. We followed the trail and had just reached the open field when we heard a vehicle coming in our direction.

Any hunter will tell you that if you are in an area where there are few places of concealment such as open woods or fields, the prime consideration is to be perfectly still. The slightest movement can be detected, most often by peripheral vision.

"Get down," Hugh warned. We immediately scattered and fell flat on the ground. The truck stopped about 150 feet from us. Two men got out and started walking in my direction. I tried my best to be a ground hog and disappear into the sage, but I was sure they would see me any minute.

The men passed within 50 feet of us and continued on toward the distillery. In a few minutes they came back from the still, each carrying two cases of moonshine (12 gallons). They put the whiskey on the ground at the edge of the field, then disappeared again and returned with two more cases. When they had placed these on the ground, one of the men went to get the truck. He cranked it up and headed right for us!

I watched closely, trying to anticipate what the truck driver's reaction might be if he saw us. He apparently didn't and stopped at the stack of whiskey. He and the other man started loading the truck while talking quietly.

I didn't know exactly where Stinchcomb and Robinson were, but I knew they were close by. I began to crawl on my belly through the tall grass toward the truck.

When I decided I could get no closer without being seen, I jumped up and ran toward the truck shouting, "Federal officer, you're under arrest." I caught one of the men at the rear of the truck and the other managed to get about ten yards before Stinchcomb arrested him. There were 16 gallons of moonshine whiskey on the truck and both men admitted they had run the still the previous night.

Several years later on another distillery raid I found that Sheriff Stinchcomb did carry a weapon occasionally. As we were approaching a large still in another section of Fayette County, Hugh reached down and picked up a baseball-sized rock. When we made the initial move into the still yard, three violators ran. Hugh, who had the reputation of having been an outstanding baseball player in his time, threw the rock, hitting one of the bootleggers in the small of the back.

Crashing through briars, honeysuckle vines and a stream of water, I finally caught the other still hand. When I returned, I found Hugh with his man in custody, thanks to his expertise, not with a firearm, but with a primitive weapon.

When a man is running to keep from going to jail, he doesn't notice pain or exhaustion until it's all over. The same thing applied to us. In the excitement of the chase, nothing mattered but catching the moonshiner. Many times I had skin ripped off by thorns, brush and barbed-wire fences and never realized it until I got home. Adrenalin numbs the body to pain.

* * *

After a couple more illicit distillery raids in November and December, during which I became further indoctrinated into the fine art of concealment and sheer speed in running down violators, I got a chance to help in the observation of the largest distillery I had ever seen.

Just after Christmas, Koppe and I were stationed at a forest fire tower located south of the Atlanta Federal Penitentiary. It was a bitterly cold night, with light rain and a brisk wind. We were helping Regional Special Investigators McQuon and Thrasher and Investigators Merritt Scoggins, Karl Strasser and Jimmy Causey. Climbing to the top of the tower, I found Koppe.

He said, "See those lights over there? That's the place we're watching. It's a house on Bouldercrest Drive. You call on the radio if there's any vehicle traffic in or out of there. I'll wait in the car and relay any messages to the others. Maybe I can get warmed up some in the meantime." Koppe had already taken his turn on the tower and was freezing.

I wedged myself in the framework of the tower, holding on with one hand while trying to keep the heavy Navy surplus binoculars to my eyes with the other. I also had an old World War II walkie-talkie radio with a two-foot antenna slung over my shoulder.

After I had spent two or three miserable hours on my perch, someone decided that we should call off the observation for the night—much to my relief. I was so numb, I probably wouldn't have seen a tractor-trailer leave the place I was watching. I still don't know if I was watching the right house.

The next day, Jimmy Causey and I got a call on the radio. "A '39 Plymouth just left the house on Bouldercrest and headed toward Atlanta."

We fell in behind the vehicle and trailed it into town. Jimmy was driving, and when the Plymouth stopped at a red light behind another car, he pulled up tight on his bumper, blocking him in. I walked up to the car and told the driver, "Federal officer, you're under arrest!" I reached in and turned off the engine. We seized the car and 150 gallons of moonshine. This seizure, along with more surveillance, gave us enough probable cause to secure a federal search warrant for the house and outbuildings on Bouldercrest.

The next morning we executed the search warrant and found a large steamer distillery in a dairy barn at the rear of the house. It had a 10-hp commercial steam boiler with an electric-fuel oil burner. There were twenty-four 220-gallon fermenter barrels containing 4,300 gallons of fermenting mash (a mixture of water, sugar, wheat bran, yeast, and sometimes barley malt and/or rye meal). It was by far the most sophisticated distillery I had ever seen and I was impressed.

Hoses ran in every direction. There were electric pumps to bring water from a nearby stream and to pump the mash into the stills. There were 100-pound bags of sugar, barley malt and rye meal stacked on each barrel. They were using a copper preheater, two automobile radiators for the condenser and an elaborate system to package the whiskey in half-gallon jars, six gallons to a case. Most distilleries in north and west Georgia used old automobile radiators as condensers to change the alcohol steam into liquid alcohol, even though the lead solder in these radiators made the moonshine unsafe to drink.

Two still operators were arrested at the distillery and admitted knowing the tripper we had arrested the day before with 150 gallons of whiskey.

This was the first still I had seen inside a building. It was capable of running 150 gallons of whiskey a day. The federal tax alone on legal whiskey was $10.50 per gallon, not to mention state and local taxes. At 150 gallons per day, seven days a week, the violators could produce 1,050 gallons per week and defraud the U.S. government of over $11,000 per week. If the distillery only ran three months, the fraud would total over $132,000! The loss of tax revenue had to be made up by hard-working, law-abiding Americans.

In these first five months, I had participated in still raids, chased liquor cars, worked undercover buying moonshine in the city and rural areas, made raw materials undercover buys from large wholesalers as well as small retailers, and had testified in state and federal courts.

I expect that there are other agents who were thrust into similar dangerous and tight situations during their initial few months on the job, but I don't know of any who had a more varied cross-section of ATF work before attending Treasury Law Enforcement School. This certainly wasn't due to any special talent I had, but in large part to my post of duty in Atlanta being the center of activity for the Southeast. More moonshine whiskey was made around the area and transported and sold in the city of Atlanta than anywhere else in the world. As a new and unknown agent, I was available for all types of undercover work. My supervisors seemed to like me and therefore when a job came up, I was recommended. I was in my glory!

But now it was time to go to *school.*

Photo of a liquor car seized in the Atlanta area

Racing engine in a moonshiner's trip car

Moonshine stacked in the back of a trip car

ATF Special Agents James Stratigos and Frank Lane examine a distillery in Jackson County, Georgia

Chapter III
Book Learning

In mid-February, I reported to Washington, D.C., to attend the U.S. Treasury Department Law Enforcement Officers Training School. This was five weeks of intensive training covering everything from Constitutional Law to qualifying with the .38 caliber revolver. We also had classes in photography, fingerprinting, trailing suspects, identification of drugs and counterfeit money, and various other law enforcement-related subjects. The school was for agents working for all branches of the Treasury Department, including the Secret Service, Customs, IRS, Narcotics Bureau and Border Patrol.

It was my first visit to the nation's capital and I was somewhat awed. The small allowance paid by the government for lodging made finding a place to stay difficult. Someone who had attended the school gave me the names of two boarding houses. I wrote them sight unseen and one accepted my reservation. I caught a cab from the Washington airport and arrived at the boarding house at five o'clock on a Sunday evening. It was a dreary, overcast day and I was tired.

I was stunned at the outward appearance of the house. All the houses in this part of the District of Columbia probably dated from the 1800's. They were built of stone and were two or more stories high with turrets which gave them a fortress-like appearance. I had never seen anything quite like this before and had certainly never been inside one. Checking the address twice to make sure I had the right place, I hesitantly rang the door bell. A middle-aged woman answered.

"I'm Charley Weems—I think I'm at the right place," I said.

She showed me into a parlor with a high ceiling, large drapes, fireplace and huge sliding wooden doors. The furniture was massive and old. I thought, What kind of place is this?

I managed to keep my composure. Soon a heavy-set woman about 60 years old appeared. She was the boss.

"I'll show you to your room," she said, as she led me down a flight of stairs. I had anticipated being upstairs, but we were going down! After reaching what I figured must be the basement, we walked down a narrow, dimly-lit hallway to a small room on the left. I expected to see Igor or Quasimodo jump out at any minute! It was a spooky place.

Part of the basement had been partitioned off into this room and I guessed, others. There was a single bed against the wall and a sort of dressing table with a small mirror. A make-shift closet without doors was at the far end of the room. The only other furniture was a chair.

The woman said, "The bathroom is at the head of the stairs. Dinner will be at six o'clock. We're having roast capon." With that, she disappeared into the bowels of the building.

Roast capon? Stumped again! Here I was in the basement of a house much like I had seen in horror movies. I didn't know a soul north of the Georgia line. Now I was confronted with another mystery—roast capon for supper. I tried to figure out what capon could be. Was it some kind of duck or pig, or even worse, some kind of goat? I resigned myself to trying to eat it, thinking I could always eat bread and butter if nothing else.

I sat on the bed and thought, as I had several times before, What have I gotten myself into? I wasn't satisfied with a nice, comfortable job with security, regular hours, etc.—I had to go for *adventure*.

Promptly at six o'clock I went upstairs and found the dining room. Most of the other roomers were already seated around a large dining room table. After some fumbling around to make sure I didn't have someone else's seat, I sat down and joined in. The first thing passed to me was a large roasted bird. I thought, This is too big to be a chicken so it must be turkey. Whatever it was, it was good. That was my introduction to capon.

After the first week, I became close friends with ATF Agent Oliver P. Hines from California. "O. P." was about my age. Sometime later I got up enough nerve to ask him what capon was. He laughed and said it was a castrated rooster. I had never heard of such a thing. I was from the country and had eaten chicken all my life. I didn't even know you could castrate a rooster!

I had seen my father "cut hogs" as he called it, and knew that steers were castrated bulls, but a chicken? Uhhh-uhh . . . .

That was only the beginning of my learning experience in Washington. I didn't realize then that 22 years later I would return to live and work in D.C., not quite as ignorant as I was then.

O.P. had similar problems with housing, so we talked to others in the class. He found a nice place to stay that served good food and said that although there were no more rooms available where he was, there were some next door. I could live there and eat at his boarding house. I checked it out and moved in after three days in the dungeon. I lost a little money on the deal, but it was worth almost anything to be out of that cramped room with no windows.

O.P. and I saved a little money by walking the ten blocks to the Treasury Building downtown for school each morning, except when it was raining or snowing. We enjoyed the exercise and usually had a lot to talk about on the subjects we were covering in school. Although I was at a disadvantage in the ways of Washington, my advantage was in the experience I had obtained during the five months I had under my belt working illegal whiskey transportation and distilleries.

Everything went smoothly after the initial housing problems and on March 18, I graduated. I couldn't wait to get back home and go to work. I was on top of the world.

My wife Dot, as usual, had had a tough time during my five-week absence. Both of our boys, Joe and Charles, ages six and four, had had chicken pox; the heating system (a coal stove) had given trouble; and it had not been a good time for her in general, but she never complained.

* * *

When I reported back to the office, I had several subpoenas to appear as a witness for the government in both state and federal court. I was assigned a government vehicle—a red 1952 Ford panel truck which had been seized while transporting moonshine and forfeited to the Treasury Department. ATF got most of its vehicles in this manner. There was always a lack of funds appropriated for vehicles. We drove a Duke's mixture of vehicles from late-model Oldsmobiles to old pickup trucks and everything in between.

All the nicer cars went to the regional special investigators and then filtered down as newer vehicles were seized and forfeited. I was the bottom man on the totem pole and I got what was left. This was a fair way to do it. We usually had one or two seized liquor cars in reserve which we could request for undercover work.

I went back to making undercover buys of whiskey in the Atlanta area. It wasn't that I was good at it—it was that most of the investigators either said they couldn't do it or appeared inept in this phase of the work. Most of the time I didn't particularly like it, but there were occasions when I really enjoyed working undercover.

Later in my career, I worked with the best—Jim King, Jim West, Charlie Riddle and Marshall Reece. These men were fearless and never at a loss for words or actions when the chips were down. They had the "right stuff" for undercover work. I learned from them but never came close to their abilities.

35

Being on probation (the first full year of an investigator's career is spent on probation) meant that I could be fired or asked to resign for any reason. After you make your year, then it is much harder for the government to get rid of an unproductive worker. It has often been said, "If you don't do anything, you won't make a mistake." I never operated that way, and although I worried about messing up, it didn't slow me down.

Mixed in with undercover work, I helped other investigators when they had a distillery located, a liquor car to catch, or a search warrant to serve. Searching houses was not an enjoyable experience because most of the places were filthy and we had to go through closets, dirty clothes, dirty kitchens, etc., looking for the "trap." This was a secret hiding place for illicit whiskey—sometimes it was a loose board in the floor, a trap door under a rug, an opening in the wall behind a mirror or a calendar, or a sliding door in back of a cabinet.

The bootleggers were ingenious. Many times we would search a whole house before noticing an area on the edge of a board worn smooth from use, or a rug obviously in the wrong place. You learn to think like the bootleggers, looking for little things and small details.

There was always something new to do, and I looked forward to every day.

Special Agents Charley Weems and Steve Whitlow examine an illicit distillery in Hall County, Georgia

Chapter IV
A Sly Mule

Early in April, we got word that a U.S. Coast Guard plane would be in Georgia to look for stills. During those years the Coast Guard, a branch of the Treasury Department, would occasionally send a small observation aircraft and pilot into the Southeast Region to help locate illicit distilleries. They always did this in the spring before the leaves budded out on the trees. Once the leaves were out, it was hard to see through the foliage to the ground.

I was assigned to work with the plane in north Georgia. One of the investigators from the Gainesville post of duty rode with the pilot, directing him into the most prolific still areas, then relayed the location of any distilleries to the ground units.

ATF Investigator Jim King from North Carolina was assigned to work with the aircraft, since it came from a Coast Guard station at Wilmington. Jim was one of the finest law enforcement officers I had the privilege of working with. He had been shot accidentally while a teenager, and although doctors had advised no strenuous physical activity, Jim had secretly used weight lifting to build himself up and he became a state champion weight lifter. He had been a North Carolina state trooper prior to coming with ATF and had a reputation as an excellent officer and driver.

We began by working Dawson County. On the first day we located and destroyed three large illicit distilleries within a five-mile radius of Dawsonville, the county seat. Two were in operation, but the operators fled when the airplane began circling overhead. By the time Jim and I reached one of the stills, the only living thing left there was a mule. He was used to haul raw materials in and whiskey out. The mule offered no resistance and was arrested on the spot!

Moonshiners frequently would use a rural dirt road to work these stills. They selected a cut through a dirt bank that was about the same height as the body of a truck. They would also make sure that the bank sloped away from the road and downhill to a natural water source some distance from the public road. The violators would use a still buggy (a stripped-down old vehicle) or a mule to pull a homemade sled to transport the materials and whiskey from the still to the dirt road. I had always thought that sleds were for snow, but a mule can easily pull a heavy load over the ground on a homemade wooden sled.

The moonshiners had built a small corral at the edge of the still yard and brought in feed, so the mule never left the still except to pull the sled. The violators could run the distillery during the day and walk out to their cars, hidden some distance away, at night.

They usually came back after midnight, driving without lights, with a truckload of sugar and other materials. Parking next to the bank, they would jump from the bed of the truck to the top of the bank, place 2x8 walk boards across, and then unload the materials onto the ground. Meanwhile, one of the violators would walk to the distillery and load the sled with whiskey, hitch up the mule and pull the whiskey up the hill to the area of the raw materials. The whiskey would be stacked on the truck and the sled loaded with sugar and other materials and returned to the still. In this way the truck could be unloaded and reloaded in a short time and no sign would be visible to anyone driving or walking down the road. All the sign was on top of the bank and over the lip of the hill. They hadn't counted on being spotted from the air!

This particular distillery was a nice one. It had a six-hp commercial steam boiler, a 250-gallon steel tank still, a 150-gallon wood barrel still, 150-gallon wood barrel doubler, 220-gallon heater box, copper preheater, automobile radiator condenser, thirty-six 220-gallon barrel fermenters, 5,940 gallons of mash, and 200 gallons of moonshine. It had a utilized mash capacity of over 8,000 gallons and was capable of running about 300 gallons of whiskey a day. If all the mash was run at one time it could make over 900 gallons of whiskey.

Large distilleries were operated daily and the mash was usually set up to reach the proper fermentation stage on a three-day cycle. In this way, a third of the fermenters were set up (mashed in) and the next day another third were set up; and the next day the last third were set up. Thus, every day one of the batches was ready to run and be mashed in again. This made for a continuous, assembly line liquor-making operation.

Jim and I had a big problem—the mule. One of the charges usually made against the moonshiners was working at the still. (We would observe the distillery until we saw the violators jarring up whiskey, transferring mash or moving a bucket so we could testify that they worked at the still.) We hadn't seen the mule do any work at the still. Another charge was possession of the still. Since the mule was apparently being kept against his will, we could hardly charge possession, and since he refused to make any statement whatsoever, even refusing to give his name, we had no choice but to release him with a warning.

38

Anyway, he probably would have gotten some jackass to represent him in court if we had pressed charges.

I took the mule by his halter and walked him out into the woods and released him. I noticed a sad look in his large brown eyes as Jim began to break up the barrels with an axe.

He was guilty all right! I just couldn't prove it.

Jim and I brought in a half-case of dynamite, fuse and detonating caps to use in destroying the distillery. It was common practice to have a case of dynamite in the trunk of the government car, along with fuse and detonating caps. We kept the caps in the glove compartment because they were much more sensitive than dynamite and a sudden jar could set off the fulminate of mercury inside the thin metal container. One man would carry the dynamite and the other the caps to keep them separated until they were ready to use. Dynamite (or an acetylene cutting torch) was about the only way you could destroy a steam boiler. The other parts of the distillery could normally be torn up with an axe and after some demonstrations by Ted Cone and Jimmy Causey, I became proficient at turning over the big 220-gallon hogshead barrels and cutting the steel bands that held them together. It was fun watching the barrels collapse into a pile of wooden staves.

Before coming to work for ATF, I had never seen a stick of dynamite, but after five months I was preparing it for use and setting it off to blow up stills. Sticks of dynamite are wrapped in a wax-like paper and are eight inches long and an inch in diameter. I had watched other investigators prepare the charges and had learned to cut a small sprig of wood about the size of a pencil and eight inches long and to sharpen one end. I then punched a hole in one end of the dynamite.

I would push the stick into the side of the dynamite on a 45-degree angle about three inches, leaving a hole for the cap. The cap was hollow at one end and had the explosive, fulminate of mercury at the other end. The fuse was pushed into the hollow end of the cap and the edge of the cap was crimped around the fuse with a special tool. Most agents used their teeth as a crimping tool—not very smart, but who wants to carry around a crimping tool? The fuse comes in rolls and we always cut off about 18 inches, which had a burning time of 1 1/2 minutes, or a foot a minute. I then slid the cap into the stick of dynamite and taped it. Sometimes I taped two or three or more sticks together when blowing a big boiler.

"Fire in the hole!" Jim shouted. The dynamite went off, blowing huge chunks of sheet metal in all directions. The despondent mule bolted and disappeared into the woods.

Twenty-two years later, in Washington Headquarters, I caused an ATF "expert" lawyer to almost have a heart attack when I told him of driving through downtown Atlanta and parking in a public lot on a daily basis with a case of dynamite in the trunk of the government car. In those days, almost everyone who worked stills thought nothing of it. Later we used the military explosive C-4, TNT and Nitromon. They were all much safer than dynamite.

We made two more unknown seizures (seizures in which no arrests were made) of illicit distilleries in Dawson County, then temporarily discontinued use of the aircraft. I didn't know it then, but some nine years later I would become deeply involved in the use of aircraft, locating and making known seizures of distilleries. Later in our careers, Jim King and I were both promoted to regional special investigator and worked together as close friends in the Atlanta office. He was one of the best agents ATF ever had. Jim could do it all and always maintained a wonderful sense of humor.

Jim enjoyed telling about the time he was working under-cover in a small south Georgia town, hauling moonshine for some of the largest liquor law violators in the U.S. It was about noontime as Jim drove through a restaurant parking lot with Sam, a local moonshiner. They were spotted by Virgil, a large-scale moonshiner.

"There goes Sam, but who's that nozzle-nosed son of a bitch with him?" Virgil asked his companion. Virgil didn't know at the time that the man with him was a paid government informer who later told Jim what the moonshiner had said. Jim got as much fun out of jokes about his nose as anyone. He told this story many times and continued to laugh about his nozzle-nosed moniker.

Chapter V
Regional Specials

The last week in April, Ted Cone asked me to help serve a federal search warrant at a farm in Butts County near Indian Springs State Park.

"This should be a good one," Ted said as we drove to the state park to meet Investigator Brack Poe and State Agents Jim Robinson and Billy Moore. We walked through the beautiful woods to the farm, then split up with Ted and Jim to make the initial move on the distillery. I was concealed in the woods behind the barn and at six-thirty, someone shouted, "He's running!" A man ran from the barn and across a small dam. I broke from the bushes. After a sprint of 20 yards, I was about to grab the man when Moore sprang out of the woods in front of us.

Henry Morgan, the man I was chasing, threw a flashlight at Moore. Billy threw up his arm to deflect the flashlight and I grabbed Morgan. "Federal officer, you're under arrest." Billy was mad as hell about being hit and I was busy for the next few minutes trying to calm Billy and hold Morgan. Meanwhile, Ted and Poe had arrested Francine Whit and Joe Arthur in the barn. It was not unusual to find a woman living at a still with her husband or boyfriend, but this was the first time I saw one working at the still.

"I expect someone will come in after dark to get the whiskey," Ted commented. The still hands had 534 gallons of liquor ready to go. We took the prisoners to the house, concealed ourselves and waited. At eight o'clock a Chevrolet panel truck drove into the yard and stopped at a gate which opened into the barnyard. I quickly approached from the rear and when the driver opened the door of the truck, I was there to arrest him. He struggled to escape, but I got a good grip on his belt and brought him to the ground with my other arm.

"You're under arrest, dammit." That was enough for him.

"What's your name?" I asked.

"Doug Archer."

If you are firm without being abusive with a violator, you can control his actions with less effort, but when someone is confronted unexpectedly, especially at night in a remote area, you can expect a violent reaction. That's why I always made an immediate statement, "Federal officer, you're under arrest," as I grabbed the subject and held on. I was taught in Treasury Law Enforcement School never to draw my pistol unless my life or someone else's was threatened. It really helped in making an arrest because you had both hands free to hold on to the violator. Most of the moonshiners knew that you weren't going to shoot them anyway and usually responded by doing their best to get away without getting into more trouble by attacking the officers.

During questioning, Archer stated that he had brought in 4,000 pounds of sugar the night before and was going to haul out the whiskey from the still. "There won't be anyone else coming in tonight," he said.

We believed him.

After all the prisoners were lodged in the Bibb County Jail, we returned to the house. By midnight we were all asleep. Early the next morning, there was a one-ton stake-body truck parked at the gate.

"We had company last night and didn't even know it," I remarked to no one in particular. There were 3,000 pounds of sugar and 100 cases of half-gallon fruit jars on the truck. Apparently the driver had come in sometime in the early morning hours and discovering the government cars in the rear of the house with his friends gone, he had decided this was no place for him. He left on foot. It goes to show you can't believe everything you hear.

SLIPPIN' AND SLIDIN' (PEEPIN' AND HIDIN')

During the summer of '55, while working transportation in Atlanta, I became familiar with the names of several notorious liquor car drivers such as "Crash" Waller, Ben Hall, L. D. "Legs" Law, and others. I heard stories of wild chases both in and out of the city when these men eluded officers by skillful driving. I secretly hoped that one day I might catch one of these legendary drivers with a load of whiskey, but this remained a dream.

In June, I was working transportation with Fulton County Deputy Richard K. Jones (who later became a special agent with ATF and still later, Chief Special Agent for the U.S. Agriculture Department in the Atlanta Region). Jones was a great guy to work with. He was a former Atlanta city police officer and knew Atlanta almost as well as Carl Koppe. Both men were excellent officers but had different personalities.

Some agents believed that an officer is only as good as his information—in other words, if you don't have good informers, you aren't much good. I found this to be true in some cases and untrue in others. Some of the best officers I worked with used their intelligence, eyesight and memory, along with long hours and dedication, to make many solid cases.

A good example of this was Koppe. He would receive information occasionally. However, most of his seizures and arrests were due to his "being out there," as he put it. His specialty was the many black neighborhoods which were a hotbed for moonshine whiskey activity. He knew the city by heart and could spot a whiskey car by the way it bounced on the street. He had a fantastic memory for license numbers, vehicles and violators, and worked the city 12 to 14 hours a day almost every day. He got results by "being there." Koppe lived his job—it was almost his entire life.

Jones was also knowledgeable about the city and liquor law violators, but he was more on the wild side. He liked to kid around and have fun while doing his job. I appreciated his attitude and his ability to keep things light while getting the job done.

Richard was a tall, slender man, 26 years old with twinkling light blue eyes. He could do a good impromptu dance to Little Richard's "Slippin' & Slidin." Koppe, on the other hand, was 6'1" weighed 210, and was quiet-natured. Both worked as my partners at different times and both were easy to get along with. I will admit, though, I was glad to get away from Koppe as a partner. He almost worked me to death!

On June 12, Regional Special Investigator Wylie Hutto called on the government radio and asked us to meet him at Hal Sims' service station on Piedmont Avenue. This was a meeting place for federal and state agents and Hal Sims loved it.

Hal operated a Gulf station across from Piedmont Park and did a lot of mechanical work on the government cars. He enjoyed associating with us and was always ready to help us in any emergency. He was available for anything we needed done to the vehicles and if the agency was low on operating funds, he would hold the bill until the next month. He was a real friend to all of us and to ATF.

When Richard and I arrived at the station, Koppe, Frank Lane, Karl Strasser and Hutto were already there. We gathered around Hutto and began to make plans.

"Now listen," Hutto said, "My informer says that whiskey is being delivered just after daylight, about six-thirty, on a parking lot between Castleberry and Fair Streets, west of Spring Street. The whiskey car comes into Atlanta with the early morning work traffic to avoid detection and usually meets another car on that parking lot."

We made plans to set up our surveillance the next morning before daylight, then checked out the area, which was within seven blocks of Five Points, the heart of downtown Atlanta. We found not one, but two parking lots. These were unpaved areas on the side of a slope. The land had been flattened out on the upper slope and then again at a lower elevation, leaving an area in between on which bushes and high grass had grown up.

Since I was junior man, I volunteered to hit the ground. The others would wait some distance away for a call on the radio when and if the car showed.

Arriving in the area about five-thirty the next morning, Richard and I dropped out near the lots. The other officers took the cars out of the area to keep them from being spotted. Jones and I concealed ourselves in the bushes between the two parking lots. We could watch both lots and call if the liquor car came in.

Finally, a few minutes before seven o'clock, a couple of vehicles came in and parked in the lower lot. The drivers got out with their lunch boxes, and walked toward a nearby building. At a little after seven, more vehicles began arriving. Workers continued to park in ever increasing numbers until we finally had to crawl through the bushes to the edge of the lot to keep from being seen. We radioed Strasser and told him to pick us up—there was too much activity for anyone to bring whiskey in now.

On the way back to Hal Sims' service station, I told the other officers what we had seen. "It's not likely that anyone will bring whiskey into that area after seven o'clock because all the other cars come in around seven," I explained.

"Listen, even though you didn't see anything this morning, how about trying it again tomorrow? This man is usually right," Hutto said convincingly.

Not having anything else going, we agreed.

As planned, the next morning Jones and I hid in the small bushes between the two parking lots and waited. Just before seven o'clock, one of the vehicles we had seen the previous day drove in and stopped in the lower lot. The man headed toward the same building with his lunch box.

It was almost seven o'clock and we were ready to leave the area when a blue '53 Oldsmobile pulled into the upper lot. I tried to burrow myself into the ground as the car came directly toward me. It turned and backed up to within eight feet of where I was hunkered down in the bushes. I kept thinking, If the driver didn't see me when he drove by, he sure will when he walks around the car. What's he going to do when he sees two grown men crouching in the bushes?

I held my breath and remained perfectly still. The man got out of the car and looked around. He was a big man, but I didn't realize how big until later. He walked to the trunk of the car and unlocked it. The trunk was filled with half-gallon fruit jar cases. We had a load of whiskey!

We were too close to radio the other officers and I didn't figure we would need them anyway. The man reached inside the trunk and took out a case, which was obviously heavy. He turned and set it on the ground no more than three feet from where I was hiding, almost in my face.

He went back to the trunk and picked up another case and as he turned back toward me, I sprang from the bushes and caught him by both wrists. "Federal officer, you're under arrest...put down the liquor."

"What the hell?" he stammered, dropping the whiskey.

Richard was at my side almost immediately, calling the other officers on the radio. "We've got him, come on in."

"What's your name?" I asked.

He replied, "Ben Hall." I was pleasantly surprised. We had caught one of the best drivers in the Southeast "sitting down." What a great catch!!

Karl Strasser took Ben to jail and I remained to help destroy the 144 gallons of moonshine and process the seized automobile. Sometime later that day when I met Strasser, I was reminded of the difference in size between Hall and me. He weighed 240 pounds and I weighed 160. Strasser said that on the way to jail, Ben had asked, "Who's that wild-eyed little fellow who grabbed me?" Ben was to see that same little wild-eyed fellow again under similar circumstances several years later.

* * *

Later that day, working undercover with Regional Special Agent Vic Bernhardt in the Cove section of Meriwether County, and Columbus, Georgia, 100 miles southwest of Atlanta, we bought whiskey from Henry Belton and made arrangements for the delivery of more whiskey. There was never time to rest on your laurels. There was too much work to do.

Although we assisted regional specials in "jacketed," or conspiracy case work, these cases were made exclusively by the regional special investigators. This involved making a case for presentation in federal court showing connections by association, actions and overt acts performed by the conspirators in further-ance of an illegal activity. To make cases against the backers of these large illicit whiskey operations, the officers usually had to spend long hours on observation work, interviews and surveillance of these individuals.

The regional special was assigned a suspected violator and it was his responsibility to gather enough evidence to build a case against the individual(s) if he was engaged in illegal activity. Help from other officers was needed to accomplish this and most of the field investigators like me were anxious to help.

This participation was valuable in learning how to make a conspiracy case and prepared us for possible promotion to regional special, which is what every field man dreamed of. The regional specials were an elite group. They worked region-wide and nation-wide on occasions.

They were given a free hand in how they approached their particular cases, and although they had supervisors, they were left alone as long as they produced good, solid cases. They wore wing-tip Florsheim shoes and nice suits instead of green kangaroo boots and work clothes. They drove the best cars in the region, sometimes new convertibles. They were looked up to by the field investigators. It was a job that I hoped one day I would be good enough to get.

The undercover buy in June from Belton in Meriwether County with Bernhardt was to be included in a jacketed case, but now it was August and we were doing extensive surveillance work in Atlanta for a jacketed case assigned to Regional Special Jesse Thrasher.

Richard Jones, Koppe and I were watching a Cities Service station at the corner of Hanes and Walker Streets. We made notes of the activity of several well-known liquor law violators—Legs Law, David Boswick and others—and observed the activities of several trucks used by known violators who frequented this service station. Some of these trucks would be seized at a later date transporting large amounts of moonshine as well as raw materials used to make whiskey.

One of us would park an old panel truck several blocks away and observe from a distance through binoculars. If we were unsure of the identity of a person or vehicle license plate, we would radio our partner to drive by and check it out. We always used vehicles which we thought were unknown to the violators. Since the regional specials got most of the good cars seized by ATF for official use, we were usually left with rough vehicles, including pickup trucks; so we had "clunkers" we could use for surveillance. We changed license plates about as often as we changed underwear.

Georgia had license plates on which the first number denoted the county of issuance in order of population, from 1 to 159. When we were working in the Atlanta area we usually sported a number "1" tag, meaning Fulton County. If we were working in some other area of the state we would change to a tag showing the number of a county in that area.

We saw a great deal of suspicious activity at the service station, including the meeting of known liquor law violators and the exchange of various vehicles, some bearing out-of-state license plates. Materials used to make illicit whiskey were transferred from one vehicle to another and we made notes of the vehicle descriptions and license numbers. On August 13, Leroy Hill loaded several sections of 14-inch galvanized pipe, similar to pipe used as smokestacks on upright steam boiler distilleries, onto a 3/4-ton pickup truck and left the station.

That same day, we trailed a large green Chevrolet stakebody truck from the service station to a big warehouse at the corner of Whitehall and Murphy Streets in Atlanta. Waiting until after midnight, Koppe and I quietly parked our car several blocks away in an alley and then proceeded on foot to the warehouse.

During the first four or five years of my career, I seldom wore a suit, except when I had to appear in court or go to a conference or school. We usually wore dark green work pants and shirts and sometimes in the summer, khaki pants and sport shirts. So, on this August night, I had on khaki pants and a sport shirt as we slipped through the dark alleys.

A railroad siding ran behind the warehouse. Koppe and I walked down the railroad tracks to the rear of the building. It had a loading platform and large roll-up doors. After trying all the doors and finding them locked, we started looking for a place to see into the building. Every window had been painted, but we finally found one that we could scratch the paint off with a pocket knife. I scratched a small area, and about 12 inches above it, scratched another small space.

By shining my flashlight through the upper opening I could look in the lower space and see a huge stack of 100-pound bags of Dixie Crystals sugar and also hundreds of cases of Ball half-gallon fruit jars. Koppe and I took turns looking. There were also what appeared to be 100-pound bags of wheat bran and barley malt—all ingredients used to make moonshine.

This was an exciting find—one of the largest raw materials stashes we had ever seen. It was possible that a large illicit distillery was located in this building or close by. We decided to check out the warehouse even further to determine if the still was there.

The only access to the four-story building was a fire escape on the outside, 75 feet further down the dark alley. The fire escape went up the side to each floor and then to the roof. One problem was that the ladder that can normally be pulled down from the first landing outside the second-story window was missing.

Since I was smaller than Koppe, I volunteered to try to climb onto the fire escape and check out the building. I tried standing on

Koppe's shoulders but couldn't reach the landing. By this time it was three o'clock in the morning.

"We've got to do something before daylight," Koppe exclaimed. "People will start coming in here pretty soon!"

I had been issued a 50-foot section of nylon tow rope. It was surplus rope used by the Army to tow military gliders into combat and was extremely strong.

"Let's try throwing one end of this rope over the corner of the fire escape platform, then pull it down and tie it," I suggested.

No luck! After trying several times to get the rope in position with no success, I tied several knots in the end of the rope, making a knot about the size of a softball.

I threw the knotted end of the rope over the platform and around an upright piece of steel used as a railing. Due to the weight of the rope I couldn't get the ball end to fall back to me, so I gently pulled the rope until it wedged itself between the upright railing and the floor of the platform. Then I pulled on the rope and swung on it, putting all my weight and then the combined weight of Koppe and myself on the rope. I hoped that the rope would stay wedged when I started up, especially when I thought of the cobblestones 20 feet below.

I started up the rope, hand over hand, thinking, What if the rope slips or a city policeman drives by and sees me climbing up a rope at three in the morning? I clambered up that rope as fast as I could without dislodging it from its precarious position.

As soon as I got a firm grip on the fire escape, I heaved a sigh of relief. I think Koppe did too. I pulled the rope up to the platform and Koppe disappeared into the shadows. Immediately, I began looking through windows trying to find a way into the building. All the windows were locked, but they were unpainted, so I could see in at each floor. There were only empty floors up through the fourth floor. I climbed up onto the roof, knowing from past experience that I could detect the odor of mash if any existed, and I smelled all the vent pipes on the roof. Law enforcement types do strange things sometimes. There were unpleasant odors emanating from most of the pipes, but no odor of mash.

Disappointed, I made my way back over the side of the building and back down the fire escape. I ran the rope through the section of platform and railing and let both ends hang down to the pavement. Koppe could hold on to the rope and keep it from moving while I came down hand over hand. Then we had only to pull on one end until the rope fell back to us.

Many times I have wondered what would have happened if city officers unaware of our identities had happened upon us while

I was on that rope or fire escape, but things like this had to be done in order to get the job done. Chances had to be taken. Most of the time we got away with it.

After the discovery of the stash of sugar and jars, we shifted our observations to the warehouse. Four nights later, the same green Chevrolet truck left the warehouse. It was heavily loaded.

Koppe called, "He's headed south!"

We were able to trail this vehicle out of the city and into Jasper County. While the truck was in traffic and even on state highways, we had no problem trailing by switching off, using different vehicles. When one of us felt that we had been on the suspect too long the other vehicle would take over.

Every vehicle looks a little different if you observe carefully. To help us trail at night without detection, most of our government cars were wired so we could turn off one of the headlights when we were out of sight of the suspect vehicle. When we returned to the trail, the violator would think the one-light vehicle was a different car. We could also turn off our stoplights or one taillight at a time. In this way the tell-tale stoplights wouldn't come on when we were trailing a vehicle without using lights, which we did quite often in remote areas. This time I almost killed Koppe and myself because of this.

Using two vehicles, we had trailed the truck into rural farmland in Jasper County. It was now around one o'clock in the morning. We were running without lights and using the truck lights as a guide, when they suddenly disappeared over a hill. We topped the hill doing about 50. There was total blackness ahead. Koppe was hanging out the right window watching the edge of the road for me. I picked up speed. Suddenly the truck lights came on about 50 feet in front of me! Instinct took over as I slammed on the brakes, almost throwing Koppe out the window. I swerved to the left around the truck, turning on my lights as I passed. Sheeee-it!

A startled-looking white man was standing alongside the truck on the driver's side. We didn't have much choice now. We could seize the truck and its contents and arrest the driver for transporting raw materials intended for use in making whiskey, or we could let him go and hope for better luck next time.

After we were out of sight of the truck driver, we parked in a side road to wait. In about 15 minutes the other government car radioed, "The truck just passed us going back toward Mansfield."

"Ten-four. Let's get out of here, Koppe." I knew it was all over for now.

We hoped we hadn't blown the stash in Atlanta, and for the next week or two we were careful in the area of the warehouse, only checking it occasionally. Two weeks later, Koppe radioed that he was trailing a 1955 Ford two-ton van truck that had just left the warehouse, loaded. Frank Lane and Richard Jones were working with me that day and we joined in trailing the truck. This time the truck was being convoyed by a '55 Olds driven by a white man.

We were successful in following the truck out of the city and it headed south. However, this time they headed toward Lake Jackson.

After crossing the dam, the truck turned off the main highway onto a dirt road on the east side of Lake Jackson. All the running lights were turned off. The Olds was still convoying the truck.

"Since we're short of vehicles and can't leap-frog him, let's pull off and the next time we'll get here ahead of him," I suggested. On the next occasion we planned to place vehicles in strategic locations around the area in order to locate the distillery without blowing our cover. When we pulled off the surveillance, the truck was eight miles south of Mansfield and four or five miles from where Koppe and I almost rear-ended the first truck driver.

We watched the warehouse periodically and less than a week later we picked up the same 1955 Ford two-ton truck being convoyed by the same 1955 Olds, going south toward Lake Jackson. Jesse Thrasher and Karl Strasser heard our radio traffic and joined in the chase.

According to plan, we didn't try to trail the vehicle, but instead rushed to the dirt road running east of Lake Jackson where we had last seen the truck a week earlier. We drove out this road and at the first intersection I dropped out of the car, concealing myself in some bushes so I could see which way the suspect truck went. Darkness had fallen and I had no trouble finding a hiding place close to the road.

Lane and Jones were dropped out at the next two intersections. Thrasher and Strasser planned to park behind a country church where they could watch the last intersection.

About 15 minutes after I dropped out, the truck, running without lights, passed me doing 60 or more. Five minutes later, the Olds raced by, headed toward the church.

A half hour later, Strasser picked me up. He said that he and Thrasher had inadvertently chosen to conceal themselves in the place where the still hands were to pick up the raw materials. When the truck was driven around behind the church, there was nothing they could do but arrest the men in the truck for transporting raw materials. Sammy Larry O'Riley was hauling over six tons of sugar, 1,600 pounds of malt and 50 pounds of yeast.

The driver of the Oldsmobile, Frank Morley, pulled behind the church before he realized what had happened. We had seen O'Riley and Morley numerous times together and with other violators at the Cities Service station in Atlanta. Later, two other vehicles were driven into the area behind the church and David Boswick, Joseph Daniel and Charles Dickson were arrested. A 1946 Ford 3/4-ton van and a 1949 Buick sedan were seized.

It was one-thirty in the morning and we were all beat. Despite our careful planning, we still hadn't found the distillery.

"The still's got to be close—we'll drive into every driveway, every field road and pasture in the area that has any sign of vehicle travel until we find it," Thrasher said emphatically.

We took the prisoners to the Bibb County Jail in Macon to await a hearing before the U.S. Commissioner. By the time we finished the processing of the prisoners and storing the seized vehicles, it was noontime. We agreed to begin looking for the distillery the following morning.

The next day, using three vehicles, we split up and began our search. We found a moonshine stash of 840 gallons three miles north of the church yard, just over the line in Newton County. Finally, about five o'clock, we located the distillery. It was being worked across a pasture, six miles northeast of the church yard and three miles from the stash.

David Cobb was arrested at the distillery. It had a utilized mash capacity (total capacity of all available fermenter vats or barrels) of 6,000 gallons and was producing 800 gallons of moonshine per day. The 15-hp steam boiler had a stack made from galvanized pipe identical to the pipe we had seen Leroy Hill loading up at the service station.

Even though we didn't achieve everything we thought we could, we wound up with seven defendants, a large distillery, five seized vehicles, over six tons of sugar and other raw materials and enough evidence against several other violators to proceed with a conspiracy case against them. Up to that time it was the largest still seizure I had participated in.

* * *

A week or so later, Howard Smith called.

"Charley, I've got reliable information that there's a still about six miles west of Hampton (Henry County). It's supposed to operate tonight."

Investigator Miles Dillard was my Resident Agent in Charge (RAC) in Atlanta. Miles was another old timer who had been through the mill in liquor law enforcement. He was a short, chubby man in his late 50's who looked a lot like Santa Claus. He had a round face, ruddy complexion and wore small wire-rimmed glasses. His appearance was deceiving, however. Miles had the reputation of being forceful when called upon in a violent situation. He had been a school teacher before coming to ATF and it had probably prepared him for the rigors of being an agent.

One of the many stories about Miles was that on a still raid in Alabama, he was grabbed from behind by a large black man, who pinned his arms and then forced his head into a barrel of whiskey, attempting to drown him. Miles somehow got one arm loose and drew his pistol. The man kept forcing Miles' head into the whiskey, but Miles placed his pistol under the man's chin and fired, saving his own life but ending the bootlegger's.

After Miles and I located the distillery that Howard had told me about, Miles suggested that we get Investigator Jim Ballard and newly-hired Investigator Forrest Kelley to go with us on the raid.

We all met at my house three miles north of Jonesboro. This was convenient since Smith lived in Jonesboro. Arriving after dark in the vicinity of the distillery, we hid our car in some woods. Using no lights and as little hushed conversation as possible, we walked about a mile to a spot 500 yards from the distillery.

"Charley and I'll go in and check it," Howard said. Slipping quietly through the woods, we heard nothing except the usual night noises of crickets, tree frogs and nocturnal creatures in the leaves.

"They're not here," Howard whispered, easing into the still yard. Placing our fingers over the lenses of our flashlights and allowing only a small sliver of light to escape, we checked the mash carefully to determine if it was ready for distillation. We would put a hand fully into the mash, being careful not to disturb the cap (a layer of wheat bran that forms on top of the mash during the fermentation process.) Then by tasting our fingers, we could tell if it was ready. If the mash was still sweet and didn't have the taste of beer, it wasn't ready for distillation. I always waited until my hand dried and then if my fingers didn't stick together, I knew the mash was ready. If the mash contained a great deal of sugar which hadn't turned to alcohol, it would be sticky and I knew it was not ready for distillation.

After checking the mash and noting several flashlight batteries and other signs of night operation, we went back to where the other officers were waiting.

Returning to the area where we had left Miles, Forrest and Jim, I saw something shining in the dark. When I got closer, I could see it was Forrest's wristwatch. It had a radium dial.

"Forrest, turn that watch over or at least turn the dial to the inside of your arm," I said.

He seemed quite offended, but grudgingly complied. I was no old timer, but I knew that on a surveillance you couldn't be too careful with your conversation and anything that reflected light, especially in an environment as quiet and remote as this.

We moved to within 300 yards of the still and settled in for a long wait. An hour or so later, we heard sounds from the still area. Dillard, Kelley and Ballard went around to the opposite side of the still site. Howard and I were to make the initial move, or "flush" the still. We waited for 30 minutes for the other officers to get in position and then started moving in.

It was a dark night with no moon. Two men were working by the eerie light of the gasoline burner. We could also hear them talking, despite the low rumble of the burner. My body tensed as I got ready to flush. I heard someone whistle.

"Whit wooo, whit wooo."

One of the men at the still returned the whistle and a third man appeared from the woods. He was carrying a flashlight and started shining the light in all directions into the woods surrounding the still yard.

Smith and I were in the open at the edge of the still yard, so when the light hit us, we broke for the three men. I went for the one with the light. Out of the corner of my eye I saw the other two jump into a creek next to the still.

The man with the light ran into a pile of pine tops at the edge of the still yard, apparently not seeing them in time to avoid the brush. I went in on top of him and a wild melee followed with dried broken branches crashing in every direction. I fought to get a good grip on him while he scrambled to get away. We finally broke free of the pine tops. He jumped and fell into the creek that ran through a washed-out area with a bank on each side three or four feet high. I fell in on top of him and finally got him calmed down and under arrest.

"What's your name?" I asked.

"Sam Prince," came the reply. Sam was a small wiry man in his 20's, and he was one of the hardest men to hold I ever grabbed onto. The small men usually were.

Prince said he was bringing gasoline to the still for fuel and had parked his car a short distance away. Meanwhile, the other two still hands made good their escape.

We found Prince's car, a 1940 Ford coupe, with nine cases of fruit jars, parked about a mile away. Prince admitted that he had bought the jars in Griffin to put the whiskey in. The still was a ground-hog type (buried in the ground next to a stream of water) with 1,000-gallon mash capacity. There were 15 gallons of moonshine. This wound up my one-year probation period and I was proud to have made it. What a year I had experienced!

Few ATF investigators failed to survive the one-year probationary period, due to the extensive written examination, the intense oral interview and an exhaustive background check. I know of only two who didn't make probation. One was Alec Evans.

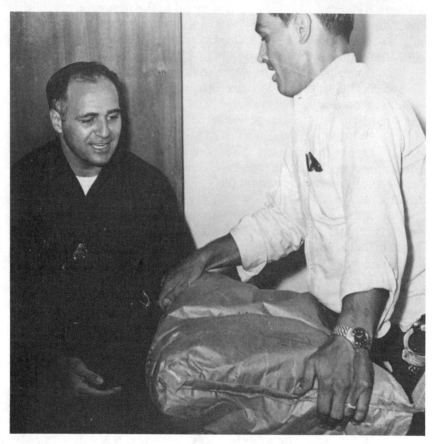

Agents Charley Weems and Charles Stanfill move seized sugar

Chapter VI
Murder and Justice

ATF investigators were sometimes assigned state revenue agents as partners. In Atlanta, State Agent Roy Gordon worked with Investigator Jimmy Causey and State Agent Jim Robinson with Investigator Ted Cone. Working together on a day-to-day basis, these officers became close friends. Many of the state agents later qualified and became excellent federal agents.

One of these was Milton Walton, a Florida state revenue agent for three years before becoming an ATF investigator in 1942. He proved himself many times not only as an excellent woodsman, field investigator and regional special investigator but also as a capable manager. He became the first regional coordinator for the Gun Control Act of 1968.

When I was promoted to regional special, Milton provided me with the evidence, information and guidance to write my first jacketed case. Frank Lane and Richard Jones were two other state officers who became excellent federal agents. I could name a dozen more, though not all were of their caliber. In every organization there is at least one bad apple and therein lies a story that I will never forget.

A former state revenue agent, Alec Evans, was hired by ATF and during his one-year probationary period, evidence was uncovered that he had collaborated with known liquor law violators. There wasn't enough evidence to prosecute him, but he was forced to resign.

I worked with Alec on a couple of occasions in north Georgia while he was a state agent, and found him easy to work with. Although he was never a close friend, I got along with him and was somewhat surprised to hear that he was under suspicion of conspiracy with bootleggers.

After leaving ATF, Evans worked for several years as a deputy sheriff in Gwinnett County and I lost contact with him. Then on a dreary morning in April, 1964, the entire state of Georgia was shocked and repulsed at the news of three Gwinnett County police officers being found brutally murdered in a remote area of the county.

A local resident called the Gwinnett police late one night about suspicious cars on a dead-end road. Two officers were on their way to respond when a third officer, who was going off duty, volunteered to go with them. All three officers—Jerry Everett, Ralph Davis and Jesse Gravitt—were handcuffed and shot several times in the head. It was a grisly, gangster-type execution. Every law enforcement officer in the area was appalled. Offers of assistance in solving the crime came pouring into Gwinnett County.

Detective John Crunkelton of the DeKalb County Vice Squad was assigned to assist in the investigation with the Georgia Bureau of Investigation and various other law enforcement agencies in the state. I had met John before and knew he was a capable, knowledgeable law enforcement officer. He proved in this investigation that he was as good as they come.

John called the ATF office and requested a meeting with investigators in the Atlanta area. I volunteered to assist in any way possible. John showed us the pictures of the crime scene—the officers handcuffed and brutally shot, a burned stolen car at the scene—and explained all the circumstances attendant to the crime. Evans came to my mind almost immediately. He had worked with the murdered officers and had been arrested just prior to this with former Sheriff Dan Heatter for liquor law violations. Evans was charged with transporting materials to a moonshine still and was out on federal bond.

I didn't voice my opinion until later when talking to John.

"The same thought crossed my mind," said Crunkelton uneasily. "The fact that three officers let someone catch them unawares and take their weapons apparently without a struggle and the fact that they didn't radio for help leads me to believe that the officers knew the killer and trusted him." This proved to be a major lead in the investigation.

After an intensive manhunt by almost every law enforcement branch in the state, three arrests were made. One of the men arrested and later convicted of murder was Alec Evans. Evans was given the death penalty, but after the ruling of the Supreme Court that death was cruel and unusual punishment, his sentence was reduced to life. (The Supreme Court has since reversed itself on the death penalty and is apparently taking into consideration the cruel and unusual punishment criminals often use in the perpetration of their crimes against innocent citizens and law enforcement officers). In Georgia, after serving seven years of a life sentence, a person is eligible for parole; however, Evans is still serving time at Reidsville State Prison where, hopefully, he will be confined forever.

Evans was the exception rather than the rule for local, state and federal officers who risk their lives daily to protect the citizens of our country. His illegal activities finally caught up with him.

After being so instrumental in bringing the killers to justice in Gwinnett County, Crunkelton was appointed chief of the Gwinnett County police. He undertook the cleanup of a county that had the reputation as a haven for law violators of all kinds, especially car thieves. John did a masterful job and held the position of chief for 16 years, during which time the county prospered and flourished. It was a suburb of fast-expanding Atlanta. The police chief in Gwinnett is appointed by county commissioners, as in numerous other Georgia counties. After the county had grown and become more urban, John suffered the fate of so many excellent law enforcement officers—he was replaced in 1985 by a man who had the favor of the commissioners. Politics is an evil of our time in every branch of government.

Crunkelton's devotion to duty, his unbiased attitude in law enforcement, his vast experience in all aspects of the job and his untiring dedication meant nothing to the politicians. This has happened more than once in all sections of this country and will continue to happen as long as people elect officials who are so short-sighted as to put political prowess ahead of experience, capabilities, past performance and dedication to law enforcement.

Crunkelton and Chief Howard Smith of Clayton County were two of the best law enforcement officers I have ever had the privilege of knowing and working with. Neither received the recognition he deserved. This often happens and although I admit I am biased, I am confident in my observations.

* * *

Smith was hired by Clayton County in 1940. He and Sam Blalock were the only two county policemen in a county that now has a police department of more than 200 men and women. I remember Howard stopping by my daddy's filling station on old 41 Highway to get a Coke and talking to me in his friendly way. Many times he told other officers how he remembered me as a little black-haired youngster.

In 1943, just after my 16th birthday, I was on my way home one night from a date. I had met the girl in Atlanta. My curfew time was 12 midnight and I was running late. The highway was almost deserted due to the late hour and the wartime rationing of gasoline. I had bought a gasoline ration stamp from a classmate for 50 cents in order to get gas and was airing out my daddy's 1937 Ford. About two miles from home, I suddenly saw a red light behind me.

My heart sank. My mother usually had to beg my father to let me use the car for any reason. It was his only entertainment and he would sometimes sit in it for hours to get out of the house and keep from listening to soap operas on the radio. I knew I had had it when Smith walked up to the window of the car and asked to see my driver's license. After checking it and looking at me closely with his flashlight, he said, "I'm not going to give you a ticket if you'll promise to slow down, but I'm going to tell your daddy about this because you could kill yourself."

I was scared, yet I could feel the compassion of Smith for a 16-year-old who was unsure of himself. I thanked him profusely and went home with the awful foreboding of what would happen when Officer Smith spoke to my daddy.

My father was an average-sized man, six feet tall, weighing 170 pounds but very strong. He was a carpenter by trade and was accustomed to hard physical labor. I was an only child and I felt he loved me dearly, although I don't recall his ever saying so. He was gone from home a lot, working in other areas of the state where work was available, but I always looked forward to his coming home. He was a quiet, fair-skinned person, and when he became angry, his face turned a brilliant red. You had better look out then, because even though he was hard to arouse, his temper made him violent.

I sweated for several days until one night at the supper table, Pop said, "I saw Howard Smith today at the store." Once more my heart sank. Then a little smile played across Pop's lips as he said, "Howard said he stopped you the other night for speeding."

I said, "He did."

Pop didn't say any more. Mom looked kind of funny, but apparently figured it was best to let it drop if Pop did. She got me later.

I don't know to this day everything Howard told my daddy, but I do know he must have told him in such a way as to make Pop's approach to me far less violent than it would have been if anyone else had given him that information. He was that way in all his dealings with people. His approach to law enforcement was a firm, no-nonsense approach and he never shirked his duty. He had compassion for people and would help them when he could. He was the ideal police officer and like a big brother to me. Years later when I worked with Howard I came to love and respect him even more.

As Keeler McCartney, a former police reporter for the *Atlanta Constitution*, has said, "Howard was one of the most respected law officers in the state of Georgia. In all the years I knew him, I never heard a breath of criticism about Howard Smith. He was an impartial officer who would lock up his grandmother if she violated the law. He'd be nice about it, but he would lock you up."

Howard Smith was truly the epitome of a police officer. We need more like him.

Groundhog-type distillery in Henry County, Georgia.

Still yard in south Clayton County, Georgia. (Note vines and undergrowth)

Chapter VII
Firelight and Fireflies

In October, Howard called me. "You won't believe this, Charley, but one of my neighbors is supposed to have a still set up on the farm in front of my house. The information is that it'll run tonight. How about helping me?" Of course, I jumped at the opportunity for two reasons: Howard was the first and second, the still was in Clayton County, not far from Jonesboro where I had grown up and lived. It was my home territory.

I contacted state agent Frank Lane, who was my partner at that time, and we met Howard at his house on Jodeco Road outside Jonesboro at eight o'clock that night.

"The still is supposed to be across the road, behind my neighbor's house," said Howard.

Since it was already dark, we left his house on foot and went across the road and into a large open field without using our flashlights. As we were circling in back of the suspect's house, Howard's German Shepherd dog came up to him.

"Go home, King! Go home!" Howard whispered.

King didn't move.

"I don't want him barking and giving us away. I'll have to use my belt as a leash," said Howard.

With the dog in tow, we continued slowly and carefully toward the still.

After ten minutes, we reached a point on the side of a hill where we could hear the roar of a gasoline burner. There was a faint glow in a wooded area close to the foot of the hill.

Since Howard had to hold the dog, he and Frank stayed put.

"I'll slip down the hill and flush the still from the other side. I don't know how long it'll take to get in position, but I'll try to flush at nine o'clock," I whispered as I faded into the darkness.

There was no moon. It was pitch dark. After skirting the distillery area, I crossed a small stream. Thinking the still must be close to this source of water, I followed the stream and the sounds of work until I was directly across from the distillery. By the glow of firelight, I could see three men working in the still yard. They moved silently. One was adjusting the pressure on the gasoline burner. This was when my adrenalin began pumping.

Crawling along the bank, I found myself entangled in a mess of honeysuckle vines. These vines grow in profusion in the South and are hard to break. I decided to try to clear the vines by jumping over the creek and scrambling up the opposite bank as fast as possible before the violators heard me. I hoped the sound of the gasoline burner would cover me.

At nine o'clock, I crouched low and leaped as far as I could toward the opposite bank. In the darkness and blinded by the firelight, I was unable to judge the distance correctly. I hit the opposite bank about halfway up and fell backward into the water. Scrambling out of the creek, I must have sounded like a bull elephant taking a bath. As I reached the top of the bank, I saw three startled men staring in my direction. The sounds of my floundering around in the creek must have frozen them momentarily.

The beam of my flashlight splashed on a white man and I shouted, "Federal officer, hold it!" A black man disappeared into the darkness toward Howard and Frank. I hollered, "He's coming toward you, Howard."

The white man stayed where he was and as the other black man started away from me, I said, "Come back—now!"

He hesitated.

"Now, dammit!" He slowly walked back.

I arrested John Moore and Claude Elwood in the still yard, and a little while later Howard and Frank came back with Harrison Stark.

I don't know if the dog participated in the arrest, but he did have a smug look on his face.

Howard was especially pleased with this seizure and arrest because he took it sort of personal that a man would set up a still so close to his residence. For several years, I kidded Howard about his neighbor, but we never had any more distilleries reported in *that* area.

LIGHTNING BUGS

Six miles southwest of Conyers, in Rockdale County, there exists something unusual for the state of Georgia and the South in general: a Trappist Monastery. It covers hundreds of acres of land and has numerous large, beautiful buildings, including a huge high-ceilinged cathedral. As I understand it, some of the monks or brothers are sworn to silence and never speak. The monastery employs outside help to operate a large farm. The monks or brothers spend all their waking hours studying and praying.

During the last week of October, SAC Frank Clark called me into his office.

"The overseer of the monastery farm called our office and reported a big still on land next to their property. Jimmy Causey's on vacation," Clark continued, "so you check it out." He handed me a telephone number. "Work the information as you see fit."

I called the number and was told by the overseer that if I would meet him at the monastery, he would show me the approximate location of the still.

On the way out of the office, I picked up Investigator Jim Ballard to help me. As I drove up to the monastery gate, I was impressed with the size and beauty of the place. We picked up the overseer. He accompanied us to a wooded area off a small dirt road. The overseer and I dropped out and continued on foot.

"I'll be back in one hour," Jim said as he left the area.

We started walking, first skirting a cultivated field and then making our way into a thick wooded area. At first, the overseer couldn't find the still. We finally came upon a creek and followed it back upstream until we almost walked into the still yard without seeing it.

The woods were thick with honeysuckle, kudzu vines and undergrowth.

I said, "Wait here."

I eased into the creek and made my way to the still yard. By walking in the water, I didn't leave tracks. Someone had been working at the still recently. It was in the process of being set up. There were two 1,000-gallon groundhog stills which had been built on the premises and filled with water and wheat bran. This type of still is circular with galvanized metal sides and a wooden bottom and top, usually made of poplar boards fitted tightly together. When poplar wood is soaked in water, it swells and forms a tight, leakproof fit. These stills were so new they were leaking a little, but I knew after another day or two they would be ready to set up and use to make moonshine.

The violators had built a small dam across the stream and prepared a flakestand box in which to place the radiator condenser.

After checking out the still area, we walked back and were picked up by Jim. We took the overseer back to the monastery.

"Don't mention this to anyone," we warned.

On the way back to Atlanta, I explained the situation to Jim. We agreed that the still wouldn't be ready to operate for at least a week.

The second week in November, Causey reported back to work and I told him about the distillery. That afternoon Jimmy and I dropped out to check the still area again. Jim Ballard was to pick us up later. As we walked through the woods toward the still, I saw several large ravines and gullies I hadn't noticed before.

Again, I had a little trouble locating the still site, but finally found it. Both stills had been mashed in and were ready to run. One of the stills had the cap barrel in place and the galvanized pipe ready to connect to the radiator condenser in the stream.

"It'll run tonight," Jimmy said. "Let's get something to eat and come back after dark."

Ballard picked us up, and we ate supper in Stockbridge, then returned to the area at eight o'clock. We hid the car on an abandoned sawmill road a mile or so from the distillery and started walking through the woods. It was one of those cool, moonless fall nights and very dark. Even in open areas we couldn't see our hand in front of our face. Usually your eyes gradually become accustomed to the darkness, but on this night it was so dark we had to feel our way through the woods.

Although we had flashlights, we didn't use them. We knew that the liquor violators would be on the alert for any sound or light anywhere around them. As we crept carefully through the woods, we stopped occasionally to listen for any sound that would help guide us. The night was quiet. Except for the sounds of tree frogs and the usual woods sounds, we heard nothing.

Finally, after about 30 minutes I heard a gasoline burner. These burners make a low roaring noise and you have to be almost on top of them to hear it. Fuel oil burners are usually force-fed by an electrically operated blower and can be heard several hundred yards away, but this one was gravity-fed and made little noise.

By moving to my left, I was able to distinguish an orange-red glow. I knew we were close. We quietly pulled back a little.

"Jim, you stay here. Causey and I'll circle the still and find the workway." (The path or vehicle trail to a still.)

The plan was to flush the still down the workway so that we would have a cleared area through which to approach the distillery quietly. As Jimmy and I began the tedious task of trying to get around the distillery, we soon discovered that the area we were trying to penetrate was covered not only with honeysuckle vines, but also "bamboo" briars. These are vine-like growths found in profusion near streams in the South. They grow to a length of eight feet, being a quarter-inch in diameter with strong thorn-like briars that cut like a razor. We both became entangled in these vines and briars and slid down into a deep ravine.

We weren't having much success getting through the area in the pitch-black darkness. I tried putting one hand over the lens of my flashlight and spreading my fingers slightly to let out a small sliver of light. Jimmy did the same thing and we eventually struggled out of the ravine and into an open sage field. We switched off our lights and hoped no one had seen them.

Usually the agent in whose territory you are working makes decisions on how to raid and as to the disposition of the case in federal or state court. This was Causey's territory and I knew from past experience that he loved to flush stills. I was a little surprised when he told me to get in front. Jimmy had a cold and probably felt that I was in better shape that particular night to run someone down. I was pleased that he placed that much confidence in me because Jimmy was known for his speed and ability to outrun violators.

The night was deathly silent. It was so dark that the only thing I could see was the vague outline of a hill on the horizon to my left. I started slowly feeling my way toward the area between the hill and the distillery. We were some distance from the still and couldn't hear the burner. We groped our way across the sage field and I eventually felt smooth ground beneath my feet.

Stooping down, I felt the ground with my hand. This must be a foot path leading toward the distillery! I started feeling my way slowly down the path toward the still. Causey was right behind me. I took one cautious step at a time and paused between steps to listen. Suddenly, I heard the sound of someone breathing in front of me! The hair on the back of my neck began to bristle and I froze.

I strained my eyes to see through the inky black darkness, but continued to hear breathing. I turned slowly toward Causey and whispered as low as I could in his ear, "I hear someone breathing."

Jimmy said, "HUH?"

I repeated a little louder, but still whispering, "I hear someone breathing."

With that, someone to my right whispered, "It's all right."

I knelt down and reached to my right. I touched the shoulder of a man.

I eased over next to him and whispered, "Is it all right?"

He said, "Yes."

My face was six inches from his and I still couldn't see him. I whispered, "We're Federal officers. You're under arrest. Don't make a sound."

Jimmy squatted down next to us and I said, "Jimmy, you stay with this man. I'll go on into the still yard and catch the others."

The black man I heard breathing by the still path was Vernon Bomar. He continued to whisper: "There's nobody at the still. We seen some lights in the woods that was too big to be lightning bugs so we decided to leave," he explained.

I left Bomar with Causey and eased on into the still yard. Bomar had told the truth. There was no one at the distillery although the burner was still on. I turned it off, walked into the branch and softly called to Ballard, "Hey, Jim, come on in. They're not here."

Ballard crossed the branch and we went back to find Causey.

Leaving Bomar in the custody of Ballard, Causey and I walked up the still path toward an old farm house on top of the hill, approaching without lights. When we got into the large dirt yard, I could see the outline of a car.

We hesitated. The flare of a cigarette lit up the car window as someone in the front seat took a draw.

"You take the driver's side and I'll take this side," I told Jimmy. As we approached the car I saw someone light a cigarette in the back seat.

The windows of the automobile were rolled up, but when I tried the door on my side, it was unlocked. Shining my flashlight into the car, I saw two black men and two black women.

"Get out!" I told the man on my side.

I identified myself and noted that he was wearing overalls and rubber boots. I asked, "Why did you leave the still?"

"Well, we seen some lights a while ago and knew they was too big to be lightning bugs, so we decided we better leave," he said.

"When did you set up the still?"

He replied, "Well, we started two weeks ago. A white man from Atlanta hired us and furnished the stuff to build the stills and sugar and stuff."

With some coaxing, Willie Evans and Ulysses Cofield admitted that this white man was paying them $50 per week and that Bomar and his wife were living in the house. They said this was the first time they had made a run. Neither of them admitted knowing the white man's name.

I left the still operators with Causey and headed back down the path. I met Ballard and Bomar coming up toward the house.

"This was on the ground where Bomar was sitting," Ballard said, handing me a .380 automatic pistol.

I have reflected many times on the fact that both Causey and I could easily have been killed by Bomar. From then on, I was careful to search violators I apprehended.

This was one of several occasions when I encountered someone with a firearm at a still. Most liquor law violators knew they could get into a lot more trouble by being armed and injuring an officer than by being caught making whiskey. But some did carry weapons.

I walked back to the distillery, reflecting on an old saying, "The Lord looks after fools and drunks." I was no drunk.

All three defendants later pled guilty in federal court. We wound up with a good still seizure and three defendants when we easily could have caught no one. If Bomar had left with the other two and the three of them had driven the car away, this would have turned out to be an unknown seizure. Sometimes you have good luck, sometimes bad.

This was a good luck story in more ways than one!!

Charley Weems examining a boiler at a moonshine distillery in DeKalb County, Georgia

Charley Weems checking mash at a moonshine distillery in
DeKalb County, Georgia

Chapter VIII
Swoop Down On 'Em

In the winter of 1955 I was working with Regional Special Investigators Ed Carswell, Vic Bernhardt and Clair Pequignot. We were investigating two retail liquor stores in Atlanta. Liquor was being sold in wholesale quantities to bootleggers in dry counties adjacent to the Atlanta-Fulton County area. It was a violation of state and federal law and had been going on a long time. Bernhardt, Carswell and Pequignot had been on the case for several weeks prior to calling me in and I was in the dark as to what we were doing.

Carswell, Jim Ballard, State Agent Owen "Sonny" Strickland and I rode together. I had not met Sonny, and although he was considered to be one of the "wild" ones, I immediately liked him. He got things done. We remain close friends to this day. Sonny's father, Owen C. Strickland, Sr., had been an ATF investigator for years in Savannah and Sonny had grown up loving both the work and ATF. Tact was not one of Sonny's strong points. You always knew when he burst into a house with a search warrant that his 230-pound presence would be made known. He would not tolerate any argument or resistance from the violators. I always felt comfortable when Sonny was along. He became an ATF investigator later on and retired in his hometown of Savannah. He's one of the "good 'uns."

Carswell was an old-timer in his middle 50's—a fine, honest man. He was kidded a lot about carrying a briefcase. Some said that the only things in it were a *Saturday Evening Post* magazine and a fifth of whiskey. Ed did drink when off duty, but as far as I knew, it never interfered with his work.

Henry Gastley once told a story about Carswell that I never forgot. There was a north Georgia moonshiner named Wally Steed who had a bad reputation for fighting. He was known as a man who would kill you in a minute.

An undercover agent had been working for some time in this liquor violator's area and had bought whiskey from Steed. A federal arrest warrant had been issued and Carswell was in a group of officers assigned to pick up subjects in a roundup of several bootleggers in the area. When Steed's name was called, Ed spoke up.

"I'll take that one."

Most of the others felt that whoever attempted to serve a warrant on Steed was sure to have trouble. He was dangerous.

Ed and his partner drove to Steed's house located back in the foothills of the Appalachians. Ed sent his partner to the back door and knocked on the front screen. It was summertime and the house was open, air conditioning being unheard of in those days. After knocking twice, Ed opened the door and walked into the small frame house. He saw that a door leading into the back room was closed, and knocked on that door.

Steed's voice boomed out from inside, "Who is it?"

Ed replied, "Ed Carswell with an arrest warrant for you, Steed."

Steed shouted, "You come through that door, Ed, and I'll kill you."

"You'd better cock your pistol then, because I'm coming in," replied Ed calmly. And he did.

He found Steed in bed and promptly arrested him. Under Steed's pillow Ed found a loaded .45 automatic. After his arrest, Steed was submissive and caused no problem at all. Ed was a refined, mild-mannered man who was fearless when the chips were down.

While we were observing the rear of the Harris Liquor Store in Atlanta, a blue '55 Ford drove into the parking area in the rear. Two white men began loading the car with cases of whiskey from the rear of an electrical supply company next door. Georgia had a state law that required all retail liquor stores to sell and load all distilled spirits through the front door of the establishment. Retail liquor stores were prohibited from having any type of back entrance. Anyone buying would have to receive the spirits through the front door where he could easily be seen. This law was designed to keep large quantities of taxpaid whiskey out of the hands of bootleggers in dry counties.

In order to get around the law, Harris moved whiskey by the case next door to the electrical supply store and then loaded it out the back. We watched as the Ford was loaded with 20 cases of taxpaid whiskey. The whiskey was covered with a blue blanket. We made notes of the license number and description of the vehicle and returned the following day with federal warrants for the electrical supply store and the Harris Liquor Store.

Sitting in Carswell's big Buick Roadmaster government car awaiting the raid time of eleven o'clock, I kept wondering why we were about to raid a legal liquor store and what to expect. Ed put me at ease with his casual manner, saying that we would just "swoop down on 'em." He explained that these people were violating federal and state laws requiring a federal wholesale or retail license to sell legally distilled spirits. Possession of large amounts of whiskey in an unmarked vehicle was prima facie evidence of intent to violate the liquor laws of the state and federal governments. These vehicles would be subject to seizure the same as vehicles bearing non-taxpaid moonshine whiskey.

Ed continued, "This is a big operation. It's headed by a man who supplies most of the red liquor (taxpaid liquor from legal distilleries) to bootleggers in the dry counties (counties in which it is illegal to sell any kind of alcoholic beverage) of north and west Georgia. We've already gathered evidence involving 14 trip vehicles and six trip boys."

At exactly eleven that morning, we made our move on the liquor store on Irby Avenue. There were several cases of whiskey stacked on the sidewalk in front of the store. Ed and I went inside and served the federal search warrant on Saul Harris, the owner, and immediately began searching the premises for evidence which would strengthen the case against Harris for selling wholesale amounts of whiskey from a retail outlet.

In the rear of the store, we found two rear seats from 1955 Fords, one of which matched the blue Ford we had seen the previous day. Next door at the electrical supply store were 31 cases of whiskey of assorted brands stacked near the rear door. The serial numbers had been removed. Some of them were found in the rear of the liquor store. The clerk at the supply store told us that the whiskey belonged to Harris. There were numerous fictitious license plates and other incriminating evidence in the vehicles out back and in the liquor store. We closed the liquor store and padlocked it.

Meanwhile, other officers including Bernhardt were swooping down on the Red Circle Liquor Store on Marietta Street. They found records, license tags and serial numbers, as well as a hidden rear entrance to the store. The rear of the building had been removed and a garage door placed in the wall with room enough for an automobile to be driven into the building. From the rear of the liquor store, a hidden door led into the garage area. Vehicles were pulled in, the garage door closed and whiskey secretly moved from the liquor store into the garage area and loaded into the vehicles.

In all, 14 vehicles and the complete contents of the two retail liquor stores were seized. A total of eight arrests were made and most of the defendants pled guilty. The U.S. Attorney eventually negotiated the return of the contents of the liquor stores, but all 14 vehicles were forfeited to the U.S. Government. Some were placed in use by ATF as official government vehicles.

* * *

Shortly after the liquor store raids, I made an arrest which later led to an even larger seizure and several arrests. Sometimes, if we were lucky, we could cultivate an informer after an arrest with varying results. Most liquor law violators dreaded having a federal case made against them. In order to cultivate an informer, we would agree to make a state case if the person would promise to help us. This was especially true if it was a small violation.

Frank Lane had received information that Albert Folley, a suspected whiskey wholesaler in the College Park area south of the Atlanta airport, was using Kent Road as a route to transfer moonshine. We knew this road was in the vicinity of Folley's home, so we drove to the area and parked in a small side street to watch for suspicious activity.

At eight in the evening, a 1948 Dodge driven by a black man approached from the direction of the Folley residence. When it stopped at the intersection of Kent Road and Janice Drive, I walked up to the driver's side.

"How do you get to the airport?" I asked, looking into the car. There were two cases of liquor in the rear-seat compartment. "You're under arrest," I told the driver as I removed the key from the ignition. "What's your name?"

"Homer Lee," he replied.

In the trunk of the car Frank found three more cases of moonshine. Frank asked, "Homer, you don't want to go to federal court, do you? Weems here wants to make a federal case, but I can put the case in state court if you'll help us catch the man who sold you the liquor."

"I'll help you if you help me," said Homer.

Frank and I argued for a couple of minutes for Homer's benefit and I reluctantly agreed to put him in state court. We were going to do this anyway. Although I had my doubts about anything substantial coming from his information, I was proven wrong!

I spent the remainder of that year was making undercover buys in areas where I was not yet known and working transportation in Atlanta. My two boys, Joe and Charles, were now seven and five years old and a handful. Even though we had a good Christmas, I was ready to get back in harness and go to work. Every day was an adventure!

MAMA, THEY'RE KILLING ME!

The first week in January, I had surgery for a recurrent back problem. Dr. Frank Eskridge of Atlanta performed the surgery and told me I could expect to be incapacitated for at least four weeks, maybe more. I was in the hospital for ten days and off work until the first of February.

When I returned, I was assigned a '50 Oldsmobile that had been seized transporting whiskey. It was just what I wanted. It had a HydraMatic transmission and if you stayed on the accelerator, it would burn rubber every time it changed gears. I loved it. The car was not only fun to drive, it also got me invited to a lot of investigations pertaining to liquor cars coming into Atlanta. I also used the car to great advantage on observation work involving raw materials outlets. Since it was unknown to the violators, I could get a great deal closer to the action without being noticed. I was immediately back into the 12- and 14-hour work days.

The second week in February, Jimmy Causey called me aside. "Can you help me tonight? Legs Law is supposed to be bringing a load of liquor in on Georgia Highway 101 through Paulding County. With your '50 Olds, we should be able to catch him."

I was all for it. "Okay, we'll meet in Dallas at six o'clock and have supper."

After supper, Jim Ballard and I found a place where we could watch Highway 101. Jimmy and I had discussed the best way to handle the liquor car if it came through.

We chose a little-used side road where we could park our car and not be seen by passing traffic, but where we could observe any vehicles that passed. Jimmy and Richard Jones parked in a similar place two miles up the highway from us. When the suspect vehicle passed their location, they were to call us on the radio. We would pull onto the highway going the same direction as the whiskey car. As he approached us from the rear, we would attempt to block him while Jimmy and Richard would pull up alongside to get him stopped. If this didn't work and the car got around us, we would have to run him down. These chases usually involved high speed and dangerous situations which we hoped to avoid by careful planning. Plans don't always work out!

We had been at our location for a little over an hour and hadn't heard a word from Jimmy. We attempted to call, but our radios were probably the worst of any law enforcement agency in the country. They were old AM models which were subject to all types of interference, even when working properly. It was not at all uncommon to hear radio traffic on our frequency from Dew Line stations in Alaska and not be able to talk to someone a mile away. On one occasion, while on surveillance in the center of Atlanta, I couldn't maintain contact with another radio car three blocks away, yet I had no problem at all talking to an ATF vehicle in New Orleans. Our radios were not reliable, to say the least.

Ballard and I became impatient for some type of action, so I decided to move the car closer to the highway. When a vehicle came by going toward Atlanta, I would switch on my headlights as he passed and see if we could jump a liquor car that way. Sometimes this worked. The violator, thinking that he had been made, would pour the coal to his car and attempt to escape—a sure sign that he was hauling whiskey.

Traffic was light on 101 at that time of night and a vehicle would pass about every 15 minutes. The first two vehicles we hit with the lights continued without slowing or speeding up, so we remained where we were. When the headlights hit the third vehicle, a 1953 Chevrolet, it slowed, stopped and backed up to the entrance of the side road.

Ballard got out of our car and said, "He might be meeting someone here to switch a load. I'll go check him."

I stayed with our car and left the headlights on the vehicle.

Ballard reached the driver's side, said something to the driver and went toward the rear of the car. He hesitated and returned to the driver. He asked the driver for the key to the trunk and when the car started moving away, Ballard reached inside. The car jumped forward with a roar.

"Let him go," I shouted, "we'll get him." I got into the Olds and fired it up. Ballard was still hanging on to the Chevrolet and it was gaining speed. As I started forward, Jimmy and Richard came over the rise in the road. Seeing Ballard hanging onto the side of a suspect car, they got into the action.

When Ballard saw their vehicle and my car bearing down, he finally let go and shouted to Causey and Jones, "Get him!"

Jimmy and Richard, thinking that the suspect was trying to hurt Ballard, sped after the Chevrolet. I reached Ballard, picked him up and floorboarded the Olds. In seconds we were behind Causey's car. As Causey pulled alongside the suspect, I saw four flashes followed by "Pow, pow, pow, pow." I thought, Oh, shit! The suspect immediately turned right into a long driveway leading to a farm house on top of a hill.

Causey was almost up against the back bumper of the Chevrolet and we were on Causey's bumper. The driveway was rough and as we reached the front yard, the Chevrolet ran under the front porch without slowing down. The hood flew up, steam poured from the burst radiator and all hell broke loose.

The driver sprang from the car and took off around the house shouting at the top of his lungs, "Mama they're killing me! Mama they're killing me!"

Jones was in hot pursuit on foot and I drove around the house, keeping my headlights on the fleeing suspect. Sliding to a stop, I bolted from the Oldsmobile as lights began to come on all over the house. I knew we were on thin ice and I was prepared for the worst. As Richard caught the suspect in the back yard, he swung his fist at Richard, which was a mistake. Jones immediately was on top of him. As they continued wrestling on the ground, the back porch of the house began to look like the grandstand at the World Series.

People of all sizes, shapes and ages boiled out of the house onto the back porch. During this time, the black boy was still shouting, "They're killing me!" When Richard finally got him under control, the boy said, "You shot me!"

Richard stammered, "Where, where?" and began looking him over carefully.

An old black woman had fallen to her knees, crying, "I knew this was goin' to happen. He's no good. I knew this was goin' to happen."

I watched the back door closely in case someone appeared with a gun. I also began talking to the black woman and the six or seven others (it seemed like more at the time) on the porch, trying to calm everyone down and reduce the tension. This accomplished, and with the suspect under control, I saw Jimmy coming from the direction of the suspect's Chevrolet.

"He doesn't have a drop," Jimmy said.

I thought, Why did he run??? I left the others in the yard to try to find some violation we could charge the suspect with because we were indeed on thin ice. I got everyone back into the living room and continued talking to the older woman, the boy's mother.

She said that the boy's father was not at home, but that he had told the boy not to take the car anywhere. The boy's driver's license had been revoked for drunk driving. The mother told me, "Take him on, take him to jail." She said this several times and I kept wondering how we were going to get out of this mess. Jimmy joined the conversation. After hearing the mother's story about the boy disobeying his father, having no driver's license and considering the fact that he was also driving drunk on this occasion, we decided to leave the boy in his mother's custody despite her protestations and pleas for us to "take him to jail."

Not only did the suspect have no whiskey, but Richard had shot down both left side tires. We were lucky that the suspect had not been hit as he had claimed, and was only suffering from a severe case of fright (which probably did him a lot of good.) On the following day, Causey took the boy's father two good tires that had been replaced by new ones on a government vehicle. That was the last we heard of it. We were lucky.

My daily report had a short notation that we had checked a 1953 Chevrolet fitting the description of a known illicit whiskey vehicle with no results. Shooting the tires down was not mentioned. We were glad to forget that part.

* * *

In February, we concentrated on observation of a large wholesale sugar outlet on Washington Street near the State Capitol; and Piedmont Feed and Grocery on Piedmont Avenue just off Decatur Street. Both these outlets were known to be major suppliers of sugar and other materials to moonshiners and both were under demand to report large sales. We used these observations and undercover buys to gather evidence in order to prosecute the owner of the business if he failed to make a report, or made a false report. Failure to report was a misdemeanor; a false report was a felony.

Any time we were not involved in other activities we would drive by these establishments or park and watch for suspicious activity. This paid off, but like all police work it involved a great deal of patience and boredom.

About the middle of February, our periodic observations of Piedmont Feed and Grocery bore fruit. My '50 Olds was running rough and that morning I had met Investigator Merritt Scoggins at Jenkins Garage in Fairburn. Merritt and I had become good friends almost immediately upon meeting. In the years to come, I came to love him like a brother. Merritt was an ex-Marine and one of the most intelligent and respected men I have ever known. Our families became close, and my two sons still talk about "Scoggins" and the time and effort he put into the Little League football team he coached. Scoggins and his wife, Juanita, are the type people everyone would want to have for neighbors and friends. They both were meticulous in their dress and Juanita kept their home spotless. I have found on many occasions what a privilege it is to be Merritt Scoggins' friend.

After leaving the Olds at Jenkins' Garage, Merritt and I returned to the Atlanta office. I picked up a 1950 Ford that had just been forfeited and placed in government service and Jim Ballard and I decided to see what was going on at Piedmont Feed. We parked two blocks away on busy Piedmont Avenue. At four o'clock a man named Moran who worked for Piedmont Feed, loaded a large amount of sugar onto the truck, then parked it in the lot of a nearby service station.

We watched the truck until it left the station 30 minutes later. We let the truck get a block ahead of us and then followed. The truck turned into an alley between Meldrum and Kennedy Streets. We stopped before we got to the alley and I walked to a house on Meldrum Street. I knocked on the door and identified myself to a heavy-set black woman. The smell of supper cooking drifted from the house.

"Could I watch someone from your back porch?" I asked the woman, showing her my badge.

"Yes, sir," she smiled, and led me through the house to the back porch.

By standing just inside the kitchen door, I could see the Piedmont truck. Moran and a black man, Willie Ogletree, were loading sugar and other materials off the Piedmont truck onto a red International truck. I watched until the transfer of materials was finished, all the while smelling the wonderful aromas of food in the kitchen. Most women in the South are great cooks. My mouth watering, I thanked the woman and ran back to the government car.

The empty Piedmont truck left the alley and turned away from us. We drove past the alley and, not seeing the red truck, floorboarded the accelerator to get to Kennedy Street at the other end of the alley.

As we made the corner, Ballard shouted, "There he is!"

We followed at a safe distance. Ogletree drove for three blocks and pulled into a driveway on Paines Avenue. This turned out to be his residence.

In order to make a good raw materials case, we had to establish intent. This was not hard if the seizure was made at or near an illicit distillery, but if the seizure was made in some other area, intent must be proven by circumstantial evidence.

When we pulled into the driveway behind the International truck, Ogletree didn't realize who we were and walked back to us. I said, "Federal officer, what do you have on the truck?"

He replied, "Sugar."

I asked, "What else?"

"Yeast," replied Ogletree.

We examined the truck and found 1,800 pounds of sugar, 100 pounds of wheat bran and 18 pounds of yeast. We had two elements of intent—suspicious movement and a combination of materials.

Ballard asked Ogletree, "Who are you hauling this stuff for?"

Ogletree said, "I was hauling the materials for a white man. His name's Mr. Roy. I don't know his last name."

Ballard asked, "When are you supposed to meet him and where?"

"I'm supposed to meet him tonight on a highway to Dallas, Georgia."

I asked, "Which highway?"

"I don't know which highway and I can't remember what time," Ogletree replied.

"Have you ever hauled for him before?" I asked.

"Yeah, I've hauled for him two times before."

At first Ogletree said that the International truck belonged to him, but when asked for a license tag receipt, he said he was in the process of buying the truck from Mr. Roy.

Ogletree said that he knew sugar, yeast and wheat bran were used to make moonshine, but that he didn't know if this particular load would be used for that. He also said that he suspected there was something illegal about the whole deal by the transfer in the alley and the meetings at night.

This was typical of the various stories moonshiners used to try to shift the blame for their illegal actions to some fictitious person. One of my favorites that was used quite often by moonshiners caught at a still was "the only reason I'm here is that I was looking for a cow that got out."

We arrested Ogletree and seized the vehicle and materials. The evidence was also used at a later date to bring charges against Piedmont Feed Company.

We were never at a loss for something to do!

Chapter IX
Grand Slam

One February morning, Ted Cone asked me to help raid a large distillery in Fayette County. It turned out to be one of the best and most memorable days of my career.

Roy Kelly had recently been assigned as supervisor in charge of all federal alcohol tax agents in the state. He was a fine, likeable, handsome man who had spent several years in Washington, D.C., prior to coming to Atlanta.

The 1950 Oldsmobile was back from the garage and it would run like a scalded dog. Jim Ballard, Miles Dillard and I met Kelly, Cone and Jim Robinson four miles west of Fayetteville. Since Kelly was along, I was anxious to do well and hoped I wouldn't goof up. We hid our vehicles on an old abandoned sawmill road and walked to the vicinity of the still, arriving at one in the afternoon.

Ted made the raid assignments. "Charley, you wait here until you hear us flush. I'll take Robinson and Kelly with me. Miles, you and Charley and Ballard spread out around this side." He swept his hand across the right edge of the woods.

It was a beautiful, bright clear day, not too cold, and the warm sun had brought out the smell of the woods. As on so many occasions, I thanked the Lord for the blessing of nature and my being a part of it. This sure was better than office work.

Hearing occasional sounds from the direction of the still, I moved cautiously, trying not to make a sound. Sound travels long distances in rural areas and the snap of a small dead tree limb breaking can spook moonshiners to run now and ask questions later. I had been carefully moving, then listening, for about 45 minutes when I heard Ted shout from the direction of the distillery—"Hey! Stop! Hey!" The raid was on!

The adrenalin flowed as I started down the hill through open woods toward the sound of someone crashing through the undergrowth. Near the bottom of the hill, I saw two men running toward me. They caught my movement, turned to their left, and ran harder. Running downhill, I put on a burst of speed and caught and tackled the one nearest me. It didn't take long.

"You're under arrest," I said, handcuffing him to a tree. At that same moment I saw the other man disappear into a pine thicket.

I plunged in, not knowing which way to go except straight ahead. Coming out into a large cotton field on the other side of the pines, I saw my man out of the corner of my eye. He had burst out of the woods into the same field. When he saw me, he turned and re-entered the thicket. I stumbled in and fell over Sam Mayer, who was trying to hide in a pile of brush.

"You're under arrest," I said, pulling him to his feet. We walked back to the other man, who was still handcuffed to the tree.

"What's your name?"

"Henry Brown," he replied.

I hadn't seen or heard any of the other officers since the initial shout. Keeping a firm grip on Mayer with one hand, I got hold of Brown with the other and felt a little better. We walked back to the still. Ted and the others were glad to see me, especially with both moonshiners. Everyone thought they had both escaped. Kelly was impressed.

The distillery was a little unusual. There were four 1,000-gallon coffin-type stills (long, rectangular boxes with a metal bottom used to ferment mash, and also as stills above the ground); 2,000 gallons of mash and 124 gallons of moonshine. It was in operation when we raided.

The stills were located 500 yards behind a farmhouse off a state highway. The driveway to the residence ran off the paved road and into the back yard. The workway led from the yard around the edge of some woods and past a cotton field, then into the woods to the distillery.

Leaving Brown with Ted, I took Mayer to the edge of the cotton field so we wouldn't be interrupted and began talking to him. Mayer told me confidentially, "Someone will be here this afternoon to bring in sugar and take the liquor out. We're all living in that farmhouse and Brown's wife is there now."

We decided to remain as quiet as possible and wait for the vehicle to come in. Knowing that we might need to block any vehicle that showed up, Ballard and I walked through the woods back to the Olds. We drove to a location south of the farmhouse. It was situated in a low area between two hills, about 100 yards off the highway. I parked on the hill on the south side, facing north. From there I could look directly up the highway to the next hill. I knew that the driveway was between me and the next hill, although I couldn't see it.

Ballard attempted to contact the officers at the still, but our radios were unreliable as usual. After several unsuccessful attempts, we saw a car approaching from the north. It disappeared into a low area and when it didn't pass our location, we knew it had turned into the still house driveway.

Since we couldn't contact the other officers, Ballard took a walkie-talkie and headed across an adjacent cotton field on foot to try to determine if the car had gone on to the still. I drove the Olds a short distance to the crest of the hill, so I could see into the low area where the driveway entered the highway. I was about a quarter-mile from the driveway.

At the time Ballard disappeared over the hill toward the still, a black 1949 Pontiac roared out of the driveway, scattering gravel in all directions, and turned north onto the highway. I knew if I waited for Ballard the car would be long gone.

I floorboarded the accelerator, and with tires squalling, sped after the Pontiac. Within a mile, I was on his bumper. There were two people in the car. I hit the siren and started to pull alongside. The driver moved all the way over into the left lane, trying to force me into the ditch. I fell back, knowing there was no way he was going to outrun me.

We were headed toward Fayetteville at 90 m.p.h. I knew I had to get him stopped before we got into town, since it was quitting time and traffic would be at its peak. I tried once more to get by on the left. When the Pontiac veered left, I fell back and came up quickly on his right side, forcing him into the left lane as we approached another hill. Immediately he slowed down.

The passenger slid over to the driver's side as the driver jumped out of the car while it was still moving at about 15 miles per hour. I forced the Pontiac onto the shoulder of the road, where it stopped. I skidded the Olds to a stop in front of the Pontiac, got out and took my keys. When I reached the Pontiac a woman was trying to get out.

I said, "Give me the keys."

She knew I was in no mood to argue and immediately handed them to me.

The man had fallen as he hit the shoulder of the road, but quickly regained his feet and sprinted across an open field. By now, he was 200 yards ahead of me and moving fast.

I took off after him. Although this was my first foot race since returning to work, I was in pretty good shape. By the time he reached a wooded area on the other side of the field, I had closed in to within 100 yards, but I was nearly exhausted. The man was now walking, so I started walking too, trying to catch my breath. He was on an old field road and although I was within shouting distance, I couldn't gain any ground.

When I started to run, he would run, and I was getting further away from help with every step. No one had any idea where I was and the early winter darkness would be coming soon.

I decided that the next time he looked back, I would put on a sprint with everything I had left and if that didn't work, I'd let him go. When he turned his head to look back, I started sprinting with the last bit of energy I had. He seemed to collapse when he saw how determined I was. When I got to him, he was sitting on the ground.

"Federal officer. You're under arrest," I gasped. I was at the point of exhaustion. "Get up! What's your name?"

He refused to tell me. This triggered an alarm. He said, "I can't get up. Just let me rest."

"You ran all the way down here—now you can walk back. Get up!" I said, getting my handcuffs out.

My handcuffs would barely close around his wrists.

"I've got to rest," he kept protesting.

I pulled him to his feet and saw that he was about 20 years old, 6'2" and weighed 220 pounds. He was a powerful man. I knew I'd better get him out of the woods or I'd have serious trouble if he decided to fight.

I made him walk in front, keeping my left hand on his right shoulder so my right hand was free, yet I could feel any sudden movement with my left. The .38 on my right hip was comforting.

When we finally got back to the cars, they were just as I had left them, but the woman was nowhere to be found. Somehow I didn't think she would be.

I placed the man, William Bryan, in the Pontiac. There were 2,000 pounds of sugar in the rear seat area, covered with a blanket. I left the Olds on the side of the road and drove the Pontiac back to the still site.

When we arrived, the other officers had finished destroying the distillery.

"We were ready to come looking for you, Charley. Where've you been?" asked Robinson.

I showed them the Pontiac, the load of sugar and Bryan, and told them what had happened. They were pleased, to say the least. It was like hitting a grand slam. Although arrests and seizures were a matter of routine, sometimes I couldn't help feeling good when everything went well.

In trying to put together what had happened to make Bryan leave the house, we decided that the still hand's wife must have been suspicious of sounds she had heard from the still. She had thrown a few clothes into the Pontiac and tried to escape with Bryan.

Bryan, bragging in front of his still-hand friends, became cocky. "If the Pontiac had run faster, you never would have caught me," he boasted.

"If you had been faster on your feet, I never would have caught you," I replied. His friends grinned at each other.

The cockiness disappeared and Bryan wilted. Once again he was just a "caught" moonshiner. Getting outrun in a car was bad, but getting outrun on foot was even worse.

Double automobile radiator condenser used at an illicit distillery in Lumpkin County, Georgia. Barrel was continuously supplied with cool water from a nearby stream. This served to keep the radiators cool while turning alcohol steam into liquid moonshine.

Aluminum mash vats with fermenting mash

Chapter X
All in a Day's Work

Working transportation was always a lot of fun. It gave me the opportunity to experience the thrill of high-speed driving without being arrested. I was a conservative driver compared to some of the wilder ones (Jack Elrod, Red Martin and Sonny Strickland to name just a few), but when I was in a chase, I forgot about everything except catching the liquor car. Luckily I survived without hurting myself or anyone else.

Carl Koppe, one of the best transportation men I ever worked with, was a conservative driver, yet fast when he had to be. Koppe probably caught more moonshine liquor cars than anyone else in ATF. One advantage of having a souped-up car was that you could be on the liquor car before he knew it, and as in raiding stills, the element of surprise was a great asset.

* * *

One night about eight-thirty Vic Bernhardt, Howard Smith and I were patrolling Hunter Street. Vic had information that moonshine was being delivered by taxicabs in the southwest section of Atlanta.

"What's that Lincoln Cab doing, parked with that other car?" Howard asked.

"Let's check it out!" Vic said.

When we turned into Mathewson Place, the two men standing by the vehicles immediately got into the cars. The Lincoln Cab pulled out just as we arrived. I jumped out of our car and Bernhardt and Smith took off after the cab.

"What's your name?" I asked the driver of the other car.

"Ellis," he replied. There was no whiskey on the 1954 Mercury, but Ellis said he was just about to take delivery of a case of liquor when we drove up.

In a few minutes Bernhardt and Smith returned with the Lincoln Cab and Johnny Kemp in custody. There were 42 gallons of moonshine in the cab. Kemp was charged with possession of the whiskey and the cab was seized for forfeiture. The cab company got the cab back, but all Kemp got was "time." Our timing was off on this one. If we had arrived two minutes later, we would have had a '54 Mercury and another defendant, but . . . you can't win 'em all.

* * *

We had already made several arrests and seizures of liquor cars in April when Homer Lee, the informer whom Frank Lane had prosecuted in state court instead of federal, paid off his debt.

"Albert Folley will be catchin' a load of whiskey behind his house tonight. I don't know who'll make the delivery, but it's supposed to be comin' in on a big van truck."

Folley lived three miles southwest of College Park at the end of a dead-end street, in south Fulton County. We checked out the location in the daytime, then made our plans.

At nine o'clock that night, Jesse Thrasher, Lane, and Koppe dropped Karl Strasser and me out on the back side of the Folley residence. We walked through a wooded area to an open field that had once been a pasture. From our position we could watch the rear of Folley's home and two other houses. It was pitch dark. A large van and an automobile were parked in the back yard of the last house on the street. Through binoculars, we watched three men unloading cases of half-gallon jars from the truck onto the automobile.

"Drive on in—they're loading!" I called to Thrasher on the radio.

Strasser was a fine man and a good officer, but he was big and heavy, and not fast on his feet. Karl had been a DeKalb County detective for years. He and I were the only two hired by ATF the day of my disastrous interview.

I gave Strasser the binoculars and radio and got ready to run. In about two minutes the headlights of Thrasher's car lit up the street. The men at the truck looked up. Simultaneously, Jesse turned into the wrong driveway and whipped wildly around the house next door and into the adjacent back yard.

Strasser called frantically on the radio, "You've got the wrong house! It's the next house! It's the next house!"

The three violators were beginning to get nervous. I took off running across the pasture toward the truck. Almost immediately I hit a barbed wire fence, tearing up a new pair of work pants, but fortunately getting only a few gashes in each thigh. Now all three men were running around the house.

I thought, Here we go again—a chance to catch three and they'll all get away. This thought, coupled with the adrenalin of the chase, gave me an added burst of speed. Around the corner of the house, I saw two of the men ahead of me. They split up and I went after the one on the left. After a short dash, I caught the big white man. Much to my surprise, it was Ben Hall—again. He had been caught once more by that little wild-eyed fellow.

"Where've you been, Ben?"

No answer.

I arrested Hall, then walked him back to the vehicles. Meanwhile, Albert Folley and Herman Black had been arrested by the other officers. We had caught three notorious liquor law violators all together.

We destroyed the 270 gallons of moonshine whiskey and seized both vehicles. The pain from the gashes in my thighs didn't matter now. I was happy.

The deal made several months earlier in which I had agreed to place a defendant in state court rather than federal had paid off. Now we had three persistent violators with long police records to bring before a federal judge. This was much better than a case against a small-time bootlegger.

Sometimes an investment pays off.

* * *

The work was there and I enjoyed it, as did most of the other men. We were making seizures and arrests almost daily and long hours were necessary to keep up with seizure and case reports and court attendance. I averaged working ten hours a day including Saturdays and Sundays.

One typical work day began on Saturday at midnight. I checked a large still in Gwinnett County which was not in operation, then returned to Atlanta. About four in the morning with other officers, I headed to Paulding County, where we assisted the local sheriff in raiding a large 4,000-gallon still ten miles southwest of Dallas. We arrested four men, destroyed the distillery, then transported the men to Atlanta to await a hearing before the U.S. Commissioner. The workday ended at one-thirty Sunday afternoon, after 13 hours. (This was in the years before any compensation was paid for overtime work.)

HORNET STING

On May 2, an unexpected call came from an informer who had furnished some vague information in the past.

"There's a 1950 Hudson Hornet parked behind a liquor store on Marietta Boulevard. It's loaded," he said.

The informer was close to John Elmer and this was Elmer's normal area of operation. We might get lucky tonight.

After an early supper at home with my family for a change, I met Frank Lane at six-thirty. We decided to wait until traffic thinned out and darkness fell before looking for the Hudson.

The Bolton area of northwest Atlanta was a mixture of industrial buildings and blue-collar residences. The liquor store was in a line of several buildings on Marietta Boulevard, a well-used street. We drove by and checked out the area. The buildings were one-story on the front, but in the rear they were two stories high due to the slope of the land, which dropped off sharply from the street to the rear. There was an unpaved, unlighted area for parking behind them.

An unpaved driveway led down the hill to the parking area and came back out onto Marietta Boulevard at the other end of the line of buildings.

We waited until seven-thirty and Frank drove back into the area. I dropped out on foot and walked casually down the street. When I reached the entrance to the parking area, I didn't see anyone so I turned in and strolled through the lot. As I got to the bottom of the hill, I saw a 1950 Hudson Hornet parked at the back side of the lot next to an area of weeds and brush. *There it is!*

My anticipation was growing as I approached the car. I glanced in as I walked by and could hardly believe my eyes. The Hudson Hornet is a big automobile, one of the fastest production autos made at that time. It was loaded level with the back of the front seat. Although the back area was covered with a blanket, I could see a portion of a case of 1/2 gallon jars in the front seat area. I knew we had a load!

I walked as casually as possible to the prearranged pick-up point. Frank was excited when I told him about the car. We immediately called Howard Smith and Richard Jones.

"Can you meet us? We'll need another car to cover one of the entrances to the lot."

"10-4, we're on the way," came Jones' answer.

There were one or two dim lights on the back of the line of stores, but the parking area was dark. I dropped out again and concealed myself in the bushes and weeds 30 yards from the Hudson. Richard and Howard parked where they could watch the exit on one end. Frank was watching the exit on the other. We expected a car to drop someone out to drive the Hornet. One of our cars would follow the drop-off car out of the area and seize it, while the other stopped the liquor car.

As I waited in the high weeds, I was visited by a stray alley cat foraging for food. He bolted when I moved and disappeared into the weeds. My mind was occupied with the possibility of being seen by someone connected to the liquor. We tried to keep our work cars as inconspicuous as possible, but after a month or two the word usually got out among the violators as to their description. I was hoping Elmer would show up again.

In a few minutes I heard someone walking across the gravel of the lot. A man appeared out of the darkness. At first I thought it was Lane looking for me, but I made no move. When he reached a lighted area, I knew he wasn't one of ours. The man walked nonchalantly across the lot and passed within ten feet of the Hudson as if he didn't know it was there.

He kept on going and stopped at the other end of the lot, looked around, and strolled back toward the Hudson. He went around to the driver's side and, looking around again, put his hand in his pocket.

Once he got that Hornet started, he would be hard to stop. I eased out of the undergrowth and walked at a normal pace toward him. When he saw me, he looked around like a trapped animal. I kept walking toward the car and he turned away from me.

"Hold on a minute," I said. He stopped. "What are you doing?"

"Just taking a leak," he replied.

"Okay, I'm a federal officer," I said, grabbing him firmly by his belt. "Come on in," I called on the walkie-talkie.

Frank, Richard and Howard came roaring in.

"This is John Brown. Let's see what he's got in his pocket," I said, pulling a set of car keys out of his slacks.

"I don't know where those keys came from!" he blurted out. What a surprise—they fit the Hudson perfectly!

There were 200 gallons of moonshine in the Hornet. Brown had four previous felony convictions and was a known associate of Elmer. Although he maintained his innocence that night, I arrested him again nine months later with Bob Davis and Ed Peacock. That time Brown was unloading 852 gallons of moonshine from a 1950 Ford truck on Alvin Drive in Atlanta. Now he had *five* felony convictions on his rap sheet and that arrest made *six*. He didn't know when to stop.

THE ROCKMART CAPER

Just before Christmas, Special Investigator Milton Walton, working out of Rome, asked me to try to make undercover buys of moonshine from five or six persistent retailers in the Cedartown area. One was a well-known bootlegger named "Alabama" Powell. He ran a thriving moonshine whiskey business out of his home at the rear of the Moose Club. Polk County was dry, so Powell's location was convenient for the men of Cedartown.

Alabama had been caught before and Milton had his

doubts about our being able to buy from him, but Forrest Kelley and I agreed to try. We decided the best time for our initial attempt would be on a Saturday afternoon when he would be the busiest.

On December 21, at four in the afternoon, we drove around into Alabama's back yard. The place was so busy we had trouble finding a place to park. Luckily, as we reached the back door someone was leaving and we walked in. I noticed several big locks and two hooks which had to be released from the inside to open the door.

Inside, there were several men sitting and standing around in the kitchen drinking whiskey and beer. Of course, we spoke as we entered and just joined in with the crowd.

"How much do you want?" Alabama asked.

Kelley told him, "A pint of red," so I said, "A pint of white."

There were two large containers sitting on each side of the kitchen sink filled with moonshine. Alabama used some type of coloring or flavoring to change the clear white moonshine to a dull red color. He took a dipper from the sink and filled one pint bottle with red whiskey and one with clear white whiskey. We each paid Powell two dollars and left.

This was the first time I had seen moonshine artificially colored. We had seized some one time that had been aged in a charred barrel. It was a reddish color, but this whiskey was colored just for looks and sold for the same price as the straight white whiskey.

We met Walton and Joe Burton and turned the whiskey over to them for evidence. They were both glad to get buys off Alabama.

Four months later, Kelley and I went back to Powell's home to make another buy. This time Alabama was not present, but Sam Jessee let us in and sold us two more pints of whiskey. The house was the meeting place for most of the drinkers in the Cedartown area and served the purpose of a local bar or pub. There was always a crowd of men in the kitchen, drinking and talking.

We waited another six weeks, then went back for a third buy. We usually made more than one buy on an undercover operation so the person selling whiskey couldn't claim it was an isolated event. It showed he was in the business.

This time we were greeted by Alabama himself. Sam Jessee was sitting in the back of the house next to the door with all the locks. Alabama began pouring up two pints. Walton and Joe Burton drove around the house into the back yard as previously arranged and I casually went to the back door. By the time they got to the door, I had all the locks off and the door open. When I got back to the kitchen, Powell was still pouring the whiskey. We paid with the badge. There were eight gallons of moonshine under the sink.

We made federal cases against Powell and Jessee. While destroying the whiskey, we had to turn away several potential customers. They were more than willing to leave when they saw the gold badge with "U.S." in the center.

* * *

While working on Alabama, we were also buying whiskey from several other retailers and wholesalers in Polk County. One of these cases was Milton and Vernon Pennell, who operated out of the Southern Cafe in Rockmart. Jim Mapes, an informer, made the necessary arrangements with the Pennells and on a Sunday in April, we made our first buy of four gallons from them. They insisted on meeting us on a dirt road a mile and a half east of the Rockmart school. They delivered the whiskey in a 1941 Ford.

Five weeks later, the Pennells made another delivery of four gallons of whiskey to us at the same place, this time in a 1947 Ford.

A week after that, we ordered eight gallons of whiskey and the Pennells brought it this time in a '49 Ford. We paid with the badge.

"I've got to go to the bushes!" Vernon blurted out. "I've got to go!"

"Go with him, Forrest, I'll stay with Milton and the car." I knew what the problem was. Every time I made several buys from someone and then flashed the badge on the final buy, there was a look of disbelief and shock on the violator's face. On two or three occasions, I thought they were going to pass out. Several of them immediately needed to go to the bathroom. Vernon Pennell was no exception.

After the arrest we seized the 1949 Ford, then went to their residences and seized the 1947 Ford and the 1941 Ford for violation of the Internal Revenue Laws. (Any vehicle used in the furtherance of a crime was subject to seizure. This included being used to transport materials or whiskey, or to accept payment for whiskey.) That made three automobiles seized for the price of eight gallons of whiskey. Not a bad trade for the government.

We told the Pennells' wives where and when bond could be made for their release.

It was always a good practice to keep the arrested moonshiners in the government car. If you let them go into the house, sometimes they became aggressive and either tried to get a gun or had to be forcibly returned to the car. This upset children and wives became unruly, cursing and fighting the officers. I would let the wife come out and talk to the violator, but I kept it short and outside the home.

A wild, upset woman was something I dreaded most of all. They were unpredictable and often dangerous.

Chapter XI
Elephant Wallow

In the spring of '56, we began a raw materials investigation on a large feed company in Ellijay, Georgia. It was to be a three-year battle which would eventually send several violators to the Atlanta Federal Penitentiary.

By May 7, we had accumulated enough evidence of the diversion of sugar and other raw materials to make a federal case against Bud Corham's brother and James Voit.

The following day, after trailing one of Bud's trucks into a prolific moonshining area, we seized the two-ton 1955 Ford, loaded with 15,000 pounds of sugar, 256 cases of half-gallon jars, 1,000 pounds of barley and 100 pounds of yeast. We executed a federal search warrant on Ellijay Feed and seized another truck loaded with 1,700 pounds of sugar, 300 pounds of yeast, 236 cases of 1/2-gallon jars, 2,400 pounds of malt and two gallons of beading oil. This is a type of oil used by moonshiners to add to low-proof moonshine to give the impression of high proof. It has an odor reminiscent of battery acid. The "bead" is the bubbles which form on top of whiskey when it is shaken up. These very small bubbles, or bead, are used by an experienced distiller to determine the approximate proof of the whiskey. The amount of bubbles and the duration of their presence after shaking is the determining factor. Most large distillers also used hydrometers to determine the proof.

Bud Corham was arrested later after indictment by a federal Grand Jury. This was my first encounter with Bud and although he was a persistent violator, he was always a gentleman and never gave anyone trouble. He weighed about 230 pounds, but was a gentle giant and very likeable. Our paths crossed again about six weeks later.

In July we were continuing the surveillance of the feed company. That led us to Coleman Newsom's house, two miles southeast of Canton in Cherokee County.

The house was in a rural area that was beginning to build up. Houses were spaced from one-fourth to one mile apart and the paved road in front of Newsom's house was used mostly by local people.

After being dropped off a half mile away, Merritt Scoggins, Warren Cagle and I walked through a patch of woods to a cornfield behind the house. We arrived just before dark and eased through the tall corn stalks to the edge of the field where we could watch both Newsom's back yard and the rear of an unoccupied house 100 yards away. A man was unloading one-gallon tin cans from a GMC pickup truck into a Ford automobile.

The man backed the car from Newsom's back yard across an open area to the back door of the unoccupied house. By now it was dark, but he didn't turn on the car lights. I couldn't see clearly, but could hear the loading of containers and occasionally could see the light from a flashlight. About nine-thirty, the loading was finished and the car drove out, heading away from Canton.

At ten o'clock all the lights at the house were turned off. There was no more activity until eleven-thirty. I was beginning to doze. Scoggins shook me.

"They're moving," he said.

A car drove into the back yard. A dog barked as a man got out of the car and began knocking on the back door, calling "Coleman!" In a few minutes Newsom came out.

"Shut up!" he shouted. The dog quieted down. The men got into the GMC truck and drove to the rear of the other house, then walked back to Newsom's residence.

Shortly after midnight there was absolute quiet. As we settled in for a long night, I heard a truck coming, headed towards Canton. The truck was pulling hard and heavily loaded and as it passed Newsom's house the driver blew the horn. A car started up and left the yard without lights, following the truck on the main road.

A short time later both vehicles returned, still running without lights. They drove around to the back of Newsom's house. The large truck was a Ford two-ton van. By moonlight, watching through the binoculars, I could see three men walk to the stash house and unload the remaining cases from the GMC pickup truck. They were quiet, working without lights except for an occasional flashlight.

We were as close as we could get without being seen and we had to be cautious with our movements. There was a thin line you had to walk on surveillance work. You had to get close enough to see, yet if you were seen or heard, the case would have to be made immediately. Any further evidence or arrests would be lost. Dogs were another problem. Once you got them stirred up, any movement would arouse them to persistent barking.

At one-thirty that morning the men finished unloading the truck, got in and drove next door. They parked near the big Ford truck, then loaded 100-pound bags of sugar from the Ford onto the pickup. Everything was done in complete darkness and as quietly as possible. About 15 minutes later, the pickup left the area without lights and headed away from Canton.

The big Ford truck was backed toward Newsom's barn. As they were backing the truck into the barn, I used the engine sound as a cover for sounds I might make and eased up close to the barn.

One of the men called out, "Come on back, Bud," and then, "Hold it, Bud." I thought,That's got to be Bud Corham driving the truck. I crouched against the side of the barn in high weeds.

One of the men said, "I've gotta go take a leak."

I thought, Uh-oh, I'm about to get pissed on, but luckily he walked to the other side of the barn to relieve himself. *Whew!*

They unloaded 100-pound bags of sugar into the barn for about 30 minutes. I could tell one of the men was large and heavy-set. It had to be Bud. They talked little and in low tones. Several times during the unloading, they would stop work and remain quiet, listening for any unfamiliar sounds.

I was beginning to wish they would get through and move on, so I could get back to a safer place. The only time I could move at all was when a car passed on the highway. At two forty-five, the GMC truck turned into the driveway. The lights went out just before they hit my hiding place. The GMC was backed alongside the Ford and more 100-pound bags of sugar were loaded from the Ford onto the pickup. They finished unloading in about 15 minutes and when the big Ford truck left, we decided to get out before daylight.

When Gastley picked us up, he asked, "How did it go?"

"Great!" was Scoggins' reply.

We filled Henry in on what we had seen. He was as elated as we were.

Henry had been assigned a jacketed case to work on the feed company and Bud Corham, so he was more or less in charge of the surveillance. ATF investigators worked under loose supervision. As long as you made good cases and produced, you were left alone. In your assigned area of operation you were free to make necessary decisions in making an arrest or seizure. It was one of the big advantages we had over other federal law enforcement agents.

The type of supervision we had, from top to bottom, made the work a joy. All our supervisors in Criminal Enforcement, from the Resident Agent in Charge to the Assistant Regional Director, started out the way I did, working as investigators in the field. They knew the advantages of being able to make decisions on the spot without having to call a supervisor. Agents knew that even if we made an honest mistake, we had every assurance that ATF supervisors would back us 100 percent. This was demonstrated to me in numerous ways and I appreciated it. We were free to operate almost without constraints except for the normal protection given to citizens by the Constitution. We knew these restrictions to law enforcement and were careful to stay within the guidelines in order to make cases that would stand up in court. Of course, sometimes the guidelines had to be stretched!

Henry called a meeting with Duff Floyd, Warren Cagle, Merritt Scoggins, Glen Wojahn, Joe Burton and me. As was the normal practice, all of us had input into the planning. After we reported what we had observed on that first night, it was decided to continue the Newsom surveillance. We would drop agents off at intersections on the main road to conceal themselves and try to determine where the GMC truck was going in the early-morning hours. We all knew that these large amounts of sugar had to be going to a moonshine distillery close by.

Three nights later, Cagle, Wojahn and I dropped out just after dark and walked back to the Newsom residence. There was a small clump of young trees and bushes on one side of the cornfield that we used as our main observation point. We could see both houses and move in either direction if need be. We were also far enough away that we could move around without being heard.

Wojahn left Cagle and me and circled well around through the woods to a location across the road where he could see both driveways. Other officers were dropped off at the next two intersections on the main road in the direction in which the GMC had left with the loads of sugar.

About nine o'clock the GMC pickup truck arrived from the direction of the suspected distillery location. It appeared to be heavily loaded and was parked in back of Newsom's house for 20 minutes. Then it was backed down to the stash house and unloaded, again without lights.

At ten o'clock, the unloading was completed and the pickup was driven back to Newsom's yard and parked. A few hours later it was loaded with sugar and left the area. The violators were using this truck to bring moonshine from the still to the stash house. The whiskey would be unloaded into the house and the truck reloaded with sugar and other materials and driven back to the distillery. This method of operation was common at large distilleries. The stash house was used as a transfer point for the whiskey. Trip cars were loaded from the stash house and the whiskey transported to Atlanta or some other large market for moonshine. Thus, the man driving the trip vehicle never knew where the distillery was. In some operations he was met at a service station or other meeting place and his vehicle driven by someone else to the stash house so that he didn't even know the location of the stash.

I was tied up for several days in court and on other investigations, but early in the evening of July 19, Scoggins and I dropped out again to take up the observation point behind Newsom's house.

During our absence, other officers had been using the observation point. I remarked to Scoggins, "Man, this place looks like an elephant wallow." We had all been lying in a small area under the bushes and the ground was packed down from four nights of use. If any one of the violators had walked back there they would have immediately become suspicious.

These things couldn't be helped—we had to get in close and we were going to leave some sign inadvertently. Some of our investigators were smokers, but they were usually aware of the light created by a cigarette in total darkness. They would shield the cigarette and then cover the butt with dirt when they were finished with a smoke. Even so, we were fortunate not to be discovered.

After we had been there an hour and a half, a car drove into Newsom's yard. Cans were unloaded onto his back porch. The other officers had advised us that they had located the distillery and would probably raid it sometime that night. We were to watch the stash house and make sure no whiskey left.

The only other activity occurred shortly after midnight when a 1955 Mercury sport coupe drove into Newsom's back yard and parked. I heard another vehicle being started at the front of the house, but I couldn't see it. The man driving the Mercury left in the other vehicle and was gone about an hour. He returned at one-thirty and left in the Mercury. It was all I could do to keep from rushing in and arresting everyone in sight and seizing the Mercury. Government vehicles were hard to come by, especially new red-and-cream sport coupes.

A couple of hours later, Gastley called. "We just hit the still—we'll be there in ten minutes." Scoggins, Cagle and I moved closer to the stash house and by the time Gastley and Floyd arrived, we were in the back yard.

In the stash house we found 756 gallons of whiskey. Next door we found 125 one-gallon tin cans on the back porch and arrested Coleman Newsom and Gordon Smith.

Driving to the distillery, Henry commented, "This will just about tie Bud up."

At the still site was the GMC pickup truck we had seen being loaded with sugar and jars at Newsom's. They were using a six-hp commercial steam boiler, a 400-gallon steel still, two radiator condensers, thirty 220-gallon barrel fermenters and had over 3,500 gallons of fermented mash. There were also 213 gallons of moonshine and 1,600 pounds of sugar. It was a nice outfit.

Sometime later, we got a federal warrant for the two-ton 1955 Ford truck that was used to supply the distillery. Floyd, Cagle, Scoggins and I seized the truck at Ellijay Feed Company.

This turned out to be a highly involved conspiracy case written by Gastley and helped give me the training and experience I would need in later years. Gastley and Scoggins became my close friends and contributed more than they will ever know to my self-confidence and education in making complicated conspiracy cases.

Chapter XII
Patience and Stealth

I took annual leave the second week of August. It was time for Joe and Charles to go back to school and we hadn't spent much time together as a family during the summer. We drove to Panama City, Florida and rented a small apartment over a grocery store on the beach. The boys had a great time with the sand crabs and the water. Dot, who always loved the ocean, enjoyed the chance to get away and be together. I did too, but by the end of the week I was ready to go back to work.

"Can't wait to get back, can you?" Dot commented as we packed up to go home.

I was fortunate to train and work with some of the legendary revenue agents while they were still in the field. "Bub" Kay, stationed in Cornelia, was known in northeast Georgia not only as a fair man, but also as a true humanitarian who would buy toys and fruit using his own money and deliver them during the Christmas season to needy children. Sometimes, he was the only Santa Claus these poor mountain children ever knew. When the citizens of Cornelia found out about Bub's generosity, they, too, began to contribute to the effort, providing a little happiness to these disadvantaged children.

Another legend was Duff Floyd. His career with ATF began in 1929 and spanned 35 years as a field investigator. Duff loved the woods. He worked out of Jasper, one of the most prolific moonshine areas in the United States, for most of his career. Gilmer and Dawson counties were hotbeds of activity for liquor law violators and remained so into the '70's.

* * *

On Monday, with the vacation over, I reported back to work and checked in with Frank Clark. Good government cars were still scarce and the one I was using had "had it." Clark was aware of its condition and handed me the keys to the 1954 Chevrolet assigned to Jimmy Causey. Jimmy had been assigned this car when it was one of only three new cars allocated to Georgia. Causey was a particular man and was protective of the car.

On the previous Friday afternoon, just before Causey was to go on annual leave, he went into Clark's office and told him he would be on leave for the next two weeks.

"The government car is parked at the Cone Street Garage," Jimmy reported.

Clark replied, "Okay, Jimmy, give me the keys in case someone else needs to use the car."

"But, Mr. Clark, I don't want anyone else using my car!" Jimmy whined.

"I don't blame you, Jimmy, I don't want anyone using my car, either—now give me the damn keys to the government car!" Clark demanded tersely. He got the keys and that's how I got the keys.

"Duff Floyd needs some help raiding a big still near Blairsville. Take Jim Ballard and Richard Jones and stay as long as they need you." Clark didn't mince words.

I caught up with my paperwork and we piled into the Chevy and headed to Blairsville. In those days there were no expressways anywhere near Blairsville. The road was a typical two lane highway into the lower edge of the Appalachian Range and I was having the time of my life, squalling the tires of Jimmy's car around the sharp curves. We arrived about one in the afternoon. Floyd and State Agent Johnny Nelson briefed us and we drove into the mountains five miles southeast of Dial. We dropped out and walked to the still area. It was located on the back side of a mountain. The workway was rough and rocky and led up a steep slope alongside a small mountain stream.

When we arrived, Duff slipped in closer and determined that the operators had left for the day. We settled down 100 yards from the distillery, ate our usual still rations—Vienna sausage, crackers, pork & beans and a Coke—and began our wait. In the mountains in late summer it's hot during the day, but at night it gets uncomfortably cool.

In the wee hours of the morning Warren Cagle woke me.

"We heard somebody come in."

We got ourselves in gear. Floyd, Cagle, Nelson and Ballard had to work their way around to the upper side of the still while Jones and I moved in closer on the lower side, covering the workway area. As I got near the still, I could hear someone cutting wood. Coke has to be started with wood. Then it will burn on its own, putting out an intense heat but no smoke. There was a faint light at the still site.

Three hours later, I heard a truck crank up at the still. I moved closer to the workway and waited, thinking that the other officers, who had the prime assignment of making the initial move, surely wouldn't let a vehicle leave the still. I was wrong. They either weren't in position to raid or had decided to wait and see what would happen next. As the truck passed me, I maintained my position as planned. As the sound of the truck faded, I thought, We just lost a vehicle and a defendant.

In a little while, more sounds came from the still site. I moved in and found that two moonshiners, Everett Wilson and Robert Kirby, had been arrested by the other officers. Wilson said that he had fired up the still around four o'clock. I asked Floyd about the truck that left earlier.

"It'll be back in," he said confidently. I didn't think so, but I wasn't about to argue with the veteran. Jones and I went back to our position along the workway and waited.

Forty-five minutes later, my heart jumped as I heard the truck coming back up the workway. Floyd, the experienced old veteran, had outguessed them again! The truck was straining under a heavy load over the rocky terrain. I waited until it was past me, then jumped into the workway and ran alongside. Richard did the same thing on the other side. I jumped onto the running board on the driver's side at about the same instant that Richard jumped onto the passenger side.

The driver, scared and surprised, put the accelerator to the floor. The truck leaped forward, veering to the right at the same time. Richard was hanging on that side of the truck and was dragged through the tall saplings and brush growing along the workway. I struggled to get hold of the driver without losing my grip on the truck. Richard finally had to let go, but the other officers heard the commotion and ran in our direction from the distillery. I had a firm grip on the driver's throat with one hand. My other arm was locked around an outside mirror on the door of the truck.

When the driver, later identified as Ted Reid, saw that he couldn't get away, he suddenly slammed on the brakes, almost throwing me off. The other officers thought Jones had been seriously injured.

"Get that son of a bitch," someone shouted. They exerted a great deal of physical force in dragging Reid out of the truck, but luckily for Reid, Jones was not hurt seriously.

There were 1,400 pounds of sugar, 25 cases of half-gallon fruit jars, 100 pounds of rye meal and 100 pounds of barley malt on the truck.

We followed the workway back down the hill to Reid's home and found more materials stored in his chicken house. By following a trail from the house across Noontoetla Creek along the edge of a corn field, we found 500 gallons of moonshine in two caches in the edge of the woods.

At the distillery was an additional 16 gallons, making a total of 516 gallons of liquor and 4,600 gallons of mash. The 3/4 ton truck was also seized. All three defendants later pled guilty in federal court.

Duff Floyd had given me a lesson in patience!!

* * *

My wife, Dot, finally accepted the fact that my career would involve 12 to 14 hour work days and most weekends. It was not uncommon for me to come home after two or three days on surveillance, having raided a large distillery, smelling strongly of moonshine and mash. Anyone who is familiar with the smell of a pigpen would recognize these odors.

She would just sigh and shake her head at the sight of me. I would try to console her by saying that I had to work these long hours to get ahead—that one day I would slow down. I never did. Many times I would get cleaned up, have a good home-cooked meal and tell her I had to go back to work at three o'clock the next morning. I could see disappointment in her eyes, but she never complained and would be up at 2:30 preparing my breakfast. Although she never worked at a job outside the home, she was a full-time mother and wife and put everything into her family. I didn't know how much to appreciate it then, but I do now and I think Joe and Charles appreciate her more as they grow older. They should.

The last day of January of '57, I encountered another pistol-toting violator at a still. Jim Ballard and I had information that a distillery would operate that night two miles west of Williamson in Pike County. Ballard, Merritt Scoggins and I arrived in the area shortly after dark. We hid our vehicle a mile from the still in the remote rural area. This was farm land, with houses spaced about a half-mile to a mile apart. It was a dark, quiet night. As we walked along an unpaved public road, we approached an old farm house.

We proceeded as quietly as we could, trying not to arouse any dogs. We were just beginning to relax as we passed a small barn close to the road when "Hawwww—EEEEE—Hawww!" a mule we hadn't noticed let go with a loud bray. Momentarily startled, we kept walking, only at a faster pace. Moonshiners are well aware that a mule is one of the best watchdogs around. His ears will point toward anything unusual in the area and he *will* bray. That mule scared the starch out of us!

In spite of the mule, we managed to get to the still area without being detected and split up. Ballard went into the woods and circled the distillery, waiting for Scoggins and me to go in by the workway and flush.

"We'll give you 20 minutes," I whispered to Ballard.

Twenty minutes later, Scoggins and I started down the dirt trail workway that ran alongside the woods to the distillery.

Creeping forward through the inky darkness, I saw a faint glow up ahead. I could hear the muted sound of a gasoline burner and knew that the tiny glow I had seen momentarily was not at the still site.

I froze. Scoggins also stopped, not making a sound. There it was again: the same glow from the same spot. I realized it was the glow of a cigarette. Crouching, Scoggins and I eased up to the man.

"Federal officers. You're under arrest," I whispered in his ear. "What's your name?"

"John Bates."

I searched him and found a .380 automatic Colt pistol in one pocket and a half-pint of moonshine in the other.

"Don't make a sound," I told Bates as I slid the automatic into my pocket. Scoggins took the prisoner and we began to move toward the still site. About 25 yards from the still, we found a 1917 Ford loaded with one-gallon jugs and five-gallon gasoline cans.

"Scoggins, you stay with Bates and the car. I'll go in," I whispered. I began to creep toward the distillery. By the dull light of the gasoline burner I could see two men in the still yard. Jack Giles was sitting on a 50-gallon pressure tank used to fuel the burner and the other man was pouring whiskey from the catch container into a barrel.

They spoke in low tones. Knowing that Ballard was somewhere on the other side of the distillery, I sprang forward and caught the man on the tank. The man pouring the whiskey went berserk!

"Goddam," he screamed, "goddam!" He threw the bucket into the air and fell over backwards into the creek. Quickly scrambling to his feet, he began plunging wildly down the stream.

"He's coming toward you, Jim!" I shouted, hoping to divert his flight enough to give Ballard time to intercept him. My shouts seemed to excite him even more and he climbed out of the creek and started plowing through thick bamboo briars and dense undergrowth. I could hear him and Ballard thrashing around in the swampy area below the still site.

After 15 minutes, Ballard straggled back to the distillery. The man had gotten away, but I could tell by Jim's torn clothes and skin that the violator was probably also pretty well cut up. Maybe he would think twice before operating another still. If he wasn't scared, he sure put on a good act!

STEALTH IS A MUST

Shortly after that experience, Henry County Deputy Hiram Cook called.

"Charley, can you meet me and Son Roland tonight? I've got information that there's a still about four miles south of McDonough in Henry County. It's a night operation and is supposed to run tonight," he said.

Scoggins and I met Son and Hiram and about nine o'clock we walked into the woods near the distillery. This was all rural farm land, sparsely settled. We could hear gasoline burners and knew the still was in operation. Leaving the other officers, Hiram and I circled around the site until we hit the workway.

A lot of officers hated to raid at night, but I really loved it. You could usually get in close without being seen, but you had to be extremely careful in your movements. Stealth was the secret.

We slipped down the workway and found a 1951 International truck parked near the still.

"Look out!" someone yelled loudly from the woods nearby. I took off toward the sound and Hiram ran toward the still. As I plunged through the dark woods, I could hear someone crashing through the brush ahead of me. I followed the sounds of breaking tree limbs and brush, and fell over my quarry. I later learned he was Hanson Parks.

"Federal officer, you're under arrest."

"Yes, sir, boss," was his only comment, leading me to believe he had served time before. When I took him back to the still, Hiram had Willie Curtis in custody. Both 2,000-gallon stills were fired up and running whiskey.

Parks and Curtis said they had arrived at the still site at first dark and had been working at the distillery since then.

This was one of many still raids I made with Cook, who later was elected Sheriff of Henry County and served for many years. Hiram became a close friend and associate. He was an old-fashioned sheriff who helped those who needed help. He would buy food for needy families with money out of his own pocket, yet he had the respect of criminals because he demanded it. Being a rural county sheriff is a tough job. They have to be firm, yet compassionate when appropriate. They're called on at all hours for almost every problem that arises in the county and they are underpaid. It's a thankless job being a good sheriff, but Hiram was a good one.

Chapter XIII
Sons of Bitches, They Called Us

That spring, we began to concentrate on all the known raw materials outlets in the Southeast, taking a different approach to suppressing the manufacture of moonshine. The theory was that if the large illicit distillers couldn't get sugar, containers and other essential materials in large quantities, they would gradually be squeezed out of moonshining. This proved to be an effective tool.

Each state had a raw materials coordinator who operated under the direction of the regional raw materials coordinator, Henry Gastley. Merritt Scoggins was RM coordinator for Georgia and Bill Parker, Doug Denney, Karl Strasser, Jim Evans and I were assigned primary duties of raw materials work. The RM duties sometimes took us into other states. We were not barred from other enforcement work and assisted in still raids at every opportunity.

Our first order of business was to contact every wholesale sugar outlet in our area, asking that they cooperate with the government in the effort. We explained why we needed their cooperation in dealing with the tremendous tax fraud involved in the production of nontaxpaid whiskey. It was estimated that in 1956 and 1957 over 35,000 gallons of moonshine a week were being sold in Atlanta alone. This would amount to a federal tax fraud of $367,500 per week. In a year's time, that's over 1 1/2 million gallons and close to $5.5 million tax fraud for just the Atlanta area! When this is multiplied by the seven Southeastern states, the amount is mind-boggling, even considering the fact that more moonshine was consumed in Atlanta than any other city in the country.

After explaining the program, we would leave written materials with the wholesalers and if we received no indication that the company was diverting sugar or other materials to suspected liquor law violators, we would express our appreciation and concentrate on those who *were* diverting these materials.

On one occasion, I had made several undercover buys from a large wholesale grocer.

"Listen, I don't want my license number reported to the government," I commented to the grocer while loading sugar and yeast on an old pickup truck. "I've got enough trouble already trying to make whiskey."

The grocer charged an extra $1.00 per bag and agreed not to report my license number. During the trial of this individual, the defense attorney cross-examined me.

"Mr Weems, you've testified as to what you said and what the defendant said, in order to prove my client intended that this material be used to make whiskey! What *did you intend* to do with the sugar?"

"Retain it as evidence," I replied.

"You didn't intend to make whiskey with it?"

"No, sir."

"Then how can you imply that my client intended it for the manufacture of moonshine? This sugar was never intended to be used to make whiskey—is that right?"

With that, the U.S. Attorney objected: "Mr. Weems is not on trial. The defendant, by his actions and statements *thought* that the materials were to be used to make liquor and it was his intent, not the agent's, that has to be proven."

The judge agreed and thus we cleared one more legal hurdle in prosecuting the people who were selling to illegitimate sources and helping to perpetuate the moonshine business.

After several undercover purchases of materials on different dates to establish that this was not an isolated instance, we arrested the store owner or wholesaler and charged him with failure to report (a misdemeanor) or making a false report to the government (a felony.)

The procedure was effective and after one or two wholesalers were arrested, the word got out. We usually had their full cooperation thereafter. The large distillers (major violators) were forced to pay more for sugar and began hauling it by tractor-trailer from the refineries in Savannah. In Georgia alone, there were 56 major violators on the government's Major Liquor Law Violator list. To qualify for this dubious distinction, they produced 500 to 7,000 gallons of illicit whiskey a week. In some cases, the U.S. government was losing $73,500 per week, or over three and one-half million dollars per year ($3,822,000) for only one major violator's organization. When this figure is added to the production of more than 50 other major violators and the hundreds of other small distilleries in Georgia, the tax loss to the federal and state governments is staggering. This is a fact that is lost to many people, who think of Snuffy Smith in the comic strips as a typical moonshiner. This may be the case in some areas of the South, but it is certainly not indicative of the type of law violator ATF investigators concentrated on. Although investigators worked on small distilleries when they were reported to us, they concentrated on the large producer.

With the cooperation of Dixie Crystals, we cut off the supply of sugar from Savannah. The big operators began bringing in tractor-trailer loads from several refineries in New Orleans. The increased cost cut down on their profits. We made several seizures of tractor trailers loaded with sugar in the vicinity of large illicit distilleries.

We were putting a lot of pressure on large-scale producers of moonshine who required tons of sugar to keep their distilleries operating. The price of sugar from outlets who either were not reporting or were making false reports to the government, went up substantially. This also took some of the profit out of the illegal distiller's pocket and in some cases increased the cost of moonshine to the retailer and consumer, thus reducing the bootlegging population.

Being assigned to work raw materials gave me the opportunity to assist investigators all over the Southeast and in every section of the country. I thoroughly enjoyed these associations and came to respect and appreciate the abilities of my fellow investigators. Most were the same type men I had been associated with in the paratroopers—adventurous types who loved their jobs and would make any sacrifice necessary to perform their duties. They were a rugged bunch, much different from the typical FBI agent. They dressed as outdoorsmen with green kangaroo boots, corduroy or twill work pants and shirt and with a .38-caliber pistol under the seat of the government car except when on a raid or working transportation. The badge and credentials were usually in a shirt pocket.

I began wearing my badge on still raids and when arrests were expected after listening to a case in federal court in which the violators had resisted arrest. One of the violators was injured in the melee that followed and claimed he didn't know who the officers were because they weren't wearing badges. This defense didn't work, but I decided then and there not to leave any avenue open to any criminal I had to subdue during an arrest.

Raw materials work was quite different. One day I would be wearing a three-piece suit, contacting presidents and owners of large wholesale grocery outlets or testifying in federal court. The next day I would be dressed in rough work clothes, needing a shave and attempting to make undercover buys from a wholesale sugar outlet in another state. It was time-consuming work with little time left for anything else.

* * *

There were several large dealers who specialized in furnishing moonshiners all the materials and equipment needed to set up an illicit distillery. They made huge profits by being a one-stop market for distillery supplies.

One of these suppliers was "Punk" Word. He ran a business in Haralson County at the Georgia-Alabama line on U.S. Highway 78. We had previously contacted Word and asked that he refrain from selling these materials to known liquor law violators and had placed him under demand to report sales of sugar in excess of 50 pounds to any one individual.

Later, Jim West and Charley Hugueley, posing as moonshiners, approached Word.

"Can you furnish us everything we need to set up a ten-sack (1,000-gallon) ground hog?" Jim asked.

"I'll have everything ready tomorrow night," Word said confidently.

The following evening, West and Hugueley bought a large sheet of aluminum, a gasoline burner, cap barrel, doubler barrel, pressure tank, metal pipes and elbows, an air pump (to pump up the pressure tank) and ten 100-pound bags of sugar. Word was happy, and we were *really* happy.

Jim and Charley made a second buy from Word of 12 cases of half-gallon jars and 30 one-gallon paraffined cans. This type of can was used almost exclusively in West Georgia for illicit whiskey containers. In fact, they were not used for anything else.

"The damn federal men are really cracking down on us about sugar," Word volunteered.

"Yeah, it's getting so a man can't make an honest living making liquor these days. We got stopped the other night, but we didn't have anything," West added.

Having established intent on Word's part, we secured a search warrant for his business.

During the same period, West was buying materials from Clark Neal, who had a large warehouse located a half mile west of Tallapoosa in Haralson County. Neal had been successful in supplying the numerous large illicit distilleries in the West Georgia area. In those days, Haralson and several adjoining counties in Georgia and the Anniston, Alabama area were producing tremendous amounts of moonshine whiskey. Most of it was being sold in Atlanta and surrounding areas. It was a hotbed of distilling activity and Neal was making his money furnishing the supplies for the illegal stills.

Again, we had to establish Neal's intent to violate the law. West and Hugueley contacted Neal in the same way as Word. After they told him they were setting up a ten-sack still, he sold them aluminum, barrels, burner, pipes, pumps, pressure tank, a hydrometer to test the proof of the whiskey, a filter bag and a half pint of beading oil. On the second buy, they bought paraffined cans and half-gallon jars.

Then federal search warrants were issued for Neal's and Word's businesses. Merritt Scoggins and Henry Gastley assembled a group of investigators who hit the two places at the same time. We were astounded at the amount of materials found at the two locations.

In addition to hundreds of cases of half-gallon jars, whiskey barrels, gasoline burners and all the other materials needed to build a still, Neal had 350 pounds of dry yeast and several gallons of beading oil. All the suspect items were seized and we had to stay in the warehouse with the materials for three weeks. The federal court forfeited the materials and we were able to dispose of them. We took turns living in the warehouse and inventorying the materials.

At the same time these seizures and arrests were made, we were seizing materials and distilling supplies from several other large suppliers in Atlanta and Griffin from whom we had made similar buys.

These seizures and arrests were given a great deal of publicity and made life more difficult for the illicit distiller. Our raw materials program was off with a flourish. Everyone who participated was proud of our initial success.

For several weeks, we had an enormous amount of work to do, preparing statements, inventorying materials and contacting every wholesale grocery supply outlet in the Southeast requesting cooperation in this effort. We were also receiving large numbers of reports from wholesale sugar dealers that had to be studied for suspicious sales.

One such sale appeared on the reports of a large sugar wholesaler in Americus. Several thousand pounds of sugar were sold to a P. C. Bottling Company on two different occasions. Investigator Bill Parker, a Phi Beta Kappa graduate of the University of Florida, was working with me in South Georgia. We were in the process of contacting more than 100 different wholesale grocers when we noticed this particular sale.

We asked local officers in Americus about P. C. Bottling Company. They said it was in a run-down section of the city. We found the address. The building contained some soft drink bottling equipment and a large number of bottles, but it obviously had not been used as a bottling facility in years. There was trash everywhere and the contents of the building were scattered and covered with dust.

The owner of P. C. Bottling, a "Buck" Williams, lived in a small seedy hotel. He apparently carried on his "business" from this location. The hotel clerk was evasive when asked about Buck, but after we identified ourselves as federal officers, he said hesitantly, "Room 314." We started toward the elevator and out of the corner of my eye I saw the clerk go to the hotel switchboard. Buck didn't answer our knock. We decided to try again at a later date.

This was my first opportunity to work with Bill Parker. During the next year, working together on the raw materials program, we became close friends. Bill is a fine man, devoted to his wife and children. He later left ATF and transferred to the U.S. Department of Agriculture as an investigator, as did Richard Jones and several others. Both Parker and Jones advanced rapidly to supervisory positions. ATF lost several outstanding investigators to other federal agencies due to our financial restrictions and one supervisor in particular. Merritt Scoggins is a prime example. After he transferred to the Small Business Administration, he rose to the number two position in SBA in the Southeast region. Scoggins is one of the most capable, brilliant men who ever worked for ATF, but he left because of a supervisor who was a problem.

Parker and I worked through that summer, contacting dealers, making undercover buys and serving demand letters on people who were apparently not going to cooperate in the RM program. Not all these contacts were pleasant. Quite often the man being required to make reports of all large sales of sugar, would become angry and refuse to sign the letters, threatening to call his congressman or his friend the governor.

About a month after the initial investigation of Buck Williams and P. C. Bottling, Doug Denney and I were in Americus. We found that P. C. Bottling Company was still purchasing large amounts of sugar and decided to pay Buck another visit. This time we didn't ask the hotel clerk the room number. We walked up the stairs directly to his room and knocked.

Someone called out, "Just a minute."

The door opened a little and when I could see a portion of a man's face, I showed him my badge and said, "Federal officers, we want to talk to you."

He pushed the door shut, took off the night latch and let us in. It was about ten-thirty in the morning and Buck was in the process of preparing his breakfast. The room was piled high with clothes, papers and boxes of various sizes. He started moving things around to try to find us a place to sit. It was impossible. He had a two-eyed electric hot plate next to a small sink and dirty cooking utensils were piled on a table, along with a stack of dirty dishes. There was a small refrigerator on one side of the room and an unmade bed on the other. It was not what you would expect of a soft drink bottler's home and business office.

We apologized for interrupting his breakfast and then got down to the business at hand.

"Just where is your bottling plant located?" I asked, thinking that maybe he had another location and a legitimate operation.

He gave us the same address as the abandoned plant location.

"Is it in operation now?" Doug asked.

Sensing that we knew more than we had disclosed, Buck said, "Well, no, but I intend to begin operation soon."

We explained the raw materials program and although we knew Buck was anything but a legitimate businessman, we asked his cooperation in not diverting this sugar to moonshiners. Doug reinforced this by saying, "You could be sent to the penitentiary."

That got Buck's attention and after that, he was cooperative. "I probably won't have any use for more sugar. I appreciate your coming by to see me," he said apologetically.

As we were leaving, I noticed a stick of butter lying on the floor in its wax wrapper. The end had apparently been stepped on and butter was oozing out the other end. I called this to Buck's attention. He immediately scooped it up.

"I'm sorry Doug stepped on your butter!" I said with a grin.

From that day until Doug was killed in a head-on collision with a moonshiner's son in Dawson County, Doug and I always accused each other of stepping on Buck's butter. Doug was a good friend. I miss him.

We had no more reports of Buck buying sugar.

* * *

Jim West and I later worked undercover in North Carolina. We attempted buys from over 118 different outlets in 100 different cities and towns from the east coast to the Smoky Mountains on the western border and made cases against 12 individuals. This gave us an indication that the raw materials program was generally accepted by the legitimate grocers. After the arrests and ensuing publicity about the cases, we had fewer problems with so-called legitimate businesses diverting materials to whiskey makers. It always angered me to see pillars of the community violate the law and use the excuse, "if I don't sell to them, someone else will."

West was as good as anyone at working undercover. Although his technique was different from Red Martin's, he could convince anyone of almost anything. He was never at a loss for words. When a large wholesale grocer on the coast of North Carolina accused him of being a federal officer, Jim left the man so confused that when we returned the next day he sold us sugar.

Jim is also a master at remembering names and license numbers. He kept few notes as to times and places, but could always come up with the proper answers. Like so many others, Jim became my close friend and colleague, despite the fact that I could outrun him in a footrace.

Jim had been assigned to work raw materials when he, Scoggins and I were returning to the Atlanta area from Augusta. Jim was new to the area, having been a city police officer in Chattanooga, Tennessee and an ATF agent for a short time in North Carolina. Merritt was driving. Jim was up front and I was in the back seat. Jim boasted about being on the track and football teams at a high school outside Chattanooga. He made several comments about how fast he was.

When agents got together, the conversation often turned into a discussion of who was the fastest. Scoggins, having seen me in action and hearing from others that I could run, spoke up. "I'll bet Charley can outrun you!"

Jim jumped at this. "How much? Five dollars—ten dollars?"

"Well, I'll bet you a dollar, just to make it sporting," said Scoggins.

"What about you, Charley, will you bet?" West asked.

I had kept quiet up until then, but when West challenged me, I said, "Okay, a dollar."

All the way to the GSA storage warehouse, West continued to badger us, wanting to raise the bet.

When we arrived, he insisted that the race be 100 yards. I agreed. Scoggins paced it off, making a mark on the ground on both ends. He took up a position at the finish line. West and I lined up. Jim took a sprinter's stance, which I didn't know anything about. I had attended Jonesboro High School in the 40's, when the only sport we had in school was basketball. There were eight players on the squad and the only time one of the three substitutes played was when someone fouled out. We had to give the sub our uniform top so he would have a number. There were only five complete uniforms left over from previous years. We started each season with two new basketballs. They had to last all season. At that time schools in rural areas had a hard time paying teachers and there was almost no money for sports. The only schools that had track, baseball and football teams were in rich areas, not Clayton County.

I stood bent over and got ready for Scoggins to drop his arm as the go signal. When he did, I was a little surprised that Jim, although of stocky build, was out in front of me by about a step. I gave it all I had. After 50 yards, I got even and edged ahead. About ten yards from the finish, I pulled ahead by two steps. All of a sudden, I heard an unusual noise behind me. Looking back as I crossed the finish line, I saw Jim rolling over and over in a pile of dust. He had fallen at top speed, hitting the rough parking area with such force that he tore his shirt and ripped the knees of his pants. Scoggins and I both stifled our laughter.

"Are you all right?" we asked.

Jim grumbled, handing both Scoggins and me a dollar and heading for the car. Neither Scoggins nor I ever mentioned the race to anyone else, and I know Jim didn't!

* * *

I walked into the office of one of the largest wholesale grocers in south Georgia and placed handcuffs on the owner early in 1958.

On three different occasions, I had contacted L.V. Black in an undercover role, posing as a bootlegger and bought large amounts of sugar and other materials. Black was under a letter of demand to make reports of all such sales and on two occasions he failed to make reports. On another he made a false report, which was a felony.

The thing that made this arrest so satisfying for me was that on every contact, Black had bragged about how stupid the ATF officers were and how he had found ways to violate the law. He suggested ways we could circumvent the law and stated that he was a member of the governor's staff and did a lot of business with the state.

Black's feathers wilted and he turned pale when I walked in wearing a suit and showed him the gold badge. All the bravado and self-importance melted away as we took him to the government car for transportation to our office in Dublin. There he was fingerprinted and photographed and later released under bond by a U.S. commissioner. He didn't spend any time in jail, but the news of his arrest and conviction was in all the local—and even the Atlanta—newspapers. This was the thing that he had worried about the most. That kind of publicity was devastating to the so-called upright citizen.

The arrest of someone who thinks he has too much power and too many connections to be caught does much to deter others who think they are above the law and are tempted to make that extra dollar.

After this arrest in Metter, Parker composed a poem based on our work as RM investigators:

"From Dublin to Metter

They knew our fame.

Sons of bitches they called us,

Raw Materials was our name!"

Chapter XIV
Sugar in the Morning

It was early autumn and I was feeling good one morning when Henry Gastley called me to the Regional Office. He handed me the cardboard top from a carton of cigarettes. On it was written "Howard Champion" and a telephone number. A confidential informant had been at the Farmers Market in Gainesville and was told that this man could furnish all the sugar and materials needed to make liquor to anyone who was willing to pay.

A lot of people who get into crime go through most of their lives without doing anything more illegal than parking overtime or running a stop sign. Then something comes along that looks like a sure thing—little risk and a large payoff—so they take a chance. If they get by with it, they keep on and usually end up in larger and more violent criminal activity with disastrous results. Sometimes it's better to get caught on the first attempt. A good lesson is learned with no great loss. This was what happened to Champion, a middle-aged man who owned his own bakery, had never been involved in criminal activity, and saw a chance to make a lot of money fast.

"Call him up and see what he says. It may be something and it might not," said Henry. Before calling, I looked up the telephone number in the Atlanta directory and found that it was the number of the Four-Star Bakery on Euclid Avenue. Henry and I agreed that anyone having a bakery would have access to large amounts of sugar, barley malt, rye meal and yeast, all ingredients used to make moonshine.

I discussed the proposed buy with Bill Crewe, the legal counsel for ATF, and Merritt Scoggins. We agreed that I should make the initial contact the following day, posing as a moonshiner.

Crewe warned me: "Since this is apparently a legitimate business and Champion has no criminal record, we'll have to give him plenty of information about our intent to make whiskey from these materials. You'll have to do it without arousing his suspicion."

I went into an adjoining office so that there wouldn't be any background noise such as typewriters or other office sounds, and called the number.

"Four-Star Bakery" came the answer.

"Is Mr. Champion there?"

"This is Champion," he replied.

I immediately began my role as a law violator. "I got your name and number from a friend in Gainesville."

"What do you need?" he asked.

I said, "Sugar."

"I can get you sugar. How much do you need?"

"Twenty bags," I replied, meaning 2,000 pounds.

"I understand. I get my sugar from Railroad Salvage and Crystal Sugar here in town."

"I don't want this reported to anyone," I broke in.

Champion quickly explained, "Crystal Sugar will have to make a report but it will be reported as sold to Four-Star Bakery. The government will have no reason to suspect anything. If I'm questioned, I'll say I used it in the bakery. If you want it delivered at night, I can do that too. I don't want to know your name and won't report your license tag number."

With that, I knew that Champion fully intended to violate the law by supplying moonshiners with materials to make whiskey and that even if he had just begun, he would be a good source.

Keeping Crewe's advice in mind, I told Champion I would come by the next morning and get with him on the amounts and prices.

The next day, I dressed in work boots, worn corduroy pants and an old Army field jacket and drove a seized 1953 Olds liquor car to the Four-Star Bakery. The Olds had heavy helper springs under the back and I had thrown an old Army blanket in the rear seat the way most liquor transporters covered their loads of whiskey. I was unshaven and certainly looked the part of a moonshiner.

I parked out front so Champion would be sure to see the car on which I had placed Dawson County license plates.

I walked into the bakery. One customer at the counter was being waited on by a young lady. I waited until the customer left and asked to see Mr. Champion. A middle-aged man appeared from the rear of the building.

Appearing cautious, I asked, "Can we talk somewhere else?"

He motioned to the back and led me into the area where the ovens and mixing vats were.

"I'm the one who called you yesterday about sugar," I ventured.

Champion seemed eager to get on with the deal. Knowing that I needed to have an iron-clad case proving intent to violate the law, I began my story.

"Since I talked to you yesterday, my still was raided and one of my hands was caught. I've got to make bond for him and then find another good place to set up. It's going to take me a little time," I said confidentially.

Champion was sympathetic. "Well, I haven't ordered the sugar yet, but I can get it any time you need it. I can furnish you yeast and rye meal too," he volunteered.

"How much a bag for the sugar?" I asked.

He replied, "Twenty-one bags (2,100 pounds) will be $300."

He handed me a slip of paper on which was handwritten, "21 bags - cash - $300.00." On the back of the paper were figures that indicated he had calculated the price the sugar would cost him. It showed a cost of $198.45, the normal wholesale cost of sugar, and that gave him a profit of $101.55.

"What kind of truck do you have?" Champion asked.

"A 3/4 ton pickup."

"I could put my tag on your truck and go get the sugar from the wholesaler and we wouldn't have to transfer the load from my truck to yours," he suggested.

"Okay, I don't care how you work it as long as the federal men don't get my tag number or name," I agreed.

"If anyone questions me about the sugar, I'll tell them I use it in my bakery," Champion continued.

I told Champion I would be back as soon as I got my still in operation. I checked the street before leaving.

Having established excellent intent on Champion's part, I drove back to the Regional Office in a good mood to report my progress to Gastley. We were both happy with the progress and made plans to develop an air-tight case against this man who was advertising to all liquor law violators that he would furnish the materials necessary to make moonshine.

About a month later I went back to the Four-Star Bakery. This time I had Doug Denney with me and introduced him to Champion.

"This is one of my still hands."

Champion was friendly and talkative, giving the impression that he knew a lot about moonshining.

"Do you have a tarpaulin to put over the sugar?" he asked.

"Naw, we've got a sheet of plywood that just fits the bed of the truck. We put it over the liquor when we bring it into town and over our materials when we go out. That way, if anyone glances into the truck, they only see plywood." I answered.

"Great idea—can one of you go to the wholesaler with me?" Champion asked.

"I'm afraid we might be recognized," I countered. "We'll need to get the sugar back to the still tonight. The hands are running liquor now and will need to 'sweeten back' while the mash is still warm."

"How do you get rid of the empty sugar bags?" Champion asked. "They can be traced."

"We burn them."

He seemed satisfied.

"I'm afraid Atlanta police might see us loading sugar behind your bakery. The other day you talked about putting your tag on our truck to go get the sugar. Do you still want to do that?" I asked.

With that, Champion took the license tag off his truck and placed it on our truck, leaving with $200 in government money. In 45 minutes he returned with twenty-one 100-pound bags of sugar on the truck. He removed his license tag and showed us a bill from Crystal Sugars and Coffee for the sugar.

"I'm going to charge you $3.00 per bag extra for my trouble. With the 20 pounds of yeast, you owe me an additional $71.00."

I paid Champion and looking around cautiously, stepped into the truck and took off, singing a popular song of the day, "Sugar in the Morning." I didn't realize it at the time, but during Champion's trial in federal court in front of the judge, jury and courtroom of spectators, I would hear myself again singing:

"Sugar in the morning, sugar in the evening, sugar at suppertime;

Be my little sugar and love me all the time."

I had forgotten to turn off a hidden tape recorder I was wearing to tape the entire conversation between myself and Champion. Another embarrassing moment!

About a week later, I called Champion on the telephone. This conversation was also taped. I asked, "Can I get some sugar tonight?"

"Why don't you take 35 bags this time, I have yeast and rye meal and can pick up the sugar," Champion suggested.

Not wanting to seem too anxious, I replied, "Twenty bags is all I can afford now." Keeping in mind the fact that we would need an airtight case in order to get a conviction on intent, I continued, "I can't pick up the sugar until after dark. My man is bringing a load of liquor into town and won't get here until then."

"Why don't you meet me at eight o'clock in front of my house on Page Avenue? I'll have the materials on my truck," Champion said eagerly.

That afternoon, Scoggins, Karl Strasser and I drove through Page Avenue in Henry's Buick and found the house. We went back to the Regional Office and made our plans for the knock-off buy that night. After discussing all the facts and evidence, we felt that with tonight's buy we would have an airtight case. Scoggins and Strasser would ease into the area without lights shortly after Doug and I arrived. Then during the loading of the sugar, they would drive up, identify themselves as federal officers, and question Champion about what was going on. It should be interesting.

In the same truck we had used on the previous buy, Doug and I drove up to Champion's house right on time. Champion's truck was parked at the curb in front of the house. I backed up to the rear of his truck and Champion appeared immediately.

"Start loading the sugar off my truck onto yours and I'll get the yeast and rye meal from the house," he said, scurrying back up the driveway.

Doug started loading the sugar. When Champion returned, I put the yeast and rye meal on the front seat and asked "How much do I owe you?"

"$265.00," he replied.

"Do you have the money you got for that load of liquor?" I asked Doug.

"Yeah. I'll get it as soon as we finish loading," Doug replied.

"This much sugar will make us about 250 gallons of liquor," I told the baker.

I could tell that Champion was not as comfortable as he had been at the bakery. He was beginning to get a little edgy. When Scoggins and Strasser drove up, he looked as though he was going to lose his supper. Strasser was a large, heavyset man as gentle as a kitten, but he didn't look gentle.

"What's going on here?" Strasser asked, after showing Champion his badge. Champion did his best to remain calm.

"I just hired these two fellows to help me move this sugar. I own three bakeries and I'm just transferring this sugar to one of them," he stammered.

Strasser pressed him for more information. Champion insisted he didn't know our names, had never sold us anything and this sugar was going to be used at his bakery.

After his arrest, and for sure after a hearing before U.S. Commissioner Ross Arnold, Champion knew he had lost in a game he should never have been in.

119

He lost a good pickup truck, 2,000 pounds of sugar, lawyers fees in excess of $1,000 and even worse, he lost his reputation as a law-abiding citizen and honest businessman. He was convicted and received probation. I feel sure Champion never violated the law again.

The Atlanta newspapers carried a write-up of the baker's arrest and at the end quoted Gastley: "This and other investigations involving such firms have been in progress for some time in line with the government's new preventive raw materials program. This is part of the all-out effort being made to curtail the flow of materials to violators of liquor laws."

The thread that ran through every raw materials case was greed. The opportunity to make a little extra money was too much of a temptation to refuse, even though most of these wholesale and retail grocers were well off financially. Although few received jail sentences, all were convicted or pled guilty and suffered the embarrassment of having a criminal record for the rest of their lives. It was a high price to pay for a few extra dollars and the thrill of violating the law in a *safe* way.

* * *

A few months later, Scoggins, James Stratigos, Strasser and I watched some men loading sugar at the rear of Cliff Pistol's residence in Dawson County. When they left in vehicles without license tags, we chased them into Lumpkin County and arrested the drivers. They were all liquor law violators with felony records. The vehicles and sugar were seized. This gave us enough evidence to obtain a search warrant for Pistol's residence and curtilage.

When we arrived the next day, Pistol was not at home, so we served the federal search warrant on his wife. She was a slender, wiry mountain woman who had experienced a hard life as a moonshiner's wife, bearing his children and worrying all the time. She was not friendly when we served the warrant, but accepted the situation. Only when we found a 2-ton Ford truck loaded with 27,000 pounds of sugar in the barn and seized the truck and sugar did she become upset.

"You're not going to take the goddam truck are you?" she screamed.

"Yes, ma'am," Karl told her gently.

"Goddam, don't take the truck! If you're going to take the goddam truck you might as well take the kids, too!" she cried. She was still screaming when we drove out of the yard—with the truck.

With the seizures the day before, this made a total of over 31,000 pounds of sugar and three trucks. Seizures like this put a crimp in the availability of sugar to the large distillers in Dawson and Lumpkin counties.

* * *

When the 20 undercover cases I made in North Carolina were called for trial in federal court, I was subpoenaed as a witness in Charlotte and Raleigh, where I learned a costly lesson about gambling.

I have never been a compulsive gambler, but I really enjoy it. In the military I learned to stay away from the crap games, mainly because I didn't have any money to start with. At the railroad, we would gamble on best poker hands by drawing employee pay cards from the files and using the Social Security numbers as our poker hands. This was usually a nickel and dime game and was a break in the monotony of office work.

While attending federal court in Raleigh, I participated in my first ATF poker game. One night after court, I found out that these guys played for blood and that I had no more business in this game than a one-legged man at an ass-kicking contest. It was not uncommon for a pot to contain $40 or $50, for me, a month's grocery bill. Special Agents Joe Carter, Jim West and others showed me how the cow ate the cabbage. I barely had enough money left to buy a Coca-Cola and pack of crackers the next day for lunch.

More costly education!

South Georgia steel tank stills. Mash is fermented and distilled in the same tank. Cap barrel is removed from still on left. Still on right is in operation with moonshine running out of "shotgun"-type condenser and being strained through a bucket containing cotton.

Chapter XV
Keep on Truckin'

Bootleg information came from varied sources and was sometimes vague.

One morning Gastley called. "Charley, I want you to check out some information I've just received from an Alabama source."

Law enforcement personnel are protective of their sources and sometimes in relaying information, it gets a little confused. What the man receiving the information thinks, and what the informer is saying, may be two different things. In this case, the person who received the information was not familiar with the territory in question and the informer had only been in the area once at night.

Gastley had climbed the ladder from the bottom. He had been a field agent, just as I was now, and had advanced through many phases of the job to his supervisory position. He had a nice office and a private secretary and the respect of everyone who knew him. He was a strong individual, six feet or more, and 190 pounds. He loved a good joke—you could hear his laugh a block away. Today, however, he was serious.

"We have information that a truck driver delivered a tractor-trailer load of sugar (20 tons) to a concrete block building in the middle of a large pasture somewhere in south Georgia."

I was stunned. The state of Georgia is the largest state east of the Mississippi and covers 58,500 square miles. At least half is considered south Georgia, which is 90% open farm land and woods.

I wanted to blurt out, "Are you kidding?" but I just grinned. Henry had gotten his joke and continued: "The truck driver was told to deliver the sugar from a refinery in New Orleans to Rhine, Georgia." (Rhine had a population of maybe 300 people and was barely on the map.)

"The driver was met in Rhine at midnight and told to follow a pickup truck. He did, but he's not sure in which direction they went after leaving Rhine. Several miles out of town, he was told to wait on the side of the road and the pickup disappeared down the dark road. It returned in ten minutes.

"The driver followed the pickup again and after about a mile he saw a man motion for him to turn into a large pasture. He was pretty jumpy by this time, but did as he was told. The man waiting on the ground inside the pasture gate jumped onto the side of the cab, telling the driver to go across the open pasture.

"The driver was worried that the truck with 20 tons of sugar on it would get stuck, but was assured the ground was hard and everything would be okay. He stopped at a large concrete building. Three other men appeared and began unloading the sugar. The unloading continued until just before daylight the next morning."

Unloading 20 tons of sugar in 100-pound bags is no easy task, even with four men working. Henry said that after this, the driver followed the pickup back to Rhine and was told to head north toward Macon. This was all the information we had to work on, but it was a start.

Checking the map, I found Rhine 14 miles south of Eastman. I called Bill Parker in south Georgia, and without telling him why, asked him to meet me in Eastman the next day at lunchtime.

Henry needed to get out of the office for a while. We took his air-conditioned government Buick to scout the area. Regional Special Investigator John Corbin (who later became ATF's top criminal enforcement officer in Washington) came with Gastley and we met Bill Parker as planned. We ate lunch at a local diner. Bill and I left our vehicles in a lot at Eastman and got into the Buick with Gastley and Corbin.

Our starting point was Rhine, but from there we didn't know where to go. "Let's try the road between Rhine and Milan first," Bill suggested. "I know two or three major violators who usually operate in this area."

On the way from Eastman to Rhine, we all concentrated on the left side of the road for anything that looked even remotely like a concrete building in a pasture. We had no luck.

Arriving in Rhine, we could see why the driver had been unsure of his location. Rhine had only one service station and several houses. It was in the middle of nowhere. Since the driver had said he returned to Rhine and then headed north toward Macon, we decided that Bill's suggestion was the most logical. We left Rhine going east toward Milan. The driver said that he had turned left into the pasture somewhere out of Rhine, so we concentrated on the left side of the road again. On both sides of the road were large pastures and farms—most of them uninhabited. The operators lived in town, since the few old houses in the area were mostly abandoned or used for hay storage.

We passed a pasture that might fit, but there was no building. You could see across the pasture to the woods a quarter of a mile away. The next big pasture on the left had a gate that looked right, but no block building. As we eased by, we could see fresh sign going in. We had learned early to recognize foot travel or vehicle travel and to determine if it was fresh or old. There were vehicle tracks at the entrance to the gate, but nothing discernible on the grassy pasture side.

Most moonshiners were excellent woodsmen and would scatter their sign by driving over different areas of open ground or grass in order not to create a worn area. A great deal of our investigative work boiled down to being able to recognize what was natural and what was unnatural in the woods. It required more than just practice—the best trackers were men who had grown up hunting and fishing. I loved this part of the work.

This entrance just didn't look right. "Bill, grab a radio and let's check this one out. Henry, you drive on and pick us up in half an hour," I said, quickly dropping out of the car. Bill and I headed for the only cover in the open pasture, a large shed-type cattle feeder on the hill.

As we crested the hill headed toward the feeder, I saw it— a big new concrete block building just over the hill. There was no way it could be seen from the road. We changed our course and headed for the building. When we were out of sight of the road, we slowed to a walk. I knew it, Bill knew it—this had to be the place. If only the sugar was still there! The building was north of the highway and completely out of sight. It was solid concrete block with no windows and one large wooden door. It was padlocked and sealed. No way to see in—well, maybe there was. Bill saw a small crack in the area where the roof joined the block walls.

"Charley, lean up against this wall and I'll get on your shoulders and try to see in." I did, and Bill stood on my shoulders. "It's full of 100 pound bags of Henderson's sugar," he exclaimed. "Good news!"

My first impression was that the still had to be close, either across the pasture or in an old abandoned farmhouse we had seen earlier. I looked at my watch. Half an hour had passed. I radioed Henry. "We've got the right spot. Give us another hour to check the area."

"Good deal," he said.

Bill and I began checking for sign along the edge of the woods at the back of the pasture, but "no joy."

The still wasn't there. Our hour was about up, so I called Henry.

"Pick us up at the entrance to the old house we saw just west of the pasture." We would have cover there and could wait in the bushes until Henry came by and made a fast pickup.

We drove back to Eastman and made plans for the night. Henry and John needed to go back to Atlanta, so we began making the necessary calls to get someone to drop us out. Doug Denney came from Newnan and by the time he arrived, Bill and I had bought all the provisions we needed for a long stay: Vienna sausages, pork and beans, soda crackers, cookies, candy bars and a couple of Cokes. We always had woods gear in the trunks of our cars, so we were ready when Doug arrived.

The typical government car trunk contained two or three local license plates, two out-of-state license plates, a case of dynamite, a sawed-off shotgun, surplus military clothing, binoculars, a shovel, an axe, still rations of pork and beans, Viennas and crackers. Some car trunks had items which were unmentionable at that time, but are commonly talked about now as a preventative measure against AIDS. Most ATF agents used these AIDS-preventatives as a ruse when they had inadvertently driven into a still road and left tracks. They would remove a condom from its container, throw the container in a likely place and then spit in the condom and throw it on the ground with two or three Kleenex. Sometimes it worked!

We filled Doug in on the plan on the way back to the pasture. Making sure there was no one in sight, Bill and I dropped out near the old house and immediately disappeared into the woods. We made our way through the woods until we crested the hill and only then ventured into the open pasture. By the time we reached the cattle feeder shed, it was beginning to get dark. There was still plenty of time to get situated.

The shed was about 40 x 60 feet with a metal roof. It was filled with hay and by climbing to the top we were concealed, yet had a view in all directions of the sugar building, two vacant tenant houses, U.S. Hwy. 280, the home of a known still hand and the former residence of another liquor law violator.

At eight o'clock a Ford and an Oldsmobile stopped on the highway opposite the gate. Three men got out and started talking. One mentioned $245 and that he would go get his truck. The other conversation was audible, but not understandable.

About an hour later, a heavily-loaded truck left one of the violator's homes across the road. The lights came on as it reached the highway. Sound carries unbelievably well at night in rural areas and I could hear the truck as it made its way toward Milan. The truck turned north and then back west, which put the sound to the north of us, directly behind the pasture. The truck slowed and dogs started barking as if it were going through someone's yard. Then the sounds stopped.

At ten o'clock, after a great deal of activity in the yard of one of the houses, two vehicles left with lights out. Upon reaching the highway, one turned toward Milan and the other toward Rhine.

I took the first watch till midnight and had just gotten to sleep when Bill shook me at two o'clock. I was wide awake as soon as I heard the activity. Two men were loading five-gallon cans onto a pickup truck at one of the vacant houses. We watched and listened and called Investigator Charley Covington, who had come up from Valdosta to help. I told him what time the truck left and in which direction. Charley searched the highway from Rhine, but was unable to find it. We knew then that it must have turned north before it reached Rhine.

Working successfully in a rural area infested with moonshiners and people sympathetic to them is almost impossible. Trying to run an extended investigation is difficult under the best of circumstances. We had to locate the distillery quickly. Most of the rural counties in the Southeast had local law enforcement officers who, either through sympathy or kinship to local violators, let it be known we were working in the area. In some cases, this was done for money or as a trade-off for information on a different investigation. We also had to be careful with our radio traffic.

Bill and I quit at four-thirty, just before daylight. We exchanged information with the others and then decided to go back in after dark. We had been in the area for three days and it was only a matter of time until we were discovered. There were too many strange vehicles and some of the agents working on the investigation were known in the area.

At ten o'clock that night, a heavily-loaded truck left one of the houses and turned west toward Rhine. I called Strasser who picked up the truck on the highway, but when it turned north on a dirt road, he had to continue straight for some distance. When he turned back to check the dirt road, the vehicle had disappeared.

Moonshiners are usually depicted as uneducated and stupid. Some are uneducated, but the ones who survive in the business are not, and they are certainly not stupid. Education doesn't have to be obtained in schools or from books. Most of the violators I worked on had more "education" in human nature, woodsmanship and cunning than a lot of Ph.D.'s. They also had the motivation of self-preservation. No one wants to go to jail or lose all he has in material goods. They are smart in their own peculiar

127

way—Phi Beta Kappa's of the wilderness. I always had more respect for them than for the shady businessman who put on a big show of being honest, yet who would make a dishonest dollar if he could. Even lower than this was the dishonest law officer who hid behind a badge and took money from violators for not doing his job or furnishing intelligence to them about the plans and activities of ATF or other law enforcement agencies.

While we were trying to decide what to do next, events were taking place that we didn't know about until it was too late.

A favorite tactic of large distillers was to call their local law enforcement friends and start putting together parts of any new developments in the area. This ploy was used in a number of counties where liquor law violators had contacts either with the sheriff or local state revenue officers. After the meeting, if it was determined that federal officers were working in the area and were close to making a seizure of a big distillery, the local law would seize the still, making sure not to arrest anyone. At a later date, they would sell the distillery back to the violator at a fair price. This gave the impression to the local populace that the officers were doing their job, yet the bootlegger only lost the use of his distillery and a fraction of the cost for a short time. The federal officers were denied making a case and destroying the distillery.

That is what happened on this case. The day after the truck was lost on the dirt road, we received word late in the afternoon that the sheriff and state agents had seized a large distillery and had parts of it piled on the court house lawn for everyone to see—a show put on to make the honest people in the county think they had good local law enforcement. While this is speculation on my part, I know what happened subsequent to our actions was no coincidence.

We dropped an investigator off at the block house with the sugar and told him not to let anyone, including the sheriff, take the sugar. We went on to the area where I had heard the truck go the first night of the surveillance. It took 15 minutes to find a farmhouse with dogs that barked when we entered the yard. Behind the house, there was vehicle sign leading around the edge of a pasture. We followed it and found the distillery site. As we suspected, nothing was left. The state officers had removed everything except some empty yeast cans.

The federal government's policy was that everything at an illicit distillery was destroyed. We would return a pint of mash to the chemist for analysis. They would determine the alcohol content for tax purposes (tax would be charged to the violator for the amount of mash seized and destroyed), but everything else except vehicles would be destroyed. Vehicles were seized and retained for forfeiture by the federal court. This fact alone led to problems with some state officers. They were allowed to retain a portion of the money received by the state when materials or vehicles were sold. They would fight you in order to take copper and sugar from the distillery. Most distilleries had copper radiators for condensers and these could be sold at a good price to junk dealers. The sugar could also be used or sold.

We were all dejected, disappointed and aggravated. It was neither the first nor the last time such underhanded practices interfered with our making a good case. Now we had to salvage what we could.

We made arrangements to have the 30,700 pounds of sugar remaining in the block building removed to a federal storage warehouse in Savannah, then returned to Atlanta to lick our wounds. We had lost one round, but the fight still had a long way to go. The raw materials program was having an effect. The violators had lost about $6,000 worth of sugar and suffered great inconvenience.

Next time we would be more careful.

South Georgia "box"-type still. (Note the propane fuel tanks)

Chapter XVI
Tightrope

Later in the fall of '59, Special Agent in Charge Roy Kelly told me that I was being promoted to regional special investigator and would be moving upstairs to the Regional Office. I was tickled to death. My first assignment would be as an undercover agent in Chattanooga, Tennessee, with a paid informant, "Red" Crankcase (name changed to protect the not-too-innocent). I would be making undercover buys of illegal whiskey in the Chattanooga area.

The newspaper later called this "Operation Tightrope," the best-kept secret in the history of the Chattanooga Police Department. From the beginning, I was told to keep it that way for my own safety. At the time, I thought they were being a little too cautious, but I found that the violators I would practically live with were capable of anything, including murder.

I'll never forget my first contact with Ruby. She lived on Spears Avenue in an old section of Chattanooga across the river from downtown. Her house was a modest, one-story frame bungalow on a small corner lot.

Red and I parked on the street and walked up to the back porch. Burglar bars on the windows and the elaborate lock system on the door leading into the enclosed back porch caught my eye. There were at least three locks and a bar to stop any unwanted guests. It was not unusual for bootleggers to have several door locks.

Red banged on the door. "Open the goddam door," he shouted, laughing. Obviously he knew the people inside. A man opened the door. He was about 28 years old, nice looking in a rough sort of way and likeable. He and Red cussed each other good-naturedly as we walked into the kitchen.

There was Ruby. She was in her 50's, weighed about 180 pounds and had several long scars on her face—a tough-looking woman. Her language was just as tough. "Where in hell you been, Red?"

"Shit, I had to go back to Atlanta. Jimbo left me and I had to get Charley here to help me."

I moved over to the kitchen table and sat down with my back to the wall. "Don't let that bird shit on your head," were Ruby's first words to me. A parakeet was in a cage hanging over the table. I laughed and wondered again, What am I doing here?

I was quickly accepted by Ruby and Shep. Since Red, Ruby and Shep were always drinking, I was the designated driver.

Chattanooga was probably the roughest city in the Southeast in those days. It was noted as a haven for car thieves, moonshiners, burglars and killers. I soon found that I was right in the middle of a band of car thieves and potential killers. Ruby's husband had been gunned down in a local bar some years before and one of her sons was presently serving time in a federal penitentiary. The other was a fugitive living north of Chattanooga.

During the past 12 years, Shep had been in juvenile homes and on Georgia chain gangs about two-thirds of the time. That was not due to his having been neglected as a child. He came from a well-to-do family who tried to raise him properly. Perhaps he was one of those who was "born to be bad." He never seemed to worry about the law.

"If you play, you gotta pay," he said many times. Despite this, I liked Shep and he and Ruby quickly accepted me as a "trip boy" who was hauling whiskey to the Atlanta area.

"Let's go to the Pine Pole," Shep said.

"Hell yeah," Red chimed in, and soon we were out the door, piling into the car furnished by the Chattanooga police for Red's use. My government vehicle was a souped-up Ford pickup that I was to use when buying whiskey, but I was riding with Red tonight. The Pine Pole turned out to be a typical beer joint in Red Bank, a suburb of Chattanooga, and it was as rough as they come. Again, I sat with my back to the wall.

I was there because Chattanooga Police Commissioner H. P. Dunlap had driven to the Atlanta Regional Office of ATF and asked the chief of criminal enforcement for help in gathering evidence of criminal activity. This was to be super-secret with no one knowing except the undercover agents, the chief of ATF, Commissioner Dunlap, Chief Brown and Inspector "Pee Wee" Upchurch. Arrangements were made for Dunlap to hire a confidential informant that ATF had used in the past, to work for the city of Chattanooga and attempt to gain the confidence of the underworld. Red Crankcase was the man.

Red is short and stocky and, of course, has red hair. He is also one of the wildest guys in captivity. He can drink liquor and cuss and shoot the bull as well as anyone I ever worked with and I worked with some humdingers.

Red enjoyed driving a car furnished by the city, spending expense money and playing the part of a don't-give-a-damn guy. In

132

three weeks he had developed a close friendship with Ruby and Shep and had met numerous car thieves, burglars and moonshiners.

After another request for assistance from ATF, Special Agent Jim Berry joined Red in Chattanooga and launched "Operation Tightrope." It became a joint effort of ATF and the Chattanooga Police. After two weeks, Jimbo, as Ruby called him, was pulled out due to federal court and other commitments and I took his place as Red's driver.

In ATF, and most other federal and state police agencies, less than five percent of the working agents ever do any type of undercover work. Probably less than one percent do extended undercover operations, working with violators on a day-to-day basis for a lengthy period of time. It's a job that most people don't like. First, you are away from home for weeks or months with only an occasional visit or telephone call. Second, you are almost always in danger, having to depend on your wits and the good Lord to get you out of hairy situations. Third, you have to pretend to be a car thief, moonshiner or, as in this case, a conspirator to murder. It was always a tough, risky assignment.

The longer the undercover assignment goes on, the more you tend to wonder how long the people you are working with can avoid making a mistake that will put you and the investigation in jeopardy. Of course, you also begin to wonder if you have made a comment or slip that would cause the violators to suspect you are an officer. An undercover agent must be constantly alert and able to think on his feet. These things build up over time and as more people necessarily become involved in the operation, the more chance you have of your cover being blown.

Undercover work is like the old saying, "You have to be there to understand."

Little did Ruby and Shep know what a hectic life I was leading at the time. I met with Ruby and Shep on Friday at Ruby's house in Chattanooga. We were together until past midnight and again all day Saturday, after which I drove back to Atlanta. Sunday night I left Atlanta en route to Washington, North Carolina, arriving at two Monday morning. I attended federal court until late in the afternoon and arrived home around midnight.

The following weekend, I left home on Saturday and arrived in Greeneville, Tennessee just before dark to begin an undercover assignment in Cocke County. On Sunday I made undercover buys of 24 gallons of moonshine in Cosby and Newport, Tennessee. I finished up the week making four more undercover purchases in Cocke County. After securing federal search warrants for several residences, I left Greeneville and arrived home Friday night. The following week I was working in Florida and had to rush back to Chattanooga to join Red.

We met Shep at Nicki's Drive-In. Red and I had talked to Ruby about buying some liquor and we were ready now. When we got to Ruby's house, she was glad to see us.

As we sat around the kitchen table, Ruby told us how she operated. "I've got a man that I've been buying liquor from for years. I pay $5.00 a gallon, but it's good copper liquor."

Red exclaimed, "Goddam, that's too much to pay!"

"But Red, for that price he stashes it for me and I have a key to the stash house. I can sell it for $1.50 a pint and make $8.00 a gallon profit. Sometimes I sell 15 or 20 gallons a day," Ruby replied.

Red started complaining about a load of whiskey he had bought from a man on Daisy Mountain. "That S.O.B. charged me too much the last time."

"He sure as hell did!" Shep agreed.

"Well, don't worry about this load. Jack will be running (the still) tonight and he will call me as soon as he has the liquor. Where you staying?" Ruby asked.

"We're over at the Terri Motel, room seven," I said.

"It'll be two or three in the morning before he gets through and when he calls, I'll send Shep over to wake you up and go with you."

Red and I left and tried to get some sleep. The Terri Motel was by no means a four-star establishment. Its primary customers were couples who just needed a bed for an hour or two. They must have been fast sleepers!

When the traffic in and out of the rooms had finally settled down enough for me to get to sleep, someone started banging on the door. It was Shep. I looked at my watch. It was four-thirty.

"Let's go. You wanna sleep your life away?" He was in a good mood.

Red grumbled, "You follow us, Charley." He and Shep left in the direction of Daisy. I followed in the hot-rod '56 Ford truck. Soddy and Daisy were two small towns located ten miles north of Chattanooga, at the foot of Daisy Mountain. Later they combined city governments and became Soddy-Daisy. The area was well-known for its production of moonshine, much like Cocke County.

As I followed Red's car around behind a grocery store, I wondered where the local law was. Here we were sneaking through alleys at five in the morning. I saw someone come out of the store just as we stopped. This must be Jack, I thought. He recognized Shep.

"Are you ready to load?" he asked, motioning to a 1948 Plymouth parked next to the building. We began loading the 105 gallons of whiskey onto my truck.

Jack was talkative. "I've been running liquor all night. It really gets you wet and muddy," he said, showing us his muddy pants legs and shoes. Jack owned the grocery store and when we finished loading, he said, "Come on in." We all went inside where Jack ran up a total on the adding machine of how much we owed for the liquor and containers.

In this area, the moonshiners use a lot of five and ten-gallon cola drums as containers. If you didn't have cans to trade, you were charged for the can also. This was something I hadn't encountered before.

Jack kept on talking: "I've just set up two 2,000-gallon outfits and mashed in 80 bales (4,800 pounds) of sugar. I can furnish you all the liquor you want," he boasted. "Why don't you bring a big van truck to haul it in?"

Red gave him his usual line of bull, saying we would get things lined up in Atlanta and see him the next week. After we paid Jack for the liquor, Red took Shep back to Chattanooga and I left, supposedly for Atlanta, with the liquor.

I drove to East Ridge, Tennessee and called ATF Supervisor George Pettway to join me at the race track. We destroyed the whiskey in the river. The next day it was reported that fish were jumping into local fishermen's boats!

ATF's policy was to destroy illegal liquor where we found it unless it was impractical to do so. Seldom did we retain a sample of whiskey. We were considered experts by the federal courts in our ability to testify that this was untaxpaid liquor and as to the amount seized.

If large seizures of cocaine and other illegal drugs were handled this way today, police agencies wouldn't have the problem of drugs disappearing from evidence lockers nor the attendant scandals relating to police officers.

For the next three months, Red and I were with Ruby and Shep just about every day. Shep was always coming up with something he had stolen and on some occasions after checking with Chief Brown, Red would buy the stolen goods for use as evidence later. We were also making buys from various moonshiners in the Chattanooga area.

We would have to come up with different excuses as to why we wanted to buy from different individuals, but Red always had an answer. The liquor was priced too high, or it had water in it, or we didn't like where we had to go to get it—something new every time. Thus, we were able to buy from 12 different moonshiners in three months without Ruby becoming suspicious.

When we were not at Ruby's house, we were hanging out at the Pine Pole Tavern in Red Bank. I noticed that Shep never seemed to have any money and always refused when Ruby offered it to him. He would rather steal what he wanted. Shep didn't believe in paying for anything. One afternoon at the Pine Pole, Ruby's son-in-law Eddie left our table with Shep and went into a back room. In a few minutes Shep returned and showed us a $100 bill, saying it was for a job he and Eddie did. That night Ruby showed us the same $100 bill.

She said, "I've got it now."

I think Shep did everything illegal for the thrill of getting by without being caught. He cared nothing for the monetary gain. Ruby did, though!

The second week of November, I had to attend federal court in North Carolina. Jim Berry took my place for a week.

During this time, Red rented a small concrete block house on Holly Street, across town from Ruby. We used it as our hide-out. That same week, Special Agent Jim King was sent to Chattanooga to make tape recordings of Ruby and Red's conversations. He climbed up into the crawl space above the ceiling of the hide-out living room and set up a large Tanburg recorder. Space was limited and King was cramped. The house was cheaply constructed and had no ventilation, only thin paneling for the ceiling. One false move and Jim would come crashing through the ceiling. Jim had no sooner gotten into the attic when Ruby and Shep came roaring into the house!

"Gimme a beer," said Shep. Jimbo went for the refrigerator. Ruby tried to make herself comfortable on an old sofa Red had bought, along with an old metal bed and some other worn-out furniture, at a thrift store in the run-down section of Chattanooga where the house was located.

"Where the hell have you been, Red?" Ruby asked.

Red went into his usual line of bull. "Shit, I've been working my ass off." In a few minutes, it was old home week with everyone shooting the breeze and having a good time.

Then came the surprise. Shep pulled out a long-barrelled .38 caliber revolver. Although everyone knew Shep was capable of almost anything, none of us had seen him with a gun before. "Wanna buy a good pistol, Red?" Shep asked.

Relieved, Red blurted out, "Will it shoot?"

"Hell, yes," laughed Shep, pointing the pistol toward the ceiling and cocking it.

"Don't shoot that damn thing in here," Red pleaded, knowing King was overhead. "Don't shoot that thing!"

Shep laughed. Red and Jimbo tried to laugh. King didn't think it was funny! Finally, after what seemed like an eternity, Shep lowered the pistol and continued to negotiate with Red on the price. King told me later that he was sweating bullets. Jim had a terrific sense of humor.

About a week later, I was asleep in one of the two bedrooms of our luxury accommodation when I heard someone pounding on the door. "Open the door." It was so cold in that house, I was sleeping in my clothes with two old Army blankets over me and was still about to freeze.

I jumped up and opened the door to the carport. Shep was standing there, wearing only a pair of slacks and a white T-shirt— no shirt, no coat. He burst into the kitchen and began to warm himself before the electric cook stove we had left on in an attempt to heat the flimsy house. Red came out of the other room and asked groggily, "What in the hell are you doing, Shep?"

"I just stole this truck in Rossville (Georgia) and I'm headed up to Maryville." (I learned later that Maryville, Tennessee, was where Ruby's son Tim was hiding out, operating a "chop shop" where he changed the appearance of stolen vehicles in order to resell them.) "The spare tire rack is dragging and I need some wire to tie it up."

I grabbed a coat hanger and opened it up to make a straight piece of wire. We all began working on the truck. This was about two in the morning and I wondered if a police car would be pulling in on us at any moment.

As Red and Shep worked at the rear of the pickup, I casually opened the door and wrote the serial number on a matchbook cover. As Shep left, I thought of the country music song, "Looking for Love in All the Wrong Places." Shep didn't know he was looking for help in all the wrong places. He had given me evidence against him for a federal case of transporting a stolen vehicle across state lines.

The following week, Red and I bought a truck that Shep had stolen in October. He had driven it to the vicinity of Maryville, where Tim had helped him change all the vehicle identification numbers on the motor, transmission and rear end in six hours. Shep boasted about the short time involved. Tim had also placed two large mirrors and a set of turn indicators on the front fenders. He made other changes in the appearance of the stolen vehicle, including replacing the rear bumper. Sometimes he repainted a vehicle. That was standard operating procedure for this ring of thieves, who averaged stealing two vehicles a week.

The negotiations took place at Vince's Garage on Rossville Boulevard with Vince and Shep agreeing on the price of the truck. Red paid $330 cash. Vince gave him a signed license tag receipt and bill of sale signed by Martin Miller.

Red asked, "Who the hell is Martin Miller?"

"Just a name we made up," replied Vince.

At that time the adjoining state of Georgia didn't have a strong title law. Shep would steal cars in Tennessee. Tim would change all the VIN numbers and Vince would take the car to Dalton, Georgia, where he would run it through an auto auction, buy it back and thus obtain a Georgia title to the stolen car. Then they would sell the car in Chattanooga. On one occasion, Shep told of slipping into a man's carport with the key to a truck he had stolen previously and stealing the same truck again. The man was watching TV in a room next to the carport and never heard a thing. I might have been skeptical of someone else pulling a trick like this, but Shep would try anything.

After we bought the truck, we turned it over to the Chattanooga police chief for later use as evidence by the FBI.

As Christmas approached, Red and I were buying whiskey on Daisy Mountain, Signal Mountain and Suck Creek, all rural areas surrounding Chattanooga. Shep was breaking into schools and churches in Chattanooga, cracking safes and stealing electric typewriters, among other things. Red and I were buying some of this stolen merchandise and keeping meticulous notes as to times, dates and other information inadvertently furnished to us by Ruby and Shep. The money to buy this evidence was furnished by the Chattanooga police department. ATF furnished the money for the moonshine.

Chief Brown and Inspector Upchurch had been receiving information for months that some Chattanooga police officers were taking bribes and furnishing information for money to local law violators. We were asked to carefully work this into our investigation without arousing any suspicion on Ruby's part.

Red could charm Ruby out of her shoes and in no time, she agreed to introduce us to a Chattanooga police officer she trusted. We parked at a drive-in on Rossville Boulevard. Ruby recognized a police officer parked nearby and waved to him. He walked over to our car and they appeared to be old friends. Ruby got right to the point. She introduced Red and me to the officer as Red and Charley, telling him we were doing business in Chattanooga and would appreciate his help. Red gave the officer $10. As he walked away, he smiled and said, "Be careful."

I thought, You need to take your own advice.

About a week later, after Ruby had called the officer at home, Red and I drove to his residence and talked to him in the driveway. He was cordial.

"Somebody's been watching my house on South Holly Street," I said.

"What kind of car did you see?" he asked.

I replied, "A green '57 Ford."

"The ATF agents have a car like that. If you're keeping anything (illegal) at the house, you'd better get it out of there. I'll check with the racket squad tomorrow and find out if ATF is watching your house."

I paid the officer another $10 and we left. He had accepted a bribe and had now consummated the act by furnishing information.

I felt a little sick. How could a sworn officer of the law wearing a badge of trust put in jeopardy his reputation, family and freedom for $20? I'll never understand it.

* * *

In most extended undercover operations, there comes a time when things begin to get so hairy that you have to bring it to a conclusion and fast. I had been working closely with Ruby and Shep now for three months and they thought I was one of them. The trust I had been able to instill in them became evident one December night. Ruby, Red, Shep and I were sitting in Ruby's kitchen when for no apparent reason Ruby said, "Let's go for a ride."

When we got to the car, Ruby said, "Charley, you drive." She got into the front seat next to me. Red and Shep got in the back. I knew something was up, but didn't know what. Ruby began directing me where to drive and we soon arrived in a remote area above Chattanooga near a radio tower. Ruby said, "Park here."

On the last couple of trips I made back to Chattanooga from Atlanta, I was apprehensive about returning to Ruby's house. I had been told she was "mean as hell" and knew from conversations with her that her sons were probably capable of anything. Her son-in-law, Eddie, from whom I had bought whiskey, had pled guilty in 1955 to being an accessory to an extremely violent murder and rape of a 53-year-old Chattanooga businesswoman. The murder took place on a government reservation south of Chattanooga. Two brothers named Krull (an appropriate name) were found guilty of this heinous crime and were executed. Eddie testified for the government and received a five-year sentence for being an accessory. When I met him, he had been out of the federal pen in Terre Haute, Indiana, for about a year.

Now, parked by the radio tower on that quiet winter night, no one said anything for some time. Ruby broke the silence. "Charley, my son's case comes up next month. He'll be going back to the penitentiary for sure if we don't do something about that damn Roy Smith."

I remained silent. I had heard Ruby mention that name several times, but this was something new. Smith was apparently going to testify against her son.

"Have you tried paying him off?" I asked.

"That won't work—we tried. We've got to get rid of him."

Red didn't say a word. That was the only time I ever knew Red to be at a loss for words. I anxiously waited.

"We thought maybe you might know someone in Atlanta who could do the job for us."

There it was! I was being asked to arrange a murder! I never expected anything like this, but Ruby's seriousness was unmistakable. This was no joke. Stall—that's the best tactic when you're confronted with something unexpected. My mind was racing. I knew if I refused flatly, she would probably go to someone else and the man could be killed before I could stop it.

"I know a man who might do it for the right price." I learned long ago that it's expected of you to talk price early in any negotiation.

"When can you see him?" asked Ruby. She was ready to do business.

This had to be reported immediately to my chief and also the Chattanooga police.

"I'm taking a load of whiskey to Atlanta tomorrow and I'll try to let you know something this week," I told Ruby.

"Good, let's go," she said.

Hardly a word was spoken during the drive back to Ruby's, but my mind was still racing. First, I had to determine if her son indeed was to go on trial in January, and second, if this man Smith was a witness against him. But how? Officers have been set up before and I didn't want to get myself into a position of being involved in a murder or be killed myself. I spent another sleepless night.

The next morning, I called my supervisor, William N. Griffin, the number three man in the Southeast Region. I advised him that I was in a position that would require top-level decisions from ATF and the Chattanooga police department.

Bill Griffin played professional football for the Chicago Bears and the Los Angeles Rams after graduating from college. He is a giant of a man both in size and in heart. He has the physical and mental toughness to be outstanding in anything he undertakes. Luckily for ATF, he chose to work for the U.S. Treasury Department. He had begun his career like all special agents and had quickly risen through the ranks. In 1977 he was asked to move to Washington, D.C., to help reorganize ATF. A man of action like Griffin does not mix well with Washington bureaucrats and to ATF's great loss, Bill retired in the spring of '77. Griffin is a man you can depend on, who did it all and who stood behind his men through hell or high water.

When I got into the Regional Office that next afternoon, Bill told me he had called the Chattanooga police chief and arranged a meeting the following morning in Atlanta with ATF Chief of Criminal Enforcement Dale McClanahan, Bob Miller and Chattanooga Police Chief Brown.

The next morning, I found myself in the office with ATF's high rollers. I was apprehensive, since I had never been in the same room with this much brass before. Bill made me feel at ease and I began to relate to them the conversation with Ruby about "getting rid" of the witness. When I finished, there was deathly silence. Miller asked Chief Brown if the man to be killed really existed and if he was going to be a witness against Ruby's son. The chief answered in the affirmative to both questions,

"Do you think this crowd's capable of having someone killed?"

"I think Ruby's family and associates are capable of anything, including murder," answered the chief.

McClanahan told the chief that we would cooperate in any way we could, but we would have to be careful not to raise the possibility of my becoming an accessory before the fact of murder.

After much discussion as to the evidence needed and the mechanics of the operation, they authorized me to attempt to make an additional case of conspiracy to commit murder.

I had been racking my brain for someone to play the part of a "hit man" if I was given the go-ahead to try to make the additional case against Ruby and Shep. I had worked with Ralph Elam, head of the vice squad for DeKalb County, and knew he was a man of the highest integrity. I also thought he could look and play the part of a big city hit man.

As soon as the meeting was over, I called Ralph and

arranged to meet him at the Huddle House in Decatur. Ralph was interested. He called his chief of police who coordinated with ATF and the deal was all set.

I told Ralph I would go back to Chattanooga and set up a time for the first meeting between him and Ruby. King would assist us in recording the conversations and possibly making photographs of the meeting. This was Friday and it had been a busy, hectic week. I told none of this to Dot or anyone else. On Saturday, I went back to Chattanooga and found Red at the block house on Holly Street. I briefed him on the general operation and we arrived at Ruby's about noontime.

"Let's go get a barbecue," said Ruby. She crawled into the front seat with me. Red and Shep sat in the back. We loaded up on barbecue and headed back to the house on Spears Avenue.

"Did you find out anything?" Ruby asked confidentially.

I didn't want to say anything that could be used later in court to imply that this murder was my idea, so I played dumb and said, "About what?"

Ruby looked directly at me and her tone of voice became cold and threatening: "What we talked about the other night—someone to do a job for us!"

I knew I couldn't draw her out any more, so I said, "Yeah, I talked to a man who'll do it."

Then came the inevitable question: "How much does he want?"

"$1,000," I answered.

During the previous conversation and this one, Shep and Red had been strangely quiet. But now Shep uttered the most terrible statement I have ever heard. "Hell, I'd kill Jesus Christ for $1,000." It still gives me the creeps to think about it.

I was stunned! No one said anything for several minutes.

As we approached Ruby's house, she said, "Charley, I'll have to think about this. That's a lot of money."

I was committed on the price. We had apparently set it too high and now Ruby and Shep were considering an alternate plan to solve their problem. Ruby thanked me for trying, and we left. I drove back to Atlanta not knowing what might happen that weekend. Would I return to Chattanooga on Monday and read about another murder—one that I could have prevented?

I went into the Regional Office early Monday morning and repeated to Griffin and Miller what had been said. I emphasized my concern for the witness. They both agreed and called Chief Brown. It was decided that when I arrived in Chattanooga, Red and I would tie up all the loose ends of the investigation and close it as soon as possible. Hopefully, no one else would be hired to do the murder.

We made several more undercover buys of whiskey and met with Chief Brown two days before Christmas. There were people we needed to identify by their proper names, but we decided to break for the holidays and finish up early in January. I worked in the office all day Christmas Eve trying to catch up on my paperwork and then took a week of annual leave after Christmas. I'm sure I was not good company that Christmas due to the strain of the past three months and the worry over what might happen the next week.

I went back to Chattanooga on January 4, and worked with local ATF agents and Chief Brown until late that night. We secured federal search and arrest warrants for the liquor law violators and Chief Brown secured arrest warrants for the car thieves based on evidence we had developed. (These cases were later adopted by the FBI.)

The next day we began our roundup. Local ATF special investigators Hynes, McKnight and Wilkes joined Special Agent Jim Berry and me. We split up the warrants. Hynes and I took half and the other officers took the rest. We arrested 11 moonshiners, seized four vehicles and destroyed 68 gallons of whiskey found on the vehicles on Daisy Mountain.

When we returned to Chattanooga, Berry, Chief Brown, Inspector Upchurch and I drove to 800 Spears Avenue. We found only Ruby and Eddie at home. Jim and I advised them we were federal officers and they were under arrest. Then we searched the house and found a license plate of a 1955 Oldsmobile stolen from Birmingham. Shep was arrested later that day driving the stolen car. It was one of the cars Shep had asked me to help him steal, but the FBI had refused to furnish an undercover man.

As I was standing in the kitchen with Ruby, she asked, "How could you do this to me, Charley?"

"You did it to yourself, Ruby," I answered.

I hoped that after thinking over all that had happened she realized that she had been on the verge of something much more serious than bootlegging and car theft.

Several months later Ruby, still in prison awaiting trial, sent word that she wanted to see me. As I drove to the Hamilton County jail, I wondered what Ruby would have to say.

I sat in the cell with Ruby and we talked like old friends. She held no grudges and was now wanting help. I told her that I was sworn to uphold the law and would tell it like it happened. I would add nothing nor leave anything out. She seemed satisfied with my answer, although I wondered if she was feeling me out to determine if I might be a little crooked or at least give her defense something to talk about at the trial. She ended the conversation by saying that her daughter and Eddie were still selling whiskey at 800 Spears Avenue and wouldn't even bring her a pack of cigarettes.

I felt a little sorry for Ruby, being left alone at age 54, but then I thought of what Shep had said on several occasions: "If you gonna play, you gotta pay." Shep never seemed to worry about going to the penitentiary. He had served time in the state prison in Sioux Falls, South Dakota; a federal penitentiary in Tallahassee, Florida; and a Georgia chain gang. I think Shep was more at home in prison than anywhere else.

All those arrested in Operation Tightrope received long state and federal prison terms. Although Ruby had a long arrest record, this was her first extended period in prison and was long overdue.

One of the ironic twists of this undercover operation involved the FBI. Among various other enforcement activities, the Federal Bureau of Investigation is charged with enforcing laws concerning interstate theft of motor vehicles. Shep had been stealing an average of two vehicles a week and transporting them between Tennessee and Georgia. The FBI was contacted and I had met with two agents near the Chattanooga airport. I told the agents that the group of people I was involved with were transporting these stolen vehicles interstate in obvious violation of federal law. On two occasions they had asked me to go along.

I told them that I could easily work one of their agents in on the operation so they could gather evidence on one of the largest stolen car rings in the country. After my suggestion, I was surprised to hear one of the agents tell me flat out, "We don't do undercover work!"

"What?" I said, amazed.

"No, our agents do not do undercover work," he said arrogantly.

I felt like saying, "Well, excu-u-u-s-e me!" I immediately wondered about the man who "led three lives," who was the subject of a popular TV show at that time. Now I know that he was another Red Crankcase—a paid government informer. This is one of the major differences between ATF and the FBI. Without undercover participation by ATF agents, hundreds of liquor law violators would have gone unpunished.

The difference in a nut shell was that the FBI ran paper trails and adopted almost all their cases from local and state police agencies while ATF agents worked their cases themselves and put people in jail physically. The fact that the FBI was in the image-making business did not hurt them any. ATF barely had money for gasoline and was the proverbial red-headed stepchild of the federal government.

Of course, after ATF and the Chattanooga police made the arrests, the FBI was quick to come in and take over the cases. From the news accounts, readers would think they had been in on the investigation from the beginning.

The final chapter came in September of the next year, when the last man charged in the automobile theft ring pled guilty. Three others previously pled guilty and received prison terms along with Ruby and Shep. All this was accomplished because Red worked with the Chattanooga police and ATF agents. One of the members of the car theft ring had been convicted in a similar operation before and the FBI labeled that operation one of the hardest to crack in their history.

Maybe if they'd let their agents do undercover work they wouldn't have to wait so long for other agencies to make their cases for them! Dirty, difficult jobs were commonplace, especially for ATF undercover agents. Despite inadequate funding and poor equipment, the average ATF agent was second to none in getting his job done. He took a back seat to no one, including the FBI.

Newspaper articles from the 1960s

Chapter XVII
Aye, There's the Rub!

Early in 1960, I was busier than a one-armed paper hanger with the crabs. Case reports for recent undercover arrests, conferences with U.S. attorneys, commissioners' hearings and the many required paperwork procedures took a great deal of time. I was also raiding stills and working undercover in Cocke County, Tennessee.

East Tennessee, especially Cocke County, was notorious for moonshining. It wasn't so much the size of the distilleries as the proliferation of them. There was a still in every hollow and on almost every farm. Officers would sometimes destroy a distillery in a hard-to-observe area, making it an unknown seizure (UDS). This was the easy way, but it didn't do much to deter the moonshine business. ATF agents would cut four or five stills in an area and the next day the violators would be putting them back up in the same location. Most of them weren't large operators, but they were persistent.

ATF was stepping up the pressure on moonshiners by initiating a known-seizure program. This meant that we were required to connect every seizure of an illicit distillery or moonshine whiskey to an arrest. There were instances when making a UDS was unavoidable, but this was discouraged by the ATF hierarchy.

For over two months, I worked undercover in Cocke County. Although I had observed moonshining all over the Southeast, Cocke was unique in several ways.

The first time I went to the ATF office in the basement of the Post Office in Greeneville, I found everything a lot more "laid back" than anywhere else I had worked. The Greeneville post of duty was unique and an education in itself.

ATF agents Roy Tubb, Charlie Riddle, John Petre and Russell Trickey were stationed in Greeneville. What a mixture of characters! They all later became my close friends, but at the time I thought, Here I am in a different world, again!

When I walked into the squad room, the first thing I noticed was a 300-pound American Indian who was sitting in the corner. He was truly a giant.

"Charley, this is the 'Big Chief,'" Petre said. "He'll be working with you...let's go over a list of who we want to buy from."

We went into a small adjoining office where Petre produced a list of 15 names and locations. "You'll be working in the chief's car. Here's $300 to get started with."

Big Chief's car was an old Cadillac. The left side had been caved in by a collision with another vehicle, so everyone had to enter and exit by the right door—no way to get out the left side. Chief lumbered across the front seat and I crawled in next to him.

The Cadillac had not been washed in months and neither had the chief. The floorboard was six inches deep in bologna rings, peanut hulls and beer can pop-tops. Saying the odor was noxious is putting it mildly. I quickly rolled down the window on my side, even though it was freezing cold outside.

As we drove into Cocke County, Big Chief spoke. "I need to stop up here and pick up a friend of mine."

"Okay."

We pulled into a beer joint and I climbed out and waited, grateful to be out in the fresh air. Five minutes later the chief emerged from the joint with a man who would be called a "street person" these days, but at that time was called a drunk. Over the past 30 years, the terminology has changed and so have a lot of other things in our society—not always for the best.

Big Chief crawled back into the wrecked Cadillac and I made my first mistake of the day. I got in next. This put me in between the chief and the drunk. I thought it had smelled bad earlier—now I couldn't even get to the window! Phew!! As we drove through the twisting mountain roads, I wondered, as I had so many times before, What am I doing here?

For the next three days, we ate together, slept in the old Cadillac together, and bought liquor together. Some fun! By the weekend I looked and smelled just as bad as the other two.

When I made the first buy, I discovered one of the unique things about Cocke County. The moonshine was definitely different. When I tasted it, I thought, This is hot and doesn't smell exactly right. The moonshiner had eight cases of liquor (48 gallons) stacked on an enclosed back porch and was eagerly awaiting my judgment as to the quality of his whiskey.

"That ain't got no rub in it!" he said emphatically before I had time to say anything.

It hit me—rubbing alcohol! That was what I tasted and smelled in the whiskey.

"Are you sure?" I croaked.

"No sir, ain't no rub in that likker," he repeated.

We bought two cases. How people survived drinking this poisonous concoction on a regular basis, I don't know. Some didn't.

It was commonplace in Cocke to add rubbing alcohol to low-proof moonshine to make it "hot" (seem to be high proof) and also to add beading oil to make it bead. Some distillery sites had cases of empty rubbing alcohol bottles scattered about. Rubbing alcohol is made from wood products instead of grain. It is poison and if ingested can cause blindness and death. In Atlanta some bootleggers mixed Solox (a paint thinner) into moonshine for the same purpose.

By now Big Chief was getting hungry, so we stopped at a general store on the North Carolina - Tennessee line in the Great Smoky Mountains. I bought a package of peanut-butter crackers and a Coke. Meanwhile, the chief was loading up. He came out with a box of soda crackers, several cans of sardines and an onion as big as a baseball. We sat down to eat on a bench in front of the store. Watching Big Chief eat those sardines with the juice running down his chin, and then follow that up with the onion, which he peeled and ate like an apple, I dreaded more than ever getting back into the car. Then I made my second mistake.

"How about letting me drive, Chief?"

"Okay," he burped.

Music to my ears! At least now I would be next to a window. Sadly, because the door was crushed in, the window wouldn't roll down. Once more I was trapped in a hot automobile filled with indescribably bad odors. Some people don't know how to appreciate fresh air, but I do.

We made buys from about half of the 15 violators on the list. Although some were afraid to sell to us, others were talkative and friendly. Harve Fox, who lived in Newport, told of being caught by ATF agents and appealing his case all the way to the Supreme Court. He had to serve 18 months in the Atlanta Federal Penitentiary anyway.

"Hell, since I got out, I've had seven different stills up—from 24 barrels to four barrels—and haven't been caught yet," Fox bragged.

I thought, Till now!

Fox sold us two cases of liquor that night. A month or two later he pled guilty and got two more years in Atlanta—plenty of time in which to think about trading two years of his life for $60.

When these undercover-buy cases were tried, I went back to Greeneville as a witness for the government. On this trip, I saw something else unexpected. One afternoon, after finishing my testimony, I was sitting in the office when Charlie Riddle came in and looked around. All the other agents were involved with court or out in the field. I guess he figured I was better than nothing.

"Can you help me raid a still that's in operation right now in Cocke County?" he asked.

"Sure."

I was always ready to raid. Of the many things I have done in my life, raiding a still is the most fun. I borrowed a pair of boots and an old shirt that someone had left in the office and was ready to go.

Charlie knew a constable he could trust. He dropped us out in a remote area of the county. Charlie led the way. Since he didn't know me well, he probably figured he would have to do it all that day. I followed, anticipating my first still raid in notorious Cocke County. We crossed some railroad tracks and began a long trek up a hollow alongside a small stream.

The woods are always beautiful in the Smokies and I enjoyed being outdoors again. After 20 minutes, Charlie stopped.

"The still's up ahead on this branch. You wait here and I'll flush 'em toward you."

I did as I was told, not knowing exactly where the still was— only the direction. As I waited on one side of the steep hill, I was thinking, Ain't this nice? I get paid to do this, forgetting for the moment the stinking Cadillac and the close calls with Ruby.

Snap, a limb cracked near the stream of water—adrenalin pumped—then I saw Charlie coming toward me.

"What happened?" I asked.

"I've already raided the still and caught one...he said there's two more gone after jars. I handcuffed him to a tree. I'll go back and raid the still again when the other two get back."

That was the first time I had heard of raiding a still twice, but it sounded like a good idea. Why did the man tell Riddle there are two more coming in? I wondered. When I got to know Charlie better, I realized why the man had "volunteered" the information.

Riddle is a small, wiry man. A typical mountaineer, he came up hard in Claiborne County, Tennessee. He worked hard all his life and is tough as nails and completely without fear. On an earlier still raid, a moonshiner succeeded in pulling Charlie's pistol from its holster. In the struggle that ensued, Charlie wrestled the pistol back from the moonshiner and promptly pushed the pistol into the man's mouth, halfway down his throat. If another agent hadn't intervened, the man might not have lived to appear in court.

When the case came to trial in federal court, the defense attorney asked Riddle on cross-examination, "Mr. Riddle, is it true that when you arrested this man, you placed your pistol in his mouth, causing him pain and a great deal of anguish? Please tell the court and this jury why you would take such violent measures to apprehend this man?"

Charlie, with a sly smile on his face, glanced at Judge Taylor and replied, "Well, he jerked my gun out of my holster and acted like he wanted to take it, so I decided I would give it to him."

Judge Taylor was one of the most respected federal judges in the United States. No nonsense was allowed in his court, yet even he had to look at the ceiling to keep from laughing.

"No more questions, Mr. Riddle," the defeated defense attorney mumbled as he sat down.

Charlie has the quick wit and ingrained intelligence typical of most mountain people. Mere college degrees cannot compete with that natural ability. His college education is like icing on the cake.

As I waited by the stream for Charlie to flush the still a second time, I began to move carefully up the creek. I had covered about 20 yards when I heard two men approaching from the hillside to my right. They were carrying two cases of empty half-gallon jars. There they are, I thought as I crouched near the stream. But where's the still? The two men crossed the water about ten yards from me. I froze! They continued up the hill on my left and it was only then that I saw the distillery. It was about 15 yards up the side of the hill.

I had never seen a still this close to running water, yet not on the bank of the stream. Why they would carry water up the hill, leaving a three-foot wide trail to the stills, is a mystery to me. As I said, Cocke County was unique.

The two men began to look around and I crouched even lower.

"Where's Henry?" one said.

"I don't know, maybe he went to take a shit."

They placed the jars on the ground. One man walked back down the hill toward me.

I thought, This is it, I can't wait for Riddle, I'll have to catch what I can. As he came nearer, I slowly stood up. He froze, looking at me like a bird dog pointing a quail. I placed my finger to my lips and with my other hand motioned for him to come to me. All the while, our eyes were locked on each other. I expected he would break and run at any moment. The man began to walk slowly toward me. He did not utter a sound to warn the other man.

When he got to me, I placed my hand on his shoulder and whispered, "Squat down, you're under arrest." He quietly did as he was told. This was the first and only time I ever heard of a moonshiner being hypnotized—but it worked!

Hearing a shout from the stills, I looked up and saw the other moonshiner break and run toward me. With a firm grip on my man, I moved toward the trail. The other man veered away from me.

I yelled to Charlie, who was in hot pursuit, "Hold this one, I'll get him!"

After a short chase, I caught the other moonshiner and brought him back to Riddle. We were both happy. No UDS this time! A bond was formed between us that day that has lasted through the years.

The only damper on that episode came when Charlie went back to the small tree where he had handcuffed the first man and found that he had climbed the tree, somehow managed to get the handcuffs over the top, climbed back down and escaped. I felt sorry for this man if Riddle ever found him—and he did.

Chapter XVIII
Sweet Revenge

One morning in February, I was in the Atlanta Regional Office when the squad room telephone rang.

"Squad room, Weems," I answered.

"Charley, I want you to help Jim West on a highly sensitive case we're working." John Corbin, my supervisor, had a knack for placing me in highly sensitive investigations, but I was anxious to go as usual and couldn't wait to get started.

Jim came in a few minutes later. "Are you ready?" he asked.

"You bet."

"I'll check out a recorder," said Jim.

I knew then who would do the recording. On the way to the east side of Atlanta, Jim briefed me on the situation. We pulled into the driveway of a nice brick home. A small woman met us at the door. This was Louise. She was 5'2" and weighed 80 pounds soaking wet. She was frail and worn, but alert and friendly. From all appearances, she had led a hard life.

Louise had been married to a large-scale moonshiner and lived in Dawson County, Georgia. Her brother was also a large-scale moonshiner. Virtually all her friends and associates were into moonshining. After the death of her first husband, J.D., Louise remarried. Hershell was a pretty good guy, though not well educated. He drove a truck for a living and loved Louise. Hershell and Louise had one child, a small frail son, two years old. They lived on Highway 19, south of Dawsonville, a short distance from her brother Cliff.

One night shortly after Christmas, a group of local men decided that since Hershell was not a moonshiner he was no good and they were going to run him out of Dawson County. Two carloads of men drove into Louise's yard and called Hershell out. They held Louise back, beat Hershell unmercifully and left him for dead. Louise managed to get Hershell to the hospital and while he was recovering, she decided to seek revenge by catching "every damn likker man in north Georgia." She almost did!

Louise had the background and knowledge to be of valuable assistance to us. She was known by most of the large operators. She had participated in the liquor business with her first husband and knew all the ins and outs. Most of all, she was MAD!

153

Tonight, Louise was to meet Joe Crow. Louise and her first husband had been in partnership with Joe in several large distilleries and we needed corroboration to back up her testimony when his case came to trial. The plan was for me to get into the trunk of Louise's car with a small tape recorder and tape the conversation between Louise and Crow.

Back in the car trunk again! I never did like that duty. I was always wondering things like, What if I can't get the trunk lid open? What if some other car rams the rear of this one and here I am lying on top of the gasoline tank, locked in? What if carbon monoxide from the exhaust seeps into the trunk? A lot of bad things can happen when you are locked in a car trunk. I had to do this a couple more times in my career, but I never liked it.

ATF was always several years behind other federal law enforcement agencies when it came to equipment. We finally obtained FM radio equipment two or three years after most local police, so it was no surprise that our tape recorders were the cheapest available. We were using Mohawk recorders while other agencies used the Minifon wire recorder. The difference was that the Minifon was quiet, small and compact, and made clear recordings. The Mohawk was just the opposite and cost about half as much.

ATF did have one Minifon in the region, but it was always being used by the technicians for experimental (?) purposes. So, we did the best we could with what we had.

I crawled into the trunk, closed the lid and asked West, "Can you hear this thing running?"

"Naw."

I could sure hear it. The on-off switch also made an audible click. I told Louise to tell me when she saw Crow approaching the car so I could turn on the recorder. After we had everything planned, Louise and I left just after dark for south Atlanta. Curled up in the trunk, I thought, She sure is in a big hurry. I found out that was the way Louise always drove.

I braced myself as best I could, but still I was bouncing around like a ping-pong ball. About ten minutes into the trip, Louise went over a railroad crossing doing about 60.

"Slow down," I croaked.

"What?"

"Slow down, you're about to throw me out!" I repeated.

"Am I going too fast?" What a question! She did slow down a little for the remainder of the trip, but not much.

I felt the car turning and then parking. Hearing a man's voice, I quickly turned on the recorder and tried to get as comfortable as possible. I heard the door open and felt the car sag to the right as someone got in and sat down. Crow must be a heavy man. He began by saying that Louise could have met him at his house. There was more small talk about a niece who was in the hospital. Louise and Crow then switched their conversation to a place to set up an illicit distillery.

"You get to ride around any today?" Crow asked.

"Not today, I had to go to the doctor."

Crow continued, "We was all back up yonder. We rode all over Gwinnett and Rockdale (counties). These places are just hard to find."

Gradually, Louise began to talk about past locations of stills and why they were caught. Crow slid into the same line of thought, claiming that if they had followed his advice the still would still be operating at the Harper place. He told of talking to a man recently.

"I told him all the damn tricks that could be in that damn crap and I said, 'It takes a good man to stand hitched—if you don't want to stand hitched, don't talk about it', and I said, 'Now, I'll explain one more thing to you—I told you about it, but I'll tell you one more thing, you know, do you own this place? Do you own that house? Do you know that they will sell that son of a bitch for taxes if they catch an outfit on it?' 'Aw, they won't do that will they?' 'They damn shore will. They shore in hell will sell it for tax.' So, he said he better study on it for a little. I knew then he wasn't going to do nothin."

Crow talked continuously for the next 30 minutes about how they had made arrangements for distillery locations, bought sugar and jars, and on one occasion lost over 1,500 gallons of whiskey and two trucks because the still hands hadn't done as he had told them.

He verified all that Louise was going to testify to, plus giving us other information we hadn't been aware of. After 45 minutes in the cramped trunk unable to move, I did manage to move slightly when Crow shifted his body in the front seat. Just then the 30-minute tape expired and began to rewind itself—Shhhhh—Shhhhh—Louise apparently heard it and began to talk a mile a minute to cover the sound. Crow, who had been talking nonstop since Louise had gotten him started, could hardly get a word in.

Finally, the rewinding stopped and I was able to carefully move the recorder under my body, not knowing what other unexpected noises might come from this el cheapo. Crow talked for another 15 minutes. By the time Louise finally got away and back to the house, I had been in the trunk an hour and a half.

As West helped me out of the trunk, I said, "Jim, next time you get in the trunk!" I was sore for a week. But we got the goods on Crow. Louise continued her work for the government for more than a year and she was instrumental in making several cases.

Louise was not well educated, but she was a smart woman. Although her life was threatened, she stood up as a witness for the government when the moonshiners came to trial. Louise was one tough woman who got her revenge.

No one ever drank **THIS** liquor!

Chapter XIX
"Lawd Have Mercy!"

After I was promoted to regional special, I was one of the elite, but I knew better than to glory in it. I could work where I wanted, when I wanted as long as I produced. With help from old-time specials like Henry Gastley and Milton Walton, I began to do what I had been trained for.

Regional specials assigned to Atlanta worked out of an office in the Peachtree-Baker Federal Building. There were seven regular specials and four undercover investigators. It was a beehive of activity. Harry Lauderdale, Jim King, Ray Hahn, Jim West, Ed Carswell, Karl Strasser, Jim Berry, Joe Powell and George Ferguson all had special investigations going. Most of them, especially Lauderdale, worked informants in the city. I worked my own cases and helped the others, learning all the while. A lot of time was spent contacting local and state officers, obtaining statements and preparing reports for the U.S. Attorney.

Checking and raiding distilleries, which I loved, was still a large part of my work—but now even more paperwork was required.

As a result of an undercover operation run by Lauderdale, we got the goods on Ben Hall for the third time. Frank Lane and I jumped at the chance to serve a federal arrest warrant on Hall. Ben was still not glad to see "that wild-eyed little fellow."

That summer I was issued an old military surplus flare pistol. It was 18 inches long and fired a flare shell an inch in diameter—a big shell. I showed it to Chief Howard Smith one day.

"Let's use it to raid a still," he said.

"Okay, you find us a still and I'll bring it."

A week later, Howard called. "Bring that cannon, I've got a still located that will run tonight." I met Howard and we ate at Butch's in Jonesboro. After dark we drove to the distillery area.

I had never fired that thing before, so I didn't have any idea what to expect, but I was game if Howard was. If we caught anything on fire, I figured Howard, being chief of police of the county, could cover it.

It was another dark night and as Howard and I eased in on the still workway, I began to hear the familiar sound of a gasoline

157

burner. There was a faint glow in the thick woods ahead. Howard stopped and leaned against a tree. A black man was working on top of the groundhog still. He appeared to be chinking the cap barrel (placing a mixture of flour and water into the joints around the cap barrel and the still, thus sealing the opening so as not to allow alcohol steam to escape).

Howard whispered, "Get ready," as he moved to my right.

The flare gun was already loaded. I braced myself against the tree and aimed toward the only opening in the trees overhead. As I squeezed the trigger, Howard kept moving. I thought, Well, if this thing explodes, we both won't get killed.

"BLAM!" the hand-held cannon went off. Brilliant white flame shot from the end of the barrel, creating a blinding light three feet long. I couldn't see a thing! Then another bright light appeared, this time about 75 feet above us, glowing a brilliant red.

I tried to see the man at the still—no one in sight, but I could hear someone crashing through the swampy area to my right. As the red flare descended, dangling from a small parachute, I began looking for the moonshiner. In about two minutes Howard came back with the black man in custody. He looked as stunned as I felt.

"Lawd have mercy, I thought a airplane was falling on me," he stammered.

Luckily Howard had not been looking toward the flare pistol when I fired and was not blinded as I was. I never used it again. Once was enough.

* * *

One night in south Georgia, two ATF agents were on an all-night surveillance of a large distillery. They had set up camp several hundred yards from the still and at about one in the morning, one of them slid out of his sleeping bag and pulled on his boots. He cautiously moved closer to check the distillery for any activity. When he returned 15 minutes later and was removing his boots and preparing to slip back into the sleeping bag, he felt movement inside the bag. Waking his partner, the agent carefully picked up the bag and moved it to the perimeter of the camp site. He shook the bag and dumped out a four-foot rattlesnake which had sought the warmth of the sleeping bag while he was away. The snake made good his escape, but there was no more sleeping that night for either agent.

Every season had advantages and disadvantages when working stills. In summer insects were a nuisance and there was the constant threat of snakes. All the Southeastern states are inhabited by one or more poisonous species. They vary from huge rattlesnakes, cottonmouths and an occasional coral snake in north Florida and south Georgia to copperheads and rattlers in the rest of the region.

One Saturday in May, Frank Lane asked me to help raid a still in Spalding County. It was close to home and in the old territory where I had worked as a field agent. I jumped at the chance.

It was hard for Dot to understand my using weekends to raid stills when I didn't have to, but I loved it. Lane and I found the sheriff and with State Agent Bobby Imes, we hit the woods near Vaughn's Station in rural Spalding.

We walked about a mile through a wooded area and found the distillery. It was set up and ready to run. There were three ground-hog stills and over 1,000 gallons of mash. We decided to stay with it since we had brought our usual rations. We ate, then settled down to wait in a pine thicket 200 yards from the still. About 50 yards away was the vehicle workway which led from the still through the woods and across a pasture. From there it ran past a farmhouse to the public road.

It was not uncommon to hear nocturnal creatures moving in the woods throughout the night. Of the many times I slept on the ground, that was the only night that something crawled into my ear. I awoke with a loud scratching noise in my right ear. I pounded the side of my head as you do to get water out of your ear. It didn't work. This commotion woke up Frank.

"Maybe I could burn him out with my lighter!" he suggested.

Not funny! The thing was about to drive me nuts. I hoped it was not an earwig—those things with a thousand legs. As a small boy I had heard stories about the earwig getting in your ear and eating up your brain. This one *felt* like it had a thousand legs and was headed straight for my brain. I didn't like this at all.

I pounded the side of my head at every angle to try to dislodge the critter with no success. I stuck my little finger into my ear as far as possible. That must have injured whatever it was and for the rest of the night I sat up feeling only an occasional twitch in that ear.

At dawn, I heard a vehicle coming from the direction of the farm house. The others woke up immediately. The sheriff and I moved out toward the stills, leaving Frank and Bobby to cover the workway. The custom was that the officer who secured the information usually called the shots as to how it was worked. Although this was the newly-elected sheriff's first still raid, I asked him, "What do you want to do?"

The car reached the still yard and we could see movement and hear jars being unloaded. The sheriff was unsure.

"We can either get him now before he gets back in the car or let him go and catch him when he comes back," I suggested.

"He who hesitates is lost," as the old saying goes, and in this case that's what happened. The man finished unloading and started the car.

As the old Ford came out of the still yard and headed toward us, the sheriff finally made up his mind.

"Let's stop him."

Famous last words. Two men on the ground are no match for a wild, scared-to-death individual driving a hot-rod Ford.

As the sheriff stepped out into the workway in front of the car, the driver tried to put his foot into the carburetor and the Ford shot forward. The sheriff jumped to one side and the car careened past me, throwing gravel and dirt in every direction. Just as I was about to jump into the workway and give chase, I heard "BLAM, BLAM, BLAM." The sheriff had opened up with his .45. This only added to the driver's frenzy and it was all he could do to keep the Ford out of the pines.

PINGGG—the right front hubcap flew off like a flying saucer into the woods. Finally, the sheriff emptied his pistol and I took off on foot chasing the car. I was sure that any moment the driver would wrap it around a tree. I don't know what happened to Frank and Bobby—I guess they were busy dodging bullets. I finally caught up with the vehicle after it jumped a ditch, breaking the battery loose and shorting out the ignition system. The driver was long gone. We had another "unknown."

Three days later, the bug finally came out of my ear.

He was dead.

* * *

My group supervisor called me into his office one morning. I thought, What have I done wrong now? John Corbin had spent most of his ATF career in North Carolina and had recently been promoted to group supervisor in the regional special section in Atlanta. He was to become another close and trusted friend. John was all business that morning.

"Charley, I've got something I want you to handle. The Knoxville police department is without a chief right now. Information is that there may be corruption all the way to the top. We don't know this for sure, but we need to find out. Lauderdale has an informer you can use and we have plenty of PEA (purchase of evidence) money. Get with Harry and the informant and let's get started."

Harry and I met the informant that night. "Puny" turned out to be just that. He was a small black man who had worked for Harry before in a successful Atlanta undercover operation, buying moonshine from several large-scale wholesalers.

I picked up a 1955 Oldsmobile from our undercover pool and turned it over to Puny with $200 and instructions to get a room in Knoxville and get started. The plan was to let Puny become known in Knoxville and then start buying large amounts of moonshine from the local wholesalers. We hoped he could secure evidence of liquor violations and later gain information and evidence on any crooked law enforcement officers.

There was one more element that made this a touchy operation. No one, including the local ATF agents, was to know we were working in Knoxville. This was going to be difficult, since some of the agents I had worked with in Greeneville were now stationed in Knoxville.

Puny left for Knoxville the next day. Harry and I followed that weekend. Puny had rented a couple of rooms in a black section of Knoxville. In order not to arouse suspicion, I went in before daylight and got my camera equipment set up in a downstairs room. It faced the front porch and the street. Puny's room was upstairs and anyone going to his room would have to come past my window. I kept the shades drawn, but by standing on a chair I could pull back the shade at the top, make photographs and not be seen. On one occasion, I made a series of photographs that were so good, Bill Griffin thought I had staged the sequence!

Harry would come up to Knoxville occasionally to help keep Puny in line. Puny was making liquor buys from several wholesale moonshiners and he tended to try to con me also. Most of the time when he misled me it was so he could do something he wanted to do personally. Harry was more adept at dealing with him.

The investigation was going as planned. Soon we secured enough evidence to make criminal cases against three wholesale moonshiners and several of their trip boys. Then one night the "shit hit the fan." I had left Knoxville and returned home for the weekend. At one in the morning the telephone awakened me from a deep sleep.

"Charley, this is Bid Lindsey in Knoxville." There was a sense of urgency in his voice.

Lindsey was agent in charge in Knoxville. I immediately came awake.

"Does ATF have a black undercover agent named Duane Sowell working in Knoxville?"

I had been instructed to keep the undercover operation secure, even from our agents in Knoxville. Lindsey was a good agent and as nice a guy as you could meet. I could tell he was upset. "What's wrong?" I asked, stalling for time to think.

161

"The Knoxville police just called and said they have arrested a drunk Negro man who claims to be a federal officer working for you."

"What did he do?" I was fully awake now.

"Well, for starters, the police received a call about a disturbance in a cheap hotel—some guy was drunk and beating up his girlfriend. Before they got there, the man left, but the hotel clerk gave the police a description of his car. It was a 1955 Oldsmobile."

Oh, shit! I thought.

"After the description of the car was broadcast on the police radio, another call came in that a vehicle of the same description had crashed through the wall of a grocery store and was fleeing the scene," Lindsey continued. "When the police finally spotted the car, it was speeding across town. The police gave chase. The car tore down several front yard fences and hit three parked automobiles. Even though the front of the car was torn up and the right front tire was flat, the driver refused to stop. He drove on the rim until the wheel finally came apart and he couldn't go any further."

I was afraid to ask, but I said, "Anything else?"

"That's all I know of right now—is he one of ours?" Bid asked again.

"Yes, but he's not a federal officer. He's working for me as an undercover informer and is not an officer of any kind." I explained the entire operation to Bid, hoping he would understand. When I finished, he asked if I wanted him to get Puny out of jail on bond.

I was emphatic. "No, let him spend the night in jail. I'll be up there tomorrow afternoon and try to get everything ironed out. If you can, contact the acting chief of police and have him get everyone who has a claim into his office at two o'clock tomorrow. I'll try to get this mess straightened out. I'm sorry for any embarrassment I've caused you...but thanks for your help."

As I hung up, I thought, What a mess! I called Harry right away and filled him in. We agreed to meet early the next morning in the Regional Office with Corbin to plan our next move.

By the next morning Harry had it all figured out. If ever there was a master technician when it came to spending purchase of evidence funds, Harry was it. His mind was always in gear. By the time we got to Knoxville that afternoon, Harry was confident we would come out of this mess with only minor damage to our case.

Lindsey had made all the necessary arrangements with the police to have everyone with a claim present at two o'clock. ATF Agent Red Beeler, a former deputy sheriff of an adjoining county and something of a politician, had arranged for a local bondsman to sign Puny's bail when I gave the word. We had a few minutes, so we drove to the police impoundment lot to see what was left of the government undercover car. How Puny managed to drive that car one block was unbelievable—yet he had crashed through a brick wall, hit several cars and kept going all the way across town.

"Well, let's go face the music," I said.

When we arrived at the chief's office, I thought half of Knoxville must be there. I could hardly get through the outer office. People were spilling out into the hall. The chief was not in a good mood. He had surmised that ATF had an undercover operation going on in his town without his knowledge, so we were more or less at his mercy.

There are times in law enforcement, as in life, when you need to be aggressive and times when you need to be conciliatory. This was definitely not the time to be aggressive. We were over a barrel, so I told the chief I was sorry about what happened. I was sorry in more ways than he knew. "We'll take care of all damage claims," I said.

I had secured $2,000 in PEA money before I left Atlanta. Harry and I began negotiating with people in the outer office. About $1,800 later, we had everyone satisfied and as Harry and I walked out of the building, I thought, This is one time Puny's going to lose some money.

Puny was released on bond and Harry drove him back to Atlanta. Instead of receiving $1,800 in reward money for the eight suspects he had bought moonshine from, Puny received receipts and releases from the numerous people we had settled with that day in the chief's office. We obtained receipts from Puny for the $1,800 the government "paid" him in "rewards." Somehow it all worked out. The government paid its debt to Puny and Puny paid his debt for the damages he caused innocent people.

The case that could have been a real embarrassment to ATF turned out okay after all. We arrested eight people and seized three automobiles. We put a crimp in the moonshine business and a scare into local officers who were thinking about protecting the violators. I was glad that one was over.

* * *

One Friday afternoon in May 1961, every ATF agent in the region was alerted to be on standby the following day for an emergency assignment. On Saturday, all hell broke loose in Montgomery, Alabama. The civil rights movement was in full swing and rioting erupted in Montgomery between whites and blacks. The local police were not equipped to handle such a confrontation. U.S.

Attorney General Bobby Kennedy was determined to force integration on the nation, especially on Alabama, after Governor George Wallace had vowed no integration at the University of Alabama.

I received a telephone call from Corbin at five in the afternoon.

"Pick up Jim Berry and get to the ATF office in Montgomery as soon as possible," he said.

Calls were being made to almost every ATF agent in the Southeast. I had mixed emotions. I grew up in the South and knew that there were two sides to this equation. I also knew that violence was not the answer. Although I didn't like the idea of getting involved, I couldn't wait to get in on the action. As we barrelled through the farmland of central Georgia and Alabama, Jim, a Mississippian, and I were strangely quiet.

We arrived in Montgomery at eleven o'clock that night. Since we were the first ATF agents to arrive from out of state, we were detailed to begin serving federal restraining orders on every known member of the Ku Klux Klan in Montgomery and the surrounding area. A federal judge had issued the orders in hopes of keeping down more violence the next day. It didn't work.

At midnight, we started waking people up all over Montgomery.

"Are you Kalvin K. Kline?" we would ask.

"Yes."

"This is a restraining order from the federal court!" With that, we would leave the bewildered individual standing in his door and go on to the next one. This occupied us for the remainder of the night. When we finally finished it was about eight o'clock Sunday morning. We were told to secure quarters at Maxwell Air Force Base and get some sleep. We were ready for that.

The day was wild. While we slept, there were various confrontations with unruly citizens. We had been issued tear gas canisters, U.S. Marshal's arm bands and night sticks upon arrival and we used them.

A group of black men, women and children were trapped in a church and could not leave due to the large crowd of hecklers. ATF agents arrived and in their usual "hell for leather" attitude, went careening through the crowd with sirens blasting and sticks flying.

Several tear gas grenades were thrown into the crowd and one brave soul picked up an active canister and threw it back into ATF Agent John Petre's government car. Petre really floorboarded it then and as his partner scrambled to get the grenade out of the car, Petre was swerving from right to left. People on the street scattered like chickens.

No ATF agent was seriously hurt except John Holt, who was hit on the head with a flying brick. The stranded people got out of the church.

That afternoon we were all called together in a large auditorium on Maxwell AFB. "Whizzer" White, who later became a Supreme Court justice, was the Attorney General's spokesman. After a briefing on why we were here, he asked if we had any questions. Did we have any questions! We had all kinds of questions—Were we supposed to arrest anyone? Did we have the authority to arrest someone for violation of state or city law and not federal law? Could we use force? Did we ever have questions!

The answers were all the same. After a line or two of Washington double-talk, the answer would be, "Play it by ear." That's the way it is most of the time in police work. You are sent out to do a job and when something goes wrong, the bureaucrats and politicians say, "We didn't tell you to do *that*," and fall back on the usual Washington line of bull.

We stayed in Montgomery until the end of the week. Things finally calmed down. It was an interesting experience.

* * *

When we got back to Atlanta, Jim King needed help on a case in Lumpkin County, north of Dawsonville. Jim had a paid informant, Louie, who had made two buys of large amounts of moonshine from Loy Hoyt. Once again, I volunteered to get into the trunk of the informer's car to corroborate his testimony about the buys.

Every time I crawled into the trunk of a car, I was apprehensive. Once I got in, I had no control over the situation. I had participated in car chases in which officers fired at the fleeing vehicles, leaving bullet holes in the trunks of several liquor cars. I knew this was not uncommon. In fact, it was common in most areas of Georgia.

As we pulled into Hoyt's yard, I heard dogs barking and a woman's voice. "Where's Hoyt?" Louie asked.

"He won't be back till ten o'clock," she replied. The dogs were nosing around the back of the car and as we drove out of the yard they chased us for a half mile.

King was waiting behind an old country church several miles away. We told him what happened at Hoyt's house. Jim thought it was funny about the dogs sniffing around the trunk.

"Maybe after the dogs piss on the tires, they won't have enough pressure left to pee in the trunk—how big were the dogs?"

I didn't think it was so funny.

About a quarter to ten, I was back in the trunk in Hoyt's yard. The dogs finally quieted down after smelling the tires. Hoyt arrived 30 minutes later. I was beginning to get cramped, yet I was afraid to move and stir up the dogs.

The moonshiner leaned against the back of the car. I was almost afraid to breathe. Louie shot the breeze about the weather and finally got Hoyt talking about liquor.

"I'm going to need 12 more cases next week. Will it still be $18 a case like last time?" Louie asked.

"Yeah, I can let you have it for $18," Hoyt replied.

"You want me to come here or meet you at the other place?"

"Here's okay," Hoyt said, "when you coming?"

"When will you have it?"

Hoyt fell right into it. "I'm going to run on Monday night— so Tuesday about ten o'clock will be okay." Louie was getting what we needed now.

"I want to get back to Atlanta before too late, the damn ATF starts working about eleven."

"Okay, we can make it nine," Hoyt agreed.

Louie pulled out of the yard and we had all the corroboration we needed to put Hoyt in the penitentiary. We did later.

These are some news clippings from the Montgomery riots in '61

Charley Weems checking moonshine-liquor stash in Knoxville, TN

Chapter XX
Fire in the Hole

With the help of Milton Walton and C.D. Veeder, I successfully prepared and submitted several good jacketed liquor conspiracy cases for prosecution early in '61. Veeder was a fine, distinguished-looking man. He was assigned to review all jacketed cases submitted for prosecution, and was the final authority in sending a case to the U.S. Attorney. He looked like a concert violinist—tall, 51 years old, with heavy eyebrows and a large handlebar moustache.

He was stricken with polio in his early adult years and spent months in the Warm Springs Polio Foundation at Warm Springs, Georgia. There he became friends with Franklin D. Roosevelt, who told Veeder that he could work anywhere he wanted in government. Luckily for ATF, he chose to work in Atlanta for the Treasury Department. He was a fine gentleman, and although paralyzed from the waist down, he made up for his affliction with his keen mind and astute knowledge of the laws of evidence. Veeder was an excellent example of a handicapped person making an outstanding contribution to society. He was not sorry for himself and didn't expect pity from anyone else. He supported himself physically and financially.

That summer, Corbin called me into his office.

"Charley, I'm going to give you a good one!" he said with a slight smile as he handed me a file titled "J.R. Turner". Every ATF agent in the Southeast had heard of J.R. In Georgia he was the equivalent of North Carolina's Perry Bloom.

I had mixed emotions. J.R.'s operation had been investigated by almost every ATF agent in Georgia for 20 years. Occasionally a big distillery would be seized and maybe one or two still hands caught, but for the most part, J.R. directed his illegal operation quietly and efficiently and stayed out of prison.

J.R. didn't make enemies. He was quick to help anyone in the community around Dawsonville and could be counted upon to contribute generously to every charitable cause. He always wore nice slacks and a dress shirt and an expensive fedora. He could have been the mayor or a legitimate businessman. In fact, he easily could have succeeded in any type of legitimate business that he chose. He was intelligent, nice looking and an excellent manager of men and details. Why he chose to indulge in criminal activities was a mystery. One reason could have been that by growing up in an area that was a hotbed of moonshining, he just naturally became involved. It was expected of him. J.R. certainly became the biggest major violator in Georgia and one of the largest in the nation.

I knew what was expected of me. Corbin had just given me the opportunity to match wits with a master, but J.R. had a lot of wild cards that I didn't know about. I was playing a losing hand from the start.

Special Agents Ray Hahn, Jim Berry and Joe Powell were detailed by John to help in this investigation. We began by collecting all the information we could from the Gainesville post of duty and all other sources we could find. I developed a list of known close associates, the locations of their residences and vehicles they used.

We collected case reports that could be connected to this operation, either directly or indirectly. We studied these to develop a common thread (M.O.) as to employees and areas of activity. I made trips to Detroit and New Orleans running down leads on raw materials sources for the operation. Hahn and I spent many long, tiring nights on surveillance of J.R. and his lieutenants. Berry and Powell were soon pulled out for undercover assignments in other states and after six weeks, I was pretty much on my own.

I could always get someone to drop me out to observe a road or suspect. It became more and more apparent that there was never any activity when I was in the area, yet I knew an organization as large as J.R.'s wasn't shutting down because of one little wild-eyed agent.

This continued for months, with Gainesville ATF Agent James Stratigos and Area Supervisor Doug Denney helping me all they could. Their territory encompassed Dawson, Lumpkin and several other prolific moonshining counties and they had all they could do to work their own information.

That fall, Doug and James helped me seize and destroy a large upright steam boiler distillery in Dawson County, five miles southwest of Dawsonville. It had all the earmarks of a J.R. still, but as usual when we raided, the still hands were long gone. We collected all the physical evidence we could and I started running down leads from the materials found.

I was getting discouraged. I even brought in Red Crankcase to try to infiltrate J.R.'s operation. After two weeks, I realized that J.R. was not going to talk to anyone he didn't know. His organization was so tight no one could get in without being known.

In a desperate effort to obtain information, one of the regional specials suggested we put a telephone tap on one of J.R.'s close associates. This was against ATF policy except with a federal court order and it could get you fired if it was discovered. But I was desperate.

Early in my career, I had assisted as local officers tapped a phone, but I only knew the basics. I needed an expert. "Hank" (an ATF agent I trusted with my life) volunteered to help me. He had experience in doing this sort of thing.

We cased the area of the suspect's residence from every angle. In those days, every telephone had two wires or a "pair" on the telephone pole. We determined the proper pair from driving past the residence and later picked out a pole to climb.

After preparing all the necessary equipment and wire, Hank and I loaded it up and arrived in the remote rural area after midnight. We drove past the house to make sure everyone was asleep and then found an old sawmill road where we could stash our car. We lugged all the wire and equipment through the woods to the telephone lines. They ran parallel to the public road.

Although it was now after one o'clock, we still had to be careful not to be seen. As Hank buckled on his climbing spikes, I unrolled the wire and kept a sharp eye and ear peeled for approaching vehicles.

"Hank! Hit the ditch!" Just in time I had seen headlights coming over the crest of a hill. We remained hidden until the car passed. Then Hank went up the pole in a flash. We spent most of the night hiding our additional wire, digging a trench into the woods and covering our sign. Just before daylight, we pulled out and headed back to Atlanta. The plan was for me to go into the woods the following week and monitor the telephone for any useful information. Hank and I were both committed to other work and couldn't get back until the following Monday night.

Three days later, Hank dropped me out some distance from the old sawmill road and I walked through a dense wooded area until I found the road. After getting oriented, I found the ditch where we had hidden the roll of wire running from the telephone pole. The wire was gone! I couldn't believe it. Making sure I had the correct location, I called Hank on the radio and told him to come on in. He did and we searched for the wire. When we reached the pole, we found that the wire was indeed gone. We had blown it.

This was only one of the unusual things that occurred during the many months I spent investigating the J.R. organization. At that time it didn't make sense, but much later I began to understand.

By now, all the regional specials in the Atlanta office knew I was assigned to work J.R., and most of them had participated in the investigation. We all worked together and although we were assigned different major violators, we usually had no secrets from each other. Hank and I were the only ones who knew about the attempt to tap the telephone line—we thought.

Several other undercover contacts were made by informants furnished by Duff Floyd from Jasper and Bub Kay in Cornelia. These legendary agents were two of the most respected men in ATF. Their efforts also proved fruitless.

We got our first big break early in '62. Denney called me. "Charley, we've just seized a big I.D. in Lumpkin County, north of Dahlonega. It has all the appearances of being a J.R. outfit."

"Hold everything until I can get there," I told Doug. I immediately called Graham Copeland, our fingerprint and physical evidence expert.

After a fast trip from Atlanta to Lumpkin County, we began a sweep of the distillery location. This was one of the largest distilleries I had ever seen. It had a 20-hp upright boiler, three feet in diameter, and fifty-four 220-gallon barrel fermenters. There were more than 10,000 gallons of mash, 1,260 gallons of moonshine and a new GMC two-ton truck loaded with 20,000 pounds of sugar.

This was typical of J.R.'s operation—very large, a steamer, all new equipment and an electrically-operated fuel oil burner.

We secured a few legible fingerprints and collected other evidence, then began to destroy the distillery. It was in a huge chicken house 100 feet long and 40 feet wide. It was located behind a five-room farmhouse and wasn't visible from the public road due to the slope of the land. Anyone seeing the two-ton truck coming into the driveway of the house would assume it was hauling chicken feed, since this was the largest chicken-producing area in the U.S.

Jim Stratigos broke out two cases of dynamite. After some discussion as to the labor involved in moving 54 barrels full of mash out of the chicken house, we decided that since the building was used to house an illegal operation it was subject to destruction also. The boiler was another problem due to its tremendous size. James called a local machinist to cut the boiler with an acetylene torch. This took about an hour. Meanwhile, Stratigos and I prepared 24 sticks of dynamite, each with a cap and fuse. We only hoped we had cut all the fuses the same length.

The plan was to drop one stick into every other barrel. I took 12 sticks, six in each hand and Stratigos took 12. We arranged the fuses all together. As Stratigos and I stood close together, Bill Maine lit all the fuses with a propane torch. Some didn't light the first time. There we stood with 24 sticks of dynamite, some lit and some not, trying to get them all going. Finally, all the fuses were spewing fire and Jim and I broke for the chicken house.

"Fire in the hole!" Stratigos shouted.

We had burned a piece of fuse earlier to time it. It burned at one foot per minute. We cut the fuses 18 inches long, so we had 90 seconds after they were lit before the dynamite would go off. That seemed like a very short time.

I moved as quickly as I could through the mash barrels in my line, keeping an eye on Stratigos. I knew that if either of us fell or got hung up some way, it would be up to the other one to get us both out.

By the time we reached the open end of the building, all the dynamite was in place and Jim and I ran for cover.

"Fire in the hole!" I shouted at the top of my voice.

No sooner had I gotten behind a big oak tree than the explosives began going off—Boom–boo-oo-om–boom. The roof lifted as several sticks of dynamite went off at the same time. Amber beer came pouring out of the cracks. What a sight! I thought about fire, but with 10,000 gallons of beer flying in all directions, there was no danger of that. We waited a minute or two to make sure all the dynamite had exploded, then ventured out. Mash dripped from every tree in the yard and the roof of the chicken house was split in several places. The smell of dynamite fumes and beer was overwhelming. Man, was this fun!

Needless to say, the destruction of the distillery was complete.

That night we slept at the still site and the following day we collected more evidence. I determined that the residence and distillery premises belonged to R.B. Bledsoe. Bledsoe showed me a lease agreement signed in the name of Roy Reece and later identified a photo of Wade White, a known employee of J.R., as the man to whom he had rented the property and who had signed the lease "Roy Reece." This was certainly helpful.

About one o'clock, an agent called from the house.

"Somebody is up here loading furniture and stuff into a station wagon."

When I got to the house, Attorney Rob Thomas was gathering up everything he could carry and hurriedly placing it in the back of the station wagon.

"Does this furniture belong to you?" I asked.

He replied, "It belongs to a client of mine."

As he continued loading the television, clothes and frozen food into the station wagon, Thomas looked longingly at the new

GMC truck with 20,000 pounds of sugar on it and said, "That's where we really lost money!"

"I'm glad to hear you admit that you're in partnership with the moonshiners," I said sarcastically.

"I have to make money some way other than as an attorney," he replied brazenly.

I was shocked that an attorney would stoop so low as to serve as a "gofer" for moonshiners and then admit that he was a part of the illegal operation.

I was disgusted, too, especially since Thomas had worked as an Assistant U.S. Attorney after his graduation from law school, prosecuting moonshiners. I was associated with U.S. Attorneys who were some of the finest men I have ever known, but Thomas was not one of them.

I never cease to be amazed that men who have everything going for them, succumb to the temptation to make a few extra dollars. Some get by with it at the time, but it always comes back to haunt them. They pay far more in the long run. I can understand a man who has almost nothing being tempted to violate ethics and principles, but not a man who has attained the status and prestige of a successful businessman, especially an attorney.

Due to this and several other instances, I still have difficulty respecting most criminal defense lawyers.

Investigator Bill Maine located several empty yeast cans in the still house and lifted 11 fingerprints. These prints were sent to the FBI lab in Washington with names of known J.R. associates. All the prints were identified as belonging to "Skeeter" Fields, one of the most notorious distillers in the Southeast. Skeeter was known for his ability to operate large steamer-type distilleries. Although Skeeter got his nickname by being fast on his feet, he was no problem when caught and was a likeable kind of guy.

The modus operandi, the still hands, the size and location of the distillery and the intervention of a high-priced lawyer all pointed to J.R., but we had only enough evidence to successfully prosecute Wade White (Roy Reece) and Skeeter Fields.

This was the first of many large-scale J.R. operations that I investigated. Over the next several years I found that direct evidence against J.R. was hard to come by.

Chapter XXI
Hazardous Duty

In the summer of '62, Jim Berry and I seized a truck with over 500 gallons of whiskey in Atlanta and James Stratigos and I seized over 1,350 gallons of moonshine in Dawson County.

Early in September, I was awakened by a midnight telephone call.

Half awake, I mumbled, "Hello?"

"Charley, there's been an assault on one of our agents. Gene Howell is being treated at Dr. Riley's office in Jonesboro. Get on it! It's your case!" John Corbin did not mince words at a time like this. As soon as I hung up the phone, I called Dr. Riley's office.

"Yes, Howell's here. No, I don't know how badly he's hurt," Dr. Riley replied to my questions.

"I'll be there in 15 minutes." I had lived around Jonesboro most of my life and knew Dr. Riley personally. I arrived at his office in less than 15 minutes.

Howell, a relatively young investigator, was still on the examining table when I arrived. He looked bad. There were numerous abrasions on his face and arms and he had a bad bruise on his right leg. His clothes were torn. He had a two-inch gash in his right temple and his right eye was swollen shut. Obviously he had taken quite a beating. Gene was later transported to Georgia Baptist Hospital where he was examined by neurosurgeons.

I made my questions brief. Gene told me he had emptied his five-shot revolver at three men who assaulted him.

Frank Lane met me at the doctor's office.

"The Spalding County Hospital in Griffin reported that three men were admitted a few minutes ago with gunshot wounds," Frank said.

After making several photos of Gene's injuries, Frank and I left for Griffin. We arrived at the hospital at one in the morning. We identified ourselves as federal officers and were told that three men had been admitted to the hospital at eleven o'clock with gunshot wounds.

The hospital supervisor pointed out a man sitting in the waiting room as the one who brought the men to the hospital.

"I'm Charley Weems, special agent with the Treasury Department," I told the man, who identified himself as Clyde Hill. "Tell me about what happened tonight."

Hill said that about ten-thirty Belford, Evan and Fulton Hill had appeared at his door saying they had been shot and asking him to take them to the Griffin Hospital.

"Anything else?" I asked.

"That's all I know," he said.

I stayed at the hospital until the surgeon who had been operating on the two most seriously injured men came out to the waiting room.

"Belford Hill was shot in one arm and in the center of his chest. The bullet went completely through his body and remained just under the skin of his back. Fulton was shot in one arm and another bullet entered his abdomen near his navel, lodging in his pelvis," the doctor said, handing me a bullet.

We sealed it in a glass vial and I took possession of it for evidence.

"All three men are sedated. They won't be able to be interviewed for some time," the doctor said.

"Stay here, Frank, and get all their clothing and any other evidence you can find," I said.

I left for the scene of the assault, knowing that I had to obtain as much evidence as possible to connect these men with the illicit distillery Howell had been investigating. My assault case would hinge on the fact that the men were in the act of violating the law and that they knew Howell was an officer of the law.

When I reached the scene of the encounter, several other agents had arrived to assist in the investigation. I began taking pictures of the crime scene and piecing together what had happened.

Chief Howard Smith filled me in briefly and said that they had not yet found Howell's gun. It was a dreary, overcast morning and I was anxious to get as many photographs of the scene as I could before it started to rain. Investigator Wilbur Porter was in an open field adjacent to where a truck had run off the road and torn down 100 feet of barbed wire fence. We tried to envision the previous night's events as we searched the area for Howell's pistol.

Porter called, "Charley, come over here!" About 25 feet from where Howell had been found, the pistol lay in tall grass. I made photos of the pistol and the area and carefully picked up the gun. It was a snub-nose Smith and Wesson .38 revolver. There were deep gouge marks in the wooden stock, but only on the right side. This would prove to be significant at the trial. In the cylinder were five empty shell casings. I placed the pistol in a plastic evidence bag and labeled it.

Walking back up the public road, I traced the route of the still truck. When I arrived at the distillery, John Guy was there. He too was collecting evidence. John filled me in on the events of the past several days.

Three weeks earlier, John had received information from a confidential informant about the location of the distillery in the Panhandle section of Clayton County. John checked the distillery and marked a shovel handle, fuel line valves and several other items with fluorescent paste. (ATF had begun to acquire a minuscule amount of technical equipment and we were anxious to try it out.) John gave the information to Jimmy Satterfield and Frank Lane to work.

Lane and Satterfield later checked the distillery and found it to be set up and ready to operate. This led up to the night of the shooting and assault.

The movies usually show stakeouts with surveillance teams sitting in new automobiles or in comfortable surroundings. This was certainly not the setting for most ATF surveillance operations. The common practice was to be dropped out of a slow-moving vehicle some distance from the violation area where we silently slipped into a place of concealment to set up observation—usually on the cold, hard ground.

Around eight o'clock, Howell, Lane and Smith were dropped out by Frank Kendall and Lt. Bill Murray. They walked in complete darkness through a wooded area. They were aware that anything could happen that night in this prolific moonshining area. They also knew that the Hill clan of six brothers and numerous cousins and other relatives controlled virtually every activity in the rural community.

The Hills were notorious for moonshining, trapping, killing deer out of season, and their overall disdain for law enforcement. Several of them had been arrested for moonshining and one had been convicted of assaulting a federal officer after being chased from an illicit distillery. They were definitely a mean and dangerous bunch.

Upon reaching a large open pasture, the officers heard the sound of a gasoline burner. A big truck was backed up to a wooded area on one side of the pasture. Except for the sound of the burners, it was deathly quiet. Howell slipped up to within 50 feet of the truck and saw that it was parked at the workway to the stills. He withdrew

177

100 yards from the truck and distillery and continued to watch and listen.

At ten o'clock Lane left the area to meet the other officers on the public road. Thirty minutes later, three men came out of the woods carrying flashlights and got into the still truck. What to do? Howell thought. We can't let them get out—they might not come back. He and Howard split up with Howard following the truck and Gene running across the pasture toward a spot where he could intercept the vehicle.

Howell was a small man, about 5'9" and 145 pounds. He had to make an instantaneous decision. He was determined to do his job, knowing the risks involved. Although he was of small stature, he showed tremendous courage that cost him his life.

The truck, running without lights, rumbled across the open pasture. Smith attempted to keep up. Howell crouched behind a small tree adjacent to the pasture road. As the truck approached, he stepped from behind the tree in front of the truck. Turning his flashlight onto the truck, he shouted, "Stop! Federal officer, you're under arrest!"

Gears clashed as the truck lurched over the uneven ground toward Howell. The lights came on as the driver attempted to run over the ATF agent. Howell jumped aside and somehow managed to jump onto the right side of the truck, all the while telling the occupants he was a federal officer and ordering them to stop.

It only served to increase the frenzy in the cab. The driver, Fulton Hill, floorboarded the accelerator and Belford Hill started striking Howell in the face with a flashlight. The truck slammed through a barbed-wire gate and onto the public road. The gouges on the right side of the pistol's stock proved the pistol was still in its holster when the truck ran through the barbed-wire gate. Howell drew his pistol while holding onto the truck with one arm. Belford Hill was still hitting him on the head with the metal flashlight.

Howell shoved his pistol into the cab of the truck and told the Hills once again to stop, he was a federal officer. With that, Fulton Hill swerved the truck up onto a low bank and began to drag Howell along a barbed-wire fence that ran parallel to the road. Belford Hill grabbed Howell's pistol, and being a powerful man, twisted the pistol back toward the ATF agent. As the gun was being twisted out of his hand, Howell pulled the trigger. The first shot struck Belford in the center of his chest. He let go of the pistol and opened the door of the truck, pushing Howell into the barbed-wire fence.

While still being dragged along the fence, Howell fired the remaining four shots into the cab of the truck. He was slammed off

178

the truck door by a fence post and run over by the rear wheels. Of the four other shots fired, one went through Belford's arm, one went through Evan's arm, one grazed Fulton's arm and the other buried in Fulton's stomach. Despite being wounded twice, Fulton drove the truck to the home of their nephew, Clyde Hill, a short distance away. Clyde took them to the hospital.

We found the truck behind Clyde's home. It was blood-spattered and beat-up from the previous night. In the rear was the shovel from the still with fluorescent paste on the handle. (This paste is not visible to the naked eye, but under ultra-violet light it fluoresces almost like neon.) The truck was seized. After we destroyed the distillery, I left the area late that afternoon. I was worn out physically and mentally.

The next three months were spent working this time-consuming case. I left no stone unturned, preparing the most air-tight case possible with the help of John Guy, Jimmy Satterfield and Frank Lane. We were all anxious to make the best case we could, knowing that the Hills would have the best lawyer money could buy.

Although Evan Hill had no previous record, both Belford and Fulton Hill had previous liquor law convictions. Belford had been convicted of assaulting federal agents previously and had served two years in the federal penitentiary. These people were persistent violators who had little respect for the law.

We secured every scrap of evidence we could, including forensic, boot prints, statements and photographs of the area from every angle. We made aerial photographs showing the proximity of the still to Fulton Hill's home and the location of the assault and subsequent actions taken by the officers and defendants. I felt we were ready to submit the case for prosecution.

All three defendants were indicted and tried on four counts of violating federal statutes. These included count one - unlawfully, willfully and knowingly forcibly assaulting, resisting, opposing, impeding and interfering with a federal officer (Eugene Howell). The other three counts were for making illegal distilled spirits and possession of the illegal distillery and spirits.

The three defendants were convicted on all counts and given prison sentences of from two to five years, with Belford receiving the five-year term. The case was appealed through the courts and the U.S. Supreme Court upheld all three convictions.

While out on bond awaiting the appeals process, Belford Hill was again arrested while operating a large illicit distillery in the same general area. This time he had erected a large platform in the middle of a 90-acre swamp, placed the distillery on it and covered the entire setup with camouflage netting. He was working the distillery using boats. Once again, the arresting agents had to fight Belford, but luckily no one was seriously injured on this occasion.

Several months after their conviction in federal court, Howell arrived at work one morning in the federal building in Atlanta. While sitting at his desk, Howell collapsed and died from an apparent hemorrhage. He had never really recovered from the brutal attack by the Hills.

Immediately, I began my own investigation, talking to Dr. Riley and the other doctors who had treated Gene. They all had noted a large bump on the back of his head. The doctors at the hospital had reported there was fluid pressing on his brain due to the blow he had received during the encounter with the Hills.

Although I pressed to have the case reopened and the Hills tried for manslaughter, the consensus of the local prosecuting attorney and the U.S. Attorney was that since the defendants had already been tried and convicted of assault, they could claim double jeopardy and that our hands were tied. I am convinced that Howell's death was caused by the encounter with the Hills.

Gene was one of several excellent officers I saw killed or maimed in the dangerous occupation of special investigator/special agent with ATF.

Two and one-half years after their arrest, the Supreme Court dismissed their appeal and the Hills finally began serving time in the Atlanta Federal Penitentiary. They got off light.

Groundhog type stills (Hill case) Panhandle sect., Clayton County, Ga.

Groundhog type stills (Hill case) Panhandle sect., Clayton County, Ga.

Aerial photo of illegal distillery area where confrontation between Special Agent Howell and Hill clan took place.

Aerial photo of illegal distillery area where confrontation between Special Agent Howell and Hill clan took place.

Chapter XXII
Win a Few, Lose a Few

John Guy sounded excited.

"I just got information on a big still over in Douglas County. If you'll meet me at the Varsity, we can get a couple of hot dogs and I'll fill you in."

"I'll be there in 15 minutes," I told him.

Jim King was in the squad room, so I grabbed him on the way out. He was always ready for a hot dog. John brought Jimmy Satterfield with him. At the Varsity, John described the suspected location to us. Satterfield knew the area. That afternoon, Jim dropped Satterfield and me on a back road about a mile and a half from the still.

Jimmy and I had full packs and camping gear. We hit some railroad tracks and walked them a while before entering the woods. Jimmy is a natural woodsman. An hour later we reached a wooded area adjacent to a dirt road. A long driveway led from the road into an old farm. The still was behind the farmhouse. We couldn't see the farmhouse, but could see and hear any vehicle that turned into the driveway.

No sooner had we gotten into position than the bottom fell out. It started raining, as they say in south Georgia, "like a cow pissing on a flat rock." It was coming down by bucketsful. Jimmy had just fired up his can of sterno to heat up some instant coffee. Being an old Navy man, Satterfield drank coffee all the time. We quickly spread a poncho that Jimmy had brought (he was always well equipped) and tried to stay as dry as we could. It was impossible and we were drenched. By the time the rain stopped, it was dark and turning colder. We spent a miserable night, but we both had done it before.

The next morning at seven-thirty we were alerted by the sound of a truck going into the still road. As we crouched in the bushes alongside the road, I felt the same excitement and antici-pation I always experienced when this kind of action was taking place.

Three hours later, a car came to a stop in the driveway. A man walked toward the farmhouse while another man remained in the car. After a short time, a large white van truck came out of the driveway and followed the car toward Douglasville. The truck appeared to be heavily loaded. An hour later, another truck left going in the same direction.

Early that afternoon, Jim King joined us. We left Jimmy at the observation point and walked across a wooded area, skirting an open field to within 100 yards of the distillery. As we crawled on our bellies across an open sage field, a truck started up. Not knowing exactly where the workway was, we froze. The truck came out of the distillery site and headed directly toward us. I thought, Oh, shit, we're either going to blow the still or get run over! We both tried to sink into the ground like moles. Just as I thought we would have to make our move, the truck veered left and continued across the field toward the old farmhouse on the hill. We had been within ten yards of the workway and didn't know it.

As soon as the truck cleared the area, Jim and I continued crawling until we reached the other side of the distillery. The location was unique. The distillery was up against a sheer escarpment on the north side and was worked across an open field and into the woods. It was in an ideal location and was covered with camouflage netting. The distillery was in full operation and we could see one man working.

Electric and gas lines ran from the distillery back up the hill to the old farmhouse. This method of supplying large stills with electric power was commonplace, but this was the first time I had seen propane gas lines run this far. Most large distilleries used electric pumps and electrically-operated furnace burners in their operation, but not many used propane gas as fuel.

We watched until just before dark, then returned to our campsite across the road. After spending another cold night on the ground, we were glad to see Lane and John Hayes come in to relieve us. King and I were picked up by Guy. Back in our car, we remained in the area and waited for other activity.

That morning about nine o'clock, Frank called on the radio. "The car pulled into the driveway and then a 3/4-ton truck came out of the distillery road and turned toward Highway 78." A half hour later, Frank called again, saying, "The same truck just drove back into the workway."

Satterfield called about eleven o'clock. "The big truck is coming out," he whispered.

Five minutes later, Hayes reported the truck was going toward Highway 78. King and I had positioned ourselves on 78 where we could see the public road intersection. The truck turned left onto the highway. We watched until it had disappeared over a hill, then pulled out behind it. Later we found it parked at a truck stop on 78, where Guy joined us.

At three o'clock, Hayes called. "The other truck has left the still and is heading your way."

Time to start arresting people, I thought. Leaving John with the truck at the truck stop, King and I took off toward the distillery.

"We'll block him where the dirt road comes into Highway 78." Our timing was perfect. As the truck arrived at 78, I made it appear that I didn't have enough space to turn in. As I blocked the truck, Jim was out in a flash and arrested the driver, Albert Holiday, before he knew what was going on.

I radioed the other agents and told them of the arrest, then crawled into the back of the truck. With the handcuffed Holiday in the front seat, Jim drove back into the distillery workway. As we approached, the two still hands recognized the truck as belonging there and kept working. King slammed the truck into the still yard and they began to realize something was wrong. Both took off running.

I vaulted the back rail of the truck and hit the ground running. Jim was out of the cab just as fast. Out of the corner of my eye, I saw him go after one, so I took the other. It was a wild chase. A surprised and scared man is a handful. I caught my man, but he jerked away from me and plunged wildly into the brush.

"You son-of-a-bitch!" I muttered, stumbling after him. I got another grip on his belt and we both fell into a large hole filled with water. He came up sputtering, but this finally took the fire out of him. I was soaked, but happy.

By any standards, this was a large operation. It had a mash capacity of over 6,000 gallons and 250 gallons of moonshine at the still. It was also the first and only still I saw using 500-gallon aluminum airplane fuel tanks for whiskey containers. It was an elaborate setup, being well-financed and well hidden more than 400 yards from the farmhouse.

I wondered how Guy had gotten information on such a large operation. I was to be pleasantly surprised at a later date.

* * *

My investigation of the J.R. syndicate continued with long hours of surveillance that finally paid off in the seizure of a two-ton truck in Lincolnton. Using three vehicles, we trailed the truck from a raw materials outlet in Atlanta. J.R. was driving a convoy vehicle and when he stopped at a red light, I got close enough to identify him. When the truck was clear of Atlanta, J.R. disappeared. We continued to leapfrog the truck until it reached a remote area in

Elbert County. In a rural area of large pastures, we lost sight of the truck. Topping a hill at a high rate of speed, we ran past the vehicle before we had time to do anything else.

The driver had employed a much-used tactic of stopping just over the crest of a hill to check for any vehicles which might be following him. He was out of the truck, using the ploy of checking his tires. After we blew the tail job, he led us on a wild goose chase, driving into dead end roads and turning around. He finally arrived in Lincolnton after dark and parked at a truck stop.

From my vantage point behind a tombstone in a cemetery across the street, I saw him make several telephone calls. After midnight, we crawled into the parking area and examined the truck closely. It was loaded with half-gallon jars and other raw materials. The driver had disappeared.

After daybreak, we seized the truck and began back-tracking his previous route. We worked three days straight without finding the distillery. I finally drove back to Atlanta, caught up on some paperwork, then returned two days later and found the distillery location, a half-mile from where the driver had checked his tires and "made" us.

I had been driving into every driveway, field road or trail leading off the public road. Finally, I crossed a large cotton field to an old tenant house, a quarter-mile from the public road. In the yard was the usual array of chickens and a couple of black children were on the porch. I saw signs of vehicle traffic going around the corner of the old clapboard house. Behind the house, the tracks continued around the edge of another cotton field. As I followed the sign, I knew this had to be it. About 300 yards from the back of the house, the trail led into a wooded area and what was left of the distillery. Most of it had been moved out!

I figured that by our being seen in the immediate area of the distillery and later seizing the raw materials vehicle, the still was blown, but the idea that the violator would have enough nerve to move this large an operation never entered my mind. The only conclusion I could draw was that they knew when we left the area and when we would be back—a sobering thought. I'd had so many good leads go up in smoke. I began to wonder if this was all just good luck on J.R.'s part or if he had inside help. But who? I didn't want to think of the possibilities.

* * *

My weekends usually began with the phone ringing. This time it was Doug Denney.

"Charley, we've got a big still located south of Dawsonville. It's probably J.R.'s."

"I'll be there as fast as I can!" I said.

I arrived about eight o'clock and met Doug, James Stratigos and Frank Frazier at the still.

It was a typical J.R. operation, using a large 15-h.p. steam boiler and having a capacity of over 12,000 gallons of mash. There were also 1,589 gallons of moonshine, but no defendants. Doug explained that while locating the distillery, our investigators had been seen. When they arrived, the still site was abandoned. Yet, we were getting close to J.R.

His time would come!

Huge upright steam boiler used at one of J.R.'s stills, being destroyed by acetylene torch.

Chapter XXIII
. . . And Some Get Rained Out

The first six months of 1963 were filled with still raids, liquor car chases and a great deal of surveillance work on the legendary J.R. case. I worked with my old friend Howard Smith when I could and with Detective John Crunkelton of DeKalb County. I ran down information on every large seizure or suspected still location, hoping to get a break on the J.R. case. We made several seizures of trucks transporting more than 800 gallons each and numerous big distilleries in the Atlanta area, but I was stymied for concrete evidence against J.R.

Several state revenue officers had radios on the ATF frequency. I suspected that some of the liquor law violators also had monitors. Knowing that there had to be a leak somewhere, I looked into the possibility of prosecuting unauthorized persons for monitoring government radio frequencies. I found that it is perfectly legal for anyone to monitor a frequency whether it belongs to ATF, FBI, CIA or any other law enforcement agency. This bothered me and I made a request for radios on a secure frequency unknown to state officers or the violators.

I worked with some of the finest state revenue agents, sheriffs and city and county officers in the country. I was also associated with some whom I wouldn't trust for five minutes. They were the exception rather than the rule, but it was true then and it's true now.

The problem of monitoring existed not only in Georgia, but in several other Southeastern states. After the Montgomery riots, ATF began to get a little respect from the powers-that-be in Washington and received additional operating funds. Finally, we were no longer having to park the government cars due to lack of money for gasoline.

Soon we received scramblers to attach to our present radios. These attachments were a lot of fun to begin with because when they were switched on, the transmission sounded like Chinese. Radios without the attachment received the transmission, but it was unintelligible. They seemed to work pretty well, but J.R.'s group still seemed to know every move we made.

On two occasions, I hired a pilot and aircraft to make aerial photographs and attempted to trail suspect vehicles. We had varying success, but I became convinced that we could use aircraft to good advantage in our work. I had no idea that John Guy had already struck gold in this area.

* * *

Sometimes you get plain lucky. Jim Berry and I were serving as witnesses in federal court in Gainesville. After court adjourned, I asked, "Jim, do you want to ride over to Dawsonville with me to check on J.R?"

"Sure thing." Jim was always ready for action (well, most of the time). We drove over to Dawson County and checked several locations.

About six-thirty in the afternoon we headed back to Gainesville to spend the night. It was summertime, so there was still plenty of daylight. Jim and I were shooting the bull about one thing and another when I overtook a white Ford van. It was traveling at a normal rate of speed and the only thing even remotely suspicious was that it had a Fulton County license plate. An unmarked truck or van from the Atlanta area was always cause for suspicion in this moonshining area. I decided to follow for a few miles to see what happened.

The van had large rear-view mirrors on each side and the driver frequently checked the mirrors. I wasn't following closely, so I wondered about this. After a short distance, the van turned off the highway into a service station parking area. As I passed, I looked straight ahead, and then into my rear-view mirror. Instead of parking at the gas pumps or in a parking space near the building, the driver stopped away from any activity and got out.

"That's funny," I said.

"Do you think he's got anything?" Jim asked.

"Don't know," I answered.

Most of north Georgia is hilly. I drove about a mile and pulled the car into an old sawmill road. Gunning it up the narrow dirt trail, I found a place to turn around and quickly pulled back to within sight of the road. In about two minutes, the van came by. Not enough time had elapsed for him to go into the station and buy anything.

"He's got a load" I said. With that, we pulled back out on the highway and soon caught up with the vehicle. I hoped that seeing me behind him again would cause the driver to panic and try to escape.

Although he looked in the mirror several times, he was cool and unaffected by our presence. I knew that he had seen us behind him earlier and that if he was in the liquor business, he recognized the green '62 Ford I was driving. The violators knew our vehicles even better than we knew theirs.

I followed for two miles and told Jim, "Get ready, I'm going to stop him!"

Jim started complaining—"I've got on a Hart Schaffner & Marx suit and Florsheim shoes," he said, "I don't want to tear 'em up."

I pulled alongside and blew my siren—Wrrrrrrrrrr. The truck slowed. I dropped behind, thinking it was going to stop. The driver kept driving at the same speed. His window was down, so I knew he heard and had seen me. I hit the siren again and pulled alongside. The van veered toward our vehicle so I dropped back, knowing there was no way he was going to outrun me.

The van continued across the left lane of the highway, hit a shallow ditch and jumped up on a driveway, crashing into an outbuilding behind a house. I skidded up the driveway and saw someone come out of the passenger side of the truck.

"Get him," I shouted, running to the truck to arrest the driver. No one was there. The driver had gone out the passenger side and Jim was in hot pursuit.

The older couple who lived in the house were outside by this time, looking with amazement at their damaged outbuilding. I identified myself as a federal officer and explained what had happened.

Gasping for breath, his face red as a beet, Jim came staggering out of the woods behind the house. "He got away," Jim said, panting. "If I hadn't had on these leather-soled shoes I might have caught him."

Jim was angry and I didn't help any by saying, "Excuses, excuses."

We were lucky and unlucky. We got 384 gallons of liquor and the truck, but the driver got away and Jim ripped his suit.

WILD WEEKEND

The Southeast Region had a purchase of evidence account (PEA) set aside to use in undercover operations and to pay rewards for useful information furnished by informers. Regional special investigators could request reasonable amounts by submitting the proper forms and justification. A strict accounting was required for the expenditure of these funds, with signed receipts or other documentation submitted at the end of each reporting period.

Harry Lauderdale had an informer who, like most, was a con man. He had helped Harry on a conspiracy case in North Carolina. Harry asked him if he could buy from J.R. The informant was ready and willing to try, for a price. Harry had a fertile mind and he and the informant concocted a plan to lure J.R. to New York City with a half-gallon sample of moonshine. No way, I thought, but I was beginning to grasp at straws. Even though the plan seemed far-fetched, I agreed to go along. We discussed the plan with Corbin and I requested $500 to get started.

"I know Investigator Berman in the New York office. I'll call him and set it up," Harry said, as he started down the hallway of the federal building.

Harry is another of the real characters I had the pleasure of working with. He is 5'8" with short legs and a baby face—somewhat similar to Babe Ruth, only with fair skin and blue eyes. He is always full of energy and his mind is constantly working—not always on work. Harry knew how to operate with PEA money. I had found that out when we dealt with Puny in Knoxville and I was afraid this had all the earmarks of turning out the same way.

We waited for a call from Harry's informer. He was to contact J.R. and firm up the arrangements for the flight to New York. J.R. would join the informer and our undercover man. Then the New York buy of several tractor-trailer loads of illicit whiskey was to be consummated—we hoped. It all seemed too far out for me, but what did I know? Harry had made some wild schemes work in the past, but this was the wildest. J.R. was supposed to bring a half-gallon sample of moonshine with him—Hmmmmm.

Early Friday night, Harry called. "The informer just talked to J.R.—he'll be in New York tomorrow night to close the deal. We need to leave tonight to get there before J.R. does. The informer will call us tomorrow. United has a flight leaving Atlanta at two in the morning that gets into New York at five. We need to be on it."

"Okay, I'm on my way. See you at the airport," I said. Once again I was leaving in the middle of the night, at a moment's notice, for who knew how long.

Harry and I arrived in the Big Apple at five o'clock that Saturday morning. We were met at the airport by Investigators Berman and Zimmerman. Berman was another Lauderdale, only heavier (240 pounds.) With Berman driving, we quickly arrived in the city and began making plans. After breakfast, we piled back into the car and headed for Times Square. I had been in New York when I was in the Merchant Marine at age 17, but it was still overwhelming to me. Berman drove like the back of the car was on fire, dodging in and out of traffic and cursing anyone who got in his way. He wheeled up to the Waldorf Astoria Hotel in the middle of Times Square.

The hotel had just been refurbished and was one of the most expensive in New York.

"We'll get a couple of suites here!" said Berman, bouncing out of the car, which he had left in a tow-away zone at the front door. A doorman in a fancy uniform began to protest, but Berman merely flashed his badge and stormed into the plush lobby.

Fanceeee! I thought, Five hundred dollars won't go far here. I started wondering how we would explain such expenditures. It didn't faze Harry a bit. He was in his element, and anyway it was *my* PEA money.

"Where's the manager?" Berman asked the frustrated hotel clerk.

"I'll get him."

In about ten seconds a well-dressed, polite man appeared. Berman, showing his badge, said, "We need to talk privately." He and the manager disappeared into a small office. In 1963, $77 a night for a hotel room was a lot of money and that was the going rate for these rooms. Five minutes later Berman and the manager came out.

"Follow me," said the manager.

We went to the 12th floor overlooking Times Square and he showed us two adjoining suites. We agreed that these would be fine. I was afraid to ask the price. After the manager left, Berman said, "We got these rooms for $20 a night." In New York City—at that time—all police officers were respected. If you were a federal officer and needed anything, all you had to do was ask. The New York police demanded respect and had the authority and backing from the courts to get it.

Berman and Zimmerman left to prepare the other stage set we would use to impress J.R. with the size of our New York operation. I was amazed at its complexity. A large warehouse on the East Side had been borrowed for ATF's use. The "Godfather," Nick Natale, an ATF agent who dressed and looked exactly like a Mafia kingpin, was to meet with J.R. and the informer in one of the suites, while we recorded their conversation from the adjoining suite. Then the Godfather would take J.R. on a tour of the city, including fake locations of transfer points for his operations. In this way we hoped that J.R. would fall for the bait and agree to furnish truckloads of moonshine for the operation.

As the day passed, Harry kept trying to contact the informer at his home in Richmond, Va. The informer was supposed to meet J.R. in Atlanta and then fly to New York. The day ended with no contact from the informer and I became more and more apprehensive about this wild scheme. Harry and I played poker with the New York agents to pass the time, until past midnight.

Sunday morning, Harry still couldn't contact the informer. Berman took us on a sightseeing trip through Greenwich Village and the Bowery. I asked myself, What am I doing in New York City on a Sunday morning, looking at a bunch of drunks lying on the sidewalks?

Sunday passed, with Harry getting more agitated at the informer. He called the airlines. There were no flights to Richmond on Sundays. "We can charter an airplane to take us to Richmond to find that asshole," Harry suggested.

"No deal," I said. "We've already spent several hundred dollars on this fiasco—we can wait until tomorrow and catch a commercial flight."

On Monday morning, Berman took us to the Newark airport, where we caught a flight to Richmond. We arrived at two o'clock, rented a car, and started looking for the informer. After checking his home and a couple of hangouts, we found him. Then came the innumerable excuses. He had been sick—J.R. was not at home—he could still do it—on and on. We caught the next plane to Atlanta and I arrived home, much to my relief, at three-thirty Tuesday morning. As usual, Harry had all the answers for the reporting of the PEA funds spent.

What a fiasco! Just another wild weekend for Harry!

Chapter XXIV
The Beeper Caper

One day after I had recovered from the trip to New York, I received a radio call from Carl Koppe. "How about meeting us at Lakewood and the South Expressway?" Koppe said.

"I'll be there in 15 minutes," I said, winding up the engine on the '60 Pontiac. It was another fast car that had been seized hauling moonshine. Sometimes trip boys tried to slip into the city driving inconspicuous panel trucks or automobiles, but most of the north Georgia and eastern North Carolina trippers drove souped up cars. The only change I had made to this one was to replace the missing back seat. I loved it.

Koppe and I met at Lakewood and Stewart Avenue. He came straight to the point. "Charley, this is kind of borderline as to being legal, but we think it is."

My attitude was, catch the law violator, put him in jail and let the courts decide if the method we used was legal. The liquor law violators weren't hindered by rules, regulations or the law (unless caught). As long as an officer was honest, did not swear to a lie in his statement or as a witness and was not brutal or abusive, I could work with him.

"Whatcha got?" I asked.

Koppe produced a small black rectangular object about six inches long and an inch wide. It had a small magnet attached to each end and a ten-inch-long uninsulated wire on one end.

"What is it?" I asked.

"A radio transmitter," Koppe answered. He took me to Fulton County Deputy Ed Michaels' car and showed me the receiver.

Michaels was a former Atlanta police officer who knew the city well. Ed was working for the Anti-Moonshine League, an organization set up to assist in the suppression of moonshine. It was privately funded by the legal liquor industry and was run by a retired ATF agent. There were several private investigators working in the field with ATF and state agents. The AML furnished money to make undercover buys of illegal whiskey. Sometimes they would furnish equipment for our use in enforcing the liquor laws.

The radio receiver was a complicated-looking multi-banned receiver with a myriad of dials and switches. It also had to be constantly tuned, since the transmitter was of low power. As the battery became weak, the transmitter drifted off frequency, as I soon found out.

"We've got a trip car located up here behind a Gulf station. We want you to slip around back and put this transmitter on the car so we can follow it back to the still." This was something new and I was already having visions of putting them on J.R.'s vehicles and trailing them to a big outfit.

"What kind of car is it?" I asked.

"A 1958 DeSoto."

"We need to look at one before I start trying to put this thing on in broad-open daylight." We drove past the Gulf station and I saw the blue and cream DeSoto parked at the rear of the station. It was the only car there and it was going to be difficult to approach without being noticed. It would be even more difficult to put the transmitter on without being seen.

Stewart Avenue had several used car lots and we started looking for one with a '58 DeSoto. We found a '58 Dodge—close enough. I pulled into the lot and while Ed talked to the salesman, I casually walked over to the Dodge. Ed was keeping the salesman occupied, having positioned himself so that the salesman was looking away from the Dodge. I quickly slid under the back of the car.

I couldn't put the device on the frame, it might be seen by someone checking the tires. The only place would be on the metal floor of the trunk between the gas tank and the cross members of the frame. We would have to let the antenna hang down, but even if seen it would look innocent enough. I slid out and rejoined Ed in about a minute. We left the salesman still talking.

We began making plans, trying to cover every base. Most of us were known by a great many liquor people, but Koppe was probably known by more than anyone else. That meant he was out. ATF Investigator George Tumlin, who was working in the under-cover pool in the Regional Office, was assigned to help me on the J.R. investigation. He had helped me with a seizure earlier that morning. Tumlin had been stationed in Bremen and wouldn't be known to the Atlanta violators. We decided he would drive my car with Michaels and me as passengers.

At two-thirty that afternoon, business was slack at the station. We executed the plan. Tumlin drove in and told the attendant to fill it up. I got out and walked to the restroom. It was on the side of the building closest to the DeSoto. I went inside. Ed followed and waited outside the door. "Looks okay," he said in a low voice.

I came out of the restroom and not looking right or left, went straight to the DeSoto. Ed remained outside the restroom door, watching for the attendant or anyone else. I glanced at Ed. He nodded and I dropped on the ground and slid under the car. As I slapped the magnets up against the metal floor, I made sure they made good contact with the metal. Okay, antenna down—get out! I thought. Wait—make sure the switch is on! Check!

I slipped out, brushed myself off and followed Ed back to the car. Tumlin had just finished paying for the gas.

As we left, I said, "George, I hope you didn't pay for the gas with a government credit card." He hadn't.

We had two receivers for the beeper (transmitter). We checked the range of reception, which was short, and decided there was no way to stay within range without our cars being spotted by the trip boy. We decided to rent an airplane, using a contract pilot to follow the vehicle by triangulating the radio signal.

This was a new experience for all of us. Since the radio receiver was non-directional, we had to go by signal strength alone to determine when we were getting close. If the signal grew weaker, we knew the vehicle was moving away from us, but we couldn't tell in which direction. We hoped that with an aircraft overhead, the signal would be easier to intercept. By flying in one direction, say north to south, we could determine where the strongest signal was. If the signal weakened, we knew we had passed it. On the next pass, we would fly in a different direction, east to west, over the strong signal area, in order to pin down the vehicle. This method was primitive at best, but it was all we had. ATF agents were used to improvising.

We had an open contract with a charter flying service in north Atlanta. They would furnish a Cessna 172 aircraft and contract pilots if available. Some of these pilots were good, but some didn't particularly like the long hours of slow flight involved in our operations.

I thought that with the help of this beeper on the liquor car, maybe we could trail the vehicle until we got him into a rural area where the observer could see him. Little did I realize that within a year's time I would be piloting the aircraft myself, with Koppe and Michaels as two of the best observers in the business. We would be trailing vehicles by sight alone, both day and night, through all areas of Atlanta and many other major cities in all parts of the United States—but that was all in the future.

At six o'clock, Koppe called. "I'm at Fulton County Airport with the plane, ready to go."

At ten-thirty, we heard a distinct change in the signal coming from the beeper, which gave off a sound like sonar: "Pingggg—pingggg." The closer the miniature transmitter came, the stronger the signal. As the car moved away, the signal decreased and died. Buildings also interfered with the reception. We had to guess which direction the vehicle was going and anticipate our moves accordingly.

We guessed the first move correctly. The sound got louder and then began to decrease. He must be on the South Expressway heading toward downtown Atlanta. Koppe was in the air in a short time and he was receiving a strong signal. As I drove across the city, Michaels was adjusting the tuner for a better signal. City Detective Lamar Williams had joined in. I was pushing the Pontiac as hard as I could, trying to regain the radio signal. The squeal of static, traffic on the government radio, and Michaels and Williams both talking at the same time, made my job difficult, but I was really into the chase.

By eleven-fifteen, we were heading northwest on Bankhead Avenue. "Turn north on McDaniel!" Ed yelled.

Two vehicles were stopped in the right lane at a red light on Bankhead, so I swerved into a service station lot on the corner of Bankhead and McDaniel, hoping to beat the light. No such luck. The light changed and a new Ford Falcon sport model with the biggest stock engine Ford made, turned the corner and cut me off. I fell in behind. At the first opening in traffic, I pulled up alongside the Ford. We were meeting an oncoming car, but I had time to get around, I thought.

The guy in the Ford hit the accelerator, leaving me hanging out to dry. Both carburetors opened up on the government Pontiac and our front end edged about two feet ahead of the Ford's bumper. It was now or never. I jerked the wheel right and then back straight without hitting the Ford. Out of the corner of my eye, I saw the car fall back as the driver involuntarily hit his brakes. I snatched the Pontiac into the right lane just as we squeezed past the oncoming car. All three of us were cursing the Ford driver for his stupidity, but we couldn't stop now.

Koppe called and told us he had experienced some confusion as to the direction of the signal, but it was now heading north toward Mabelton, a small suburb of Atlanta in adjoining Cobb County.

I wheeled into a side street to turn around. As I finished a tight U-turn, I was blocked by the same Ford that had almost caused us all to be killed. Before I could get my door open, Williams had jumped out of the car and was halfway to the other vehicle. A uniformed Atlanta police officer came out of the Ford just as fast, but froze as Williams stuck his detective's badge in the officer's face.

"What in the hell are you doing—trying to enforce traffic laws in an unmarked car? Get the hell out of the way!"

The officer didn't say a word. He quickly moved out of our way. Williams was still fuming as we burned rubber and continued north.

Koppe had the signal pinned down in Cobb County. He guided us into the area. Soon we began to pick up the signal again. This didn't look like an area where a distillery would be located, but we had seized large distilleries in basements of $125,000 homes (in those days this was upper-class). Koppe left with the plane and we waited until about one-thirty that morning when the neighborhood had quieted down, before driving past the location of the strongest signal.

This was a new subdivision in a rural setting. There were several new homes, but a lot of open land and woods in the area. We determined that the transmitter had to be at one particular home. We could see two vehicles in the driveway, but neither was the vehicle on which we had put the beeper. Could it be in a basement garage? The only way to find out was to go in on foot.

I dropped George and Ed and parked in a woods road a half mile from the house. In 20 minutes they called to be picked up. "It's not there," said Ed.

"It's got to be—maybe it's around back?" I asked.

"We checked all around the house and didn't see it," they both replied.

"Okay, let's go meet Koppe at Peachtree-DeKalb Airport and knock off for now." It was six o'clock Saturday morning and we were all beat.

I got to bed about seven-thirty. After five hours of fitful sleep, I headed back to Cobb County with Koppe. Neither of us could rest until we solved this mystery. We checked the area and continued getting a strong signal from the same home. We ate supper in Marietta and returned to the small woods road, hiding our vehicle a quarter-mile from the house. All police work involves long hours of waiting. In law enforcement you learn early that patience is a necessity. During these times, I gave thanks to the good Lord for the opportunity to work at an occupation that was interesting, exciting and fulfilling. I still do.

We dozed a little, but it's hard to get comfortable in a car filled with radios, binoculars and other equipment. Early Sunday morning, I got out of the car and did the usual things you do after getting up. I walked around a while to stretch my legs. Koppe was drinking coffee from a Thermos and I joined him.

At ten forty-five, the signal began to get louder. The '58 DeSoto had to be leaving the house and coming toward us. We eased the car forward so we could see the public road. As the signal increased in volume, a new Chrysler station wagon passed us. The signal faded. The beeper had to be on that station wagon.

"Did you see who was in that wagon?" Koppe asked.

"I sure did—a nicely-dressed couple in their 30's and two children. How do you figure that?"

After the signal faded, we pulled out into the public road. I increased my speed until I received a strong signal again. We passed a large Baptist church on our right and the signal began to fade.

"It's in the church yard." Hard to believe—but some liquor-law violators are regular church goers. "We'll wait until after the sermon starts and check the parking lot," I ventured.

Driving through the lot, our signal was so loud that we had to turn the receiver down to keep from disturbing the service. The '58 DeSoto was not in the lot. Had the beeper fallen off the liquor car and been found by the station wagon driver? Had the trip boy found the transmitter and placed it on the first vehicle he had access to—the station wagon? Something had definitely gone wrong, but we could only speculate.

We drove back to our hiding place and waited. At twelve-fifteen, the signal became stronger once again. We moved to within sight of the road. As the same station wagon passed, the signal began to weaken.

"What're we going to do?" Koppe asked.

"We've got to do something," I said.

Koppe agreed. I pulled out behind the station wagon.

We had been without much sleep for three days and were unshaven and dressed like hunters. Imagine the surprise on the faces of the upper-class couple and their two children as I pulled into the driveway and parked behind the station wagon. They were just getting out of the car. I approached and identified myself as a federal officer. The man and his wife both looked closely at my badge and credentials. I assured them that I was indeed a federal officer.

I told them we were picking up a signal from their station wagon that was on our frequency. The man was very cooperative.

His wife said, "This is my car. I don't understand." Neither appeared to be aware of any type of transmitter on the vehicle.

"Can we check it?" I asked.

"Sure, go ahead," the man said. "You go on in the house and fix lunch," he told his wife.

Koppe and I began to look under the vehicle. We found nothing. We opened the hood and then began looking inside the vehicle itself—nothing! By now I was grasping at straws.

"Could I look in your briefcase?" I asked the lady.

"I'm a businesswoman—but look if you have to," she said. I did. Nothing but contracts and legal papers.

During the search, the husband had suggested several times that we could take the vehicle to a local service station and put it on a grease rack to look more thoroughly under it. I finally caught on and agreed. Telling Koppe to follow us, I got into the station wagon with the man.

"I'll be back shortly," he told his wife, and turned the station wagon toward Marietta. After a short distance, he asked, "What would the government do to me if I had a transmitter?"

"Not a thing," I blurted out. "All we want to do is turn it off so we can find ours. Where is it?"

The man stopped the car and started to explain. "I've been a little suspicious of my wife," he confided. "This friend of mine works at a local radio shop and told me about these new transmitters. I was hoping to trail her and find out if my suspicions are valid or not without getting anyone else involved. But I guess I did get someone else involved."

"Listen, all I want you to do is turn the transmitter off for a couple of days, so we can find ours. Then you can turn it back on and do whatever you want to. Where is it?"

"On top of the glove compartment," he said. I was under the dashboard in no time. Koppe had parked behind the station wagon. He ran up to see what had happened. We were both elated to find the transmitter. It was much more advanced than the one we were using. (This was the case most of the time, as civilians and violators usually had more advanced and better equipment than we did.)

The transmitter was well-hidden between the dashboard and the top of the glove compartment. It was plugged into the regular radio antenna. That gave it ten times more range than ours. It was supplied power by the auto battery with no small batteries to become weak and cause a frequency drift. I unplugged it and thanked the man. Koppe and I headed to Peachtree-DeKalb Airport.

I still wonder what that executive told his businesswoman-wife on returning home that Sunday afternoon.

I don't think he ever tried to use a tracking device again.

An hour later, Koppe and I were in a Cessna 172 over downtown Atlanta. No sooner had we taken off from PDK when we began picking up the beeper signal—ours this time. By triangulation, we determined the signal was coming from an area north of Georgia Tech in downtown Atlanta.

We contacted Michaels and got him into the area with another receiver. He was able to pinpoint a house on State Street, which was only five blocks from the corner of Bankhead and McDaniel. That's where our confrontation with the driver of the Ford Falcon had taken place. By three that afternoon we were back on the ground, making plans to check the location. The house fronted on a main thoroughfare and was on a high bank. The back yard was fenced and bordered around the edges with hedge, but it could be entered from an alley.

At ten o'clock, Michaels dropped us out. We walked in the shadows to the back yard. The fence was five feet high and the gate was locked. No problem. Koppe watched as I went over the fence and dropped in the yard. Then I thought, What if they have a dog? I was within 50 feet of the house. The '58 DeSoto was parked in the yard beside a 1 1/2-ton Ford truck. This must be a big stash, I thought. They're bringing in whiskey 900 gallons at a time!

The lights were on in the back of the house and I could hear a TV playing inside. Good—that would cover any noise I might make. I slid up under the DeSoto and felt for the beeper. It was right where I had placed it three days before.

Just then the back door opened. I froze. A white man walked out, looked around, and walked toward the car and truck. If he gets in the car, should I try to roll out at the last minute and maybe get run over, or should I try to make myself flat enough on the ground for the vehicle to go over me?—Nope, that's out. I made up my mind to try to roll under the truck if the car began to move. About this time, the man reached the front of the car and stopped. I held my breath. Then I heard the sound of a zipper and water hitting the ground. Just another country boy who, even though he had an inside toilet, preferred to go outside when nature called.

When he finished and went back inside, I retrieved the beeper and was back over the fence in no time flat.

The next day we secured vehicles and equipment to begin our surveillance of the stash house. The Southeast Region had recently been assigned an observation vehicle from Washington Headquarters. ATF was slowly beginning to be recognized as one of the best law enforcement agencies in the country and received a small increase in its budget along with the recognition.

The observation vehicle was a large van, having the appearance of a meat truck with the air conditioner on top of the cab. The inside was elaborate. There were small ports through which pictures could be made and even a periscope-type apparatus for scanning the area. It had a government radio installed in the rear and to cap it off, a remote switch for starting the engine and turning on the air conditioner from the rear without crawling back into the cab. The back doors had metal louvers that could be opened or closed as needed to observe without being seen. It was well-equipped, but we soon discovered it was like an oven in late-summer Atlanta.

The neighborhood of the stash house was a "fringe area," mostly black, but including some white families. I drove the cross-between-an-armored-car-and-a-meat-truck up a side street. Koppe called from the rear and said, "That's good." I pulled to the curb and parked. Several black children were playing on the sidewalk and I saw an old black woman shelling beans on the front porch of a house across the narrow street. When she looked away, I quickly slipped into the back of the truck. I looked through a small port and saw her looking up and down the street, wondering what had happened to me. As she continued shelling beans, I could see that she kept a close eye on everything that happened in her neighborhood. Good for her!

After 30 minutes with the engine and air conditioner off, the back of the truck became a furnace. Koppe and I were sweating like horses.

"Let's try out the air conditioner," he said.

After checking around the vehicle, I started the engine with the remote control. Almost immediately there were five or six children looking into the cab and trying to see into the rear of the truck. They couldn't figure out how the truck's engine had suddenly started itself. The air conditioning felt good, but now we had become the object of attention. Not good. After ten minutes their curiosity subsided. Things settled down around the truck. We've got it made, I thought.

Not quite. "Koppe, do you smell anything?" I looked at the engine gauges. The engine was overheating. All we could do now was get out of there. I saw the woman go into the house. Immediately, I slipped into the driver's seat and drove away. The woman probably still wonders about that mysterious truck with no driver.

So much for fancy equipment. Back to the old on-the-ground-in-the-bushes method. This was obviously a night operation and the only movement we would see would probably be from first dark until around midnight.

We replaced the batteries in the beeper and decided to place it on the large truck in the back yard in an attempt to trail it from the stash house to the distillery. That night Koppe and I slipped silently into the back yard. I placed the beeper on the frame near the cab. We monitored the signal until the next morning, when it began to fade. We knew the truck was now moving. Using three vehicles, we found the truck at a garage across town. We worried that someone might find the beeper while working on the truck.

I slid my pistol and handcuffs under the seat of the Pontiac. Koppe dropped me out a block from the garage and I walked nonchalantly down the street and into the three-bay truck garage. The Ford was being worked on in the last bay. The mechanic was checking the rear wheels. Waiting until he took a break, I quickly slipped under the truck, jerked the transmitter off the frame and strolled out, hoping no one had seen me take it. When I got back to the Pontiac, Koppe asked, "Did you get it?" I held up the transmitter and we resumed our stake-out.

The truck left at three that afternoon. We followed it to a well-known wholesale sugar outlet and watched as it was loaded with five tons of sugar. It left the warehouse at half past four. Using three vehicles, we leap-frogged it out of town and onto I-85. It headed toward South Carolina.

Suddenly, a late-model Mercury passed me doing about 90. "Watch it," I called to Koppe, who was in a car ahead of the truck, "I think Bud Corham is convoying the truck." A well-known supplier of raw materials to moonshiners, Corham would pass the loaded truck and check the highway ahead. Then he would slow up, let the truck pass him, and check for suspicious vehicles behind the truck.

In addition to Koppe's vehicle leading the suspect vehicle, two ATF cars were running behind, to follow if he turned off. We all scattered, but were able to keep the vehicle in sight.

By nightfall, we reached Banks County in northeast Georgia. The truck pulled into a truck stop. This gave us a chance to plan our next move. We were in a rural area known for large illegal distilleries. We decided to place one of our trail vehicles on a secondary road leading south of I-85 and the other on the same road leading north. The remaining vehicle would watch the truck, calling on the radio when it moved.

We took turns getting a bite to eat at the truck stop and settled down for a long night.

"I'll take the first watch," I said. Shortly before midnight, I was half asleep when I looked up to find the truck gone.

"670 to 422!" I screamed into the microphone. "He's gone!"

A welcomed reply came loud and clear: "He just passed our location going south."

Whew! saved again, I thought.

We waited as long as possible before pulling out onto the road. By that time, Michaels was trailing the truck and had to turn off the first side road to avoid detection. We were running without lights. I had to turn on my lights to speed up and catch sight of the truck. As I crested a hill, there he was! I reduced my speed to coincide with his.

When he disappeared over a hill, I flipped a switch under my dash to cut off my left front headlight. This way, I hoped to fool him a little longer. My car was equipped with separate switches for the headlights, stoplights and tail lights.

Trailing in this manner and running without lights when we could, we were able to follow the truck to a rural area three miles from Commerce. We pulled off the surveillance before dawn on Saturday morning and decided to let the area cool until later.

The following week we continued our surveillance of the stash house on State Street. Tumlin was taking the ground duty every night and would call when any vehicle left the stash house. Koppe and I would trail the vehicle. Michaels and Lamar Williams were assisting. Over the next week, using this method, we were able to trail different vehicles into high-volume bootlegging areas of Atlanta. We made seizures of three vehicles and 149 gallons of whiskey and arrested three trip boys—a good week's work. We decided to let the stash cool and went back to the area in Banks County where we last saw the big truck loaded with sugar.

The day after we trailed the truck to Banks County, I called Gastley in Gainesville and gave him the details. Henry had worked in Alabama, but was familiar with north Georgia violators. Henry and Investigator Bill Maine from the Gainesville post of duty located a distillery about a mile from where we had last seen the truck. We met them at noontime on Monday. Michaels and Gastley dropped out Maine, Koppe and me and we walked in. The distillery was on a big farm in a 120 x 40 foot chicken house. There were three chicken houses behind the farmhouse. The still was supplied electric power from the house and water from an electric pump in a creek.

I saw two 1 1/2-ton late model Ford trucks parked between the chicken house and the farmhouse. One was the truck loaded with sugar that we had trailed the previous week.

"Watch it," Maine whispered as a dog started to bark. I ducked and saw a man come out of the still house. He looked in all directions and then went back inside. It seemed that every farmhouse in the South had at least one dog and sometimes four or five. They are always a factor to be reckoned with. Once you get them stirred up, the only thing you can do is leave the area until they settle down.

Investigators Roy Longenecker and Leonard Mika came up with an innovative and unique solution to the dog problem while working in North Carolina. They had a large distillery located, but every time they tried to get close enough to observe, dogs all over the area started barking. They decided to put their idea into action. After buying a box of Kotex at a local drug store, they drove to the animal shelter in Raleigh.

"Do you have a bitch dog in heat?" Roy asked. The startled attendant thought he had a couple of weirdos or perverts on his hands. When he picked up the telephone to call the police, Roy and Leonard showed him their gold shields.

"This is official government business," said Mika sternly.

There happened to be a large bitch dog in heat. Longenecker and Mika proceeded with their plan. While one of them held the dog's head (both claim to have done this), the other official representative of the United States Government took a Kotex and rubbed it briskly on the dog's female genitalia. (For the uneducated, when a female dog is in heat, her reproductive organs produce a mucous-like substance which gives forth an odor that is evident to every male dog within a mile or more.) The rubbing soaked the Kotex with this odorous substance, and gave the dog no end of pleasure. Placing the Kotex in a plastic bag, they thanked the dog pound attendant and left—much to the chagrin of the dog.

That afternoon, with their unusual precious package, they walked into an area a half mile from the distillery. As Mika watched, Longenecker climbed a big tree and carefully tied the soaked, odoriferous sanitary napkin to a limb about 12 feet above the ground.

"Do you think that's high enough?" asked Mika.

"I hope so," said Roy, as he climbed down.

For the next two weeks, there was a strange absence of dogs around that farmhouse and local people complained of hearing dogs fighting on a hill about a half mile from the farm. It worked like a charm.

I never tried this technique, but I always wanted to.

Now we had our own problems. After dark we slipped through the woods and approached from the direction of a knoll behind the chicken houses. A light breeze was blowing in our faces, so we knew we were now downwind of the dog and he couldn't smell us.

Another 1 1/2-ton truck pulled into the yard alongside the chicken (still) house. Two men hurriedly began unloading cases of half-gallon fruit jars. Being downwind, we could smell the mash and hear the fuel oil burner. We had probable cause to suspect a violation in our presence, so now we could "swoop down on 'em."

"Henry, the still's in operation, come on in!" I whispered into the radio. I began crawling toward the truck. The timing was perfect. As I reached a point 40 feet from the truck, Henry came barrelling into the driveway, dropping Michaels at the house to get anyone there. He whipped into the back yard. The still hands froze for a moment. I lunged forward and caught Harold Stitts as he attempted to get into the cab of the truck. Koppe caught Dave Walton in the still house.

Gastley found us. "That's Harold Stitts," he said with a grin. I had heard of Stitts being on the major violator list, but had never seen him before. This apparently wasn't J.R.'s still, but it was a big one. The mash capacity was over 10,000 gallons.

Our long hours of trailing and surveillance had paid off again. We seized three 1 1/2-ton trucks, a half-ton truck and a nice 1956 Mercury. Henry took Stitts and Walton to jail in Gainesville and we remained at the still until the next morning. I had no trouble sleeping on the three tons of sugar stacked in the still house.

Two days later we went back to the stash house at 795 State Street. After catching another set-off vehicle and driver on Saturday night, we decided we had better hit the stash house before they moved out. I secured a federal search warrant for the premises. We hoped to catch one more set-off vehicle before hitting the stash. Ray Hahn and Michaels took the ground observations, with Koppe and me being the catch men.

Ray called. "A car just left going north toward Tenth Avenue. Looks like he's loaded. It's a red and white '57 Dodge—couldn't get the tag number."

The Dodge passed our location. We fell in behind it and after a short distance, he pulled into a shopping center.

"This is as good a place as any," I said.

Koppe blocked the Dodge and I grabbed the driver before he realized we were there. He was hauling 180 gallons of moonshine. We radioed the other officers at the stash house. Koppe followed me with the prisoner and I drove the Dodge back to State Street and into the back yard. We all hit the back door and inside we arrested Nancy Regan (yes, that's her real name) and Bill Christian.

In a back room we found another 959 gallons of moonshine. The '58 DeSoto was in the yard with 72 gallons of moonshine whiskey in the back. This made a total of 1,211 gallons of whiskey, two cars and three arrests. A good present for my 36th birthday, although I didn't get home until two in the morning and missed my own party. Another disappointment for my wife Dot.

The beeper, although confusing in the beginning, led to the seizure of 11 vehicles, a large illicit distillery and over 2,000 gallons of illegal whiskey. Not bad for two weeks' work. We were happy.

Chapter XXV
A Drip Under Pressure

Two weeks later an informant called.

"I saw 'Boxhead' driving a new Ford truck up Highway 19, in Dawson County." Boxhead was one of J.R.'s still men. A few days later, I saw a truck that fit the description parked at a service station in the edge of Gainesville. I quickly put it under observation.

The pencil pushers in Washington I.R.S. Headquarters had recently come up with an ingenious method of trailing suspect vehicles. It was nothing on the technical scale of a radio transmitter—those things cost money! This was much, much simpler and inexpensive—the drip can. I always thought it must have been named for the inventor.

The can was 8x6x2 inches. It had a screw-top cap with a small metal tube soldered into it. A small rubber hose was pushed over the tube and hung down eight inches. The can also had lengths of wire soldered to it to enable you to attach it to the underside of a vehicle quickly—or so they said. The drip can would be filled with a specially-mixed fluorescent liquid and when the can was "properly" placed beneath a vehicle, the liquid would drip onto the pavement, leaving a trail. What a brilliant idea! The agents were to pick up this trail using an ultra-violet light, specially built to ATF specifications, and follow the suspect vehicle to various clandestine locations. The light was a small rectangular box with a small purple bulb. It looked like something made in a high school shop.

Like a lot of ideas, in theory it sounded good, but actually it was as useless as tits on a boar hog. But I would try anything. I secured one of these "top secret" drip cans. Slipping into the service station lot, I wired the can to the frame of the truck, in the process getting a face full of dirt and grease and cutting my hands on the so-called quick–to-attach wires. Even though the can was painted a dull black (those guys had thought of everything) it was still hard to hide. I did my best.

At a nearby church which overlooked the parking lot, I identified myself to the minister and he agreed to give me a key to the church. From a Sunday School room at the rear, I had a great view of the truck and could enter and leave without being seen.

From the church I checked on the truck on a daily basis. Investigator Hugh Merrill also checked when he was in town. About a week later, the truck was gone. No problem. I got out my trusty fluorescent light and found a large amount of blue-green substance on the gravel lot where the truck had been parked.

Although I was the object of several questioning stares from bystanders, I crouched down with my funny-looking box and peered at the ground. Maybe I could get out of there before the guys in the white coats arrived! Aha! The trail led to the street. Now what? Would I stay crouched down and duck walk like Barney Fife down the middle of a busy street? Or, as the originators of this wacky idea had instructed, would I sit on the front of a vehicle and point the ultra-violet light at the highway, proceeding in this manner to the site of the violation. Surely I wouldn't attract attention sitting on the hood of a car moving at five miles per hour, a box in my hands, peering intently at the street.

It was apparent that used motor oil that ordinarily dripped onto the pavement from older vehicles also fluoresced. Not only that, when the suspect vehicle was driven on dirt roads, dust would immediately cover any material that dripped from the can. In short, it didn't work. Those were some of ATF's lean years. Happily, the agency is now as well equipped as most other federal law enforcement agencies, except of course, the FBI, who only have to hear of something new and it's theirs.

So much for the drip can and Washington experts. They remind me of a definition of "expert:" "X" is an unknown quantity, and "spurt" is a drip under pressure.

* * *

Howard Smith, Jimmy Satterfield, Frank Lane and I hit another large illicit distillery in the panhandle section of Clayton County that fall. We arrested five men—three Ellisons and two Morgans. It was another family operation. We seized two vehicles and destroyed more than 200 gallons of whiskey.

Someone was really coming up with a lot of information in the panhandle. I wouldn't find out the source until later. You just don't ask.

* * *

Later, Jim King and I lucked up on J.R. He was headed toward Atlanta driving a new dark blue Pontiac. We trailed him to the Howard Johnson Motel at North Druid Hills Road, where he stopped briefly before proceeding towards Atlanta. I alerted Michaels and Koppe and they headed for known raw materials outlets. J.R.

doubled back on us a couple of times, so when he didn't show up at the raw materials outlet, we were out of luck.

The next day, thinking I had nothing to lose, I drove to the motel where J.R. had stopped. Maybe this is where he meets with other violators, I thought.

The badge I carried opened a lot of doors, especially with legitimate, law-abiding citizens. The motel manager was immediately cooperative. Pulling a photo of J.R. from my pocket, I asked, "You ever see this man before?"

He looked at the photo carefully and asked, "What did he do?"

"Has he been here?" I asked impatiently.

"He checks in about once every two weeks. In fact he stayed here last night."

Great, I thought, He's probably using a room here to meet with his RM (raw materials) suppliers, and maybe the people he's supplying whiskey to.

Taking back the photo, I asked, "Will you call me the next time he checks in?"

The manager agreed. I left him my home and office phone numbers although I doubted he would call. It was a long shot.

Thinking back about this incident makes me realize that ATF was blessed not only with some of the best law enforcement agents in the country, but also with the most dedicated secretaries and office workers. Most were as loyal to ATF as the agents. Rather than continually transferring from one government agency to another for more pay as is prevalent in Washington, the women in the Southeast Region were ATF all the way.

Every agent in the region knew of Pearl Wilder (and she is a pearl). She was a legend. She started work for ATF out of high school and after a number of years rose to the position of secretary to the Chief of Criminal Enforcement in the region. Without a doubt, she knew more of the interworkings of the region than the Regional Director. She never married and ATF was her life. A more dedicated or loyal person couldn't be found. Pearl was one of many like that.

Two weeks after talking with the hotel manager, I received a radio call from the Regional Office.

"A man wants you to call him at Howard Johnson's."

Pearl had taken the call and relayed it immediately to me. As I sped across Atlanta, I was busy formulating a plan. Sure enough, J.R. had checked in at three that afternoon. He then left the motel.

I had asked the manager to give J.R. a room with a door leading to an adjoining room. They had two identical doors between them—each could only be opened from one side. This gave privacy to each room, but both could be opened to make a suite-type arrangement. At my request, the manager had also reserved the adjoining room for me.

I checked quickly for J.R.'s car, then secured keys to his room and the adjoining one. I let myself into J.R.'s room and unlocked the door between the two rooms from his side. I looked around briefly, but saw no luggage or anything unusual. I went next door and called our squad room. Luckily, Jim King answered.

"Jim, this is Charley—I need you and a tape recorder as quick as you can make it—also a small transmitter we can hide."

King never asked why when someone needed him for anything. He was always ready to help. "Where do you want me?" he asked.

After I told him, "Howard Johnson's, North Druid Hills," he knew almost everything I did.

I met Jim in the parking lot. We hurriedly unloaded the equipment into my room, then unlocked the door leading into J.R.'s room. We could slip the small microphone for the recorder under our adjoining door without it being seen, even if someone opened the other door. I watched through the peephole in the front door while Jim searched for a place to put the radio transmitter.

"The only place I can find is behind this night stand next to the bed."

"Okay, let's get out of here," I said.

Jim went into our room. I checked to make sure the transmitter was on, then closed the two adjoining doors and went out the front door and back into our room. Jim slipped out to get a couple of sandwiches and we were all set.

At seven-thirty I heard a car door slam. Jim turned on the recorder and I checked the peephole in the front door. I couldn't see anyone, but could hear the key being placed into the door of the next room. I looked across the parking lot and saw J.R.'s Pontiac. It had to be him. Then I heard it! A woman's voice! I should have known. I had no idea J.R. was fooling around. Jim and I looked at each other and he just shrugged his shoulders. Well, maybe he would still meet with some liquor people. I was grasping at straws again.

The broadcast radio in their room came on and we were getting beautiful music through our secret transmitter, but little else. Only enough to know they weren't talking about the liquor business.

"Jim, I'm going outside to see what she drove up in." By now I felt sure they wouldn't be coming out for some time. I eased our door open and stepped out. Parked directly in front of the room was a new Ford that looked familiar. Nonchalantly, I walked to the vending machine at the office, got a Coke and walked back through the lot. I made a mental note of the license number. I knew it was from Dawson County because it had 153 for a prefix.

I walked to an outside phone booth and called the license registration office at the State Capitol. Someone was on duty there 24 hours a day. This was before the days of computers, but almost immediately the registration came back. Damn, I thought, J.R.'s with the wife of a good friend of his.

J.R. had really been a thorn in my side. All I had to do was call this woman's husband, tell him his wife was in Room 124 with J.R., and give him the address. He would probably put one major violator out of action forever. It was tempting, but I decided I couldn't do that, even to my worst enemy.

I returned to the room. They definitely were not discussing whiskey in the next room! Jim and I waited until we were sure they were gone, retrieved our radio transmitter and called it a day.

I was beginning to think J.R. was the luckiest or the smartest man I had ever known, or else I was the dumbest.

J.R. had a joker in the deck I didn't know about.

RUBBER LEGS

Just after Christmas of '63, John Guy came up with information on another large distillery—this time in Haralson County. It was two miles east of Tallapoosa, a small rural town inhabited mostly by moonshiners or sympathizers. The weather was cold as whiz. Special Investigator Wally Hay (a transplanted New Yorker) and I were dropped out a mile from the distillery. Wally was a city boy, but it was soon apparent that he was game for anything. Although it was hard to get used to his New York ways, I found him intelligent and we became close friends.

We met Jimmy Satterfield and Chuck Connors in the woods adjacent to a farm house. The distillery was in a large chicken house at the rear of the dwelling. I was wearing insulated underwear, wool pants and shirt and a suede jacket. I also had a huge arctic military parka that reached to my knees, plus a military sleeping bag.

Satterfield and I took the first shift, beginning at midnight. As the night wore on, it got colder and colder, going down to 12° F. I was warm in the sleeping bag with the parka over it until about one that morning.

An automobile drove through the yard to the chicken house. I came out of the bag in a flash and quickly put on the hooded parka. As I raised the heavy Navy submarine binoculars to my eyes, I began to shake. This had never happened to me before. My jaw began to tremble violently—I couldn't control my teeth chattering. I strained to see through the binoculars. They were jumping up and down. The driver of the car wasted no time getting into the still house and then all was quiet. Back in the sleeping bag, it took another 15 minutes for me to warm up again. Great work. I loved it.

Just before daylight, O.W. Sills picked me up. We drove into a small side road across Highway 78, and began the long wait for the liquor car to leave the still. Satterfield was to let us know by radio when the vehicle was loaded and was leaving the distillery. Four hours later, the radio came to life.

"He just left—loaded," Jimmy called.

O.W. was driving. As we pulled up to Highway 78, facing the dirt road where the vehicle would have to come out, I suggested we block the liquor car at the highway. While we were discussing, or rather arguing, the merits of this idea, the liquor car appeared. It turned toward Tallapoosa instead of Atlanta.

"He's seen us—you'd better get on him—fast," I exclaimed. The old saying, "he who hesitates is lost" was completely true when chasing moonshiners.

Finally, O.W. pulled out and the violator really began to move. If he hadn't been carrying a half-ton of liquor, we probably wouldn't have gotten close. He whipped onto the first street he came to in Tallapoosa. We were nearly on him. As he topped a hill, the driver's door flew open and the driver rolled out.

"Look out," I shouted as the liquor car rolled backward down the hill toward us. I was trying to get out of the back seat to catch the driver.

We were close enough to the liquor car to keep the damage to a minimum as our car rear-ended the other vehicle. Finally, getting clear, I saw the driver running 100 yards ahead of me. In my nine years of chasing bootleggers, I had never lost a foot race. As I poured it on, the icy-cold air began to work on my body. I had been soaking up heat for four hours.

After a hard sprint of 100 yards or more, I saw the suspect walking about 75 yards ahead of me between two houses. I began to black out. My lungs felt like they were bursting and my legs turned to rubber. I fell to my knees and thought, Dammit, I'll really be kidded about someone outrunning me. I staggered back to my feet and continued toward the place where I had last seen the suspect.

It was ten o'clock. The usual crowd of local men were standing and sitting around a big pot-bellied stove in a nearby service station, a hangout for moonshiners. When I walked in, everything was quiet. No one said a word.

"Did anyone come in here in the past five minutes?"

They all looked at one another. No one spoke. The owner of the station, a big, burly guy in his late 40's, spoke up. Grinning, he said, "We've been here most of the morning—who you looking for?"

I should have known—even if he had run in here, no one would say so.

"A tall, slender boy about 19," I answered.

"Haven't seen him," came the reply. I walked out the door, almost feeling the laughter being held back until I left. But, you can't win 'em all.

O.W. picked me up and we headed back to the still site. At least, we had gotten the car with 108 gallons of liquor. Satterfield, Connors and Hay had raided the chicken house and caught "New Boy" Coleman and B. F. Desota. The distillery was a fairly large operation with over 5,000 gallons of mash.

I thought, This informer of John Guy's really gets around— he comes up with stills north, south, east and west of Atlanta. This was unusual, because an informer would only occasionally be able to furnish information on more than one particular area. Puzzling. I still didn't ask John—I was just glad he was getting the information, no matter where.

Upright steam-boiler still seized in Dawson County, GA

Chapter XXVI
Dawson County Heroes

Monday started out well.

Koppe and I had arrested John Green, a known J.R. associate. He was driving a Ford van loaded with 324 gallons of moonshine. We caught him in a black area of Atlanta and hoped to tie this seizure and arrest into a conspiracy case against J.R. I took Green before a U.S. commissioner to have bail set, then went back to the squad room at the Regional Office to prepare statements.

At three-fifteen the phone rang.

"Squad room, Weems," I answered.

John Corbin's voice was urgent. "Charley, Doug Denney and James Stratigos were involved in a wreck about 20 minutes ago. Doug's dead and we don't know if James will make it."

I was stunned. I had worked closely with Doug on raw materials. Our friendship had grown as he was promoted to area supervisor in Gainesville and I to regional special in Atlanta.

I had also worked closely with Stratigos. I respected him as a fellow agent and friend. He was the first and only resident agent in charge in Dahlonega—certainly not a job for the faint of heart. James quickly made believers out of the numerous liquor law violators in that notorious area. I loved them both.

I swallowed hard.

John went on, "Get a photographer and get up there as soon as you can. It happened on Highway 53 between Gainesville and Dawsonville. You make the investigation. It's yours."

It was January. The year was turning bad—very bad—very soon.

I grabbed photographer Ed Hunt and we headed north. The roads and highways between Dawsonville and Atlanta were as familiar as the back of my hand and by four o'clock we were on the scene. Vehicles were still parked alongside the road, but the government car and the other car involved in the crash had been removed.

Ed began making photographs of the location from every angle, while I tried to piece together what had happened. I didn't have time to mourn the loss of one of my best friends. I had to do my job and do it quickly and efficiently before someone could rethink what had happened and in some way try to blame Doug.

As soon as I began talking to witnesses, I found that it was another of many accidents that took innocent lives either because parents weren't able to control a teenager or because of the attitude prevalent in some areas that young people are just having a little fun with hot rod cars. Dawson County was noted for its liquor car drivers and strangely they were looked upon as local heroes. Today we were seeing some of the fruits of this attitude.

Doug and James had left Gainesville about two-fifteen on their way to meet some other officers. They were travelling west on Highway 53 and were two miles east of Dawsonville on a stretch of highway full of sharp curves and small hills. Double yellow lines marked the road continuously for two and a half miles, showing it was unsafe to pass.

As Doug reached the crest of a small hill, a car driven by Lloyd Spray at a high rate of speed passed Dawson County Deputy Sheriff Warren's car. Spray barely got around Warren in time to avoid the government car approaching from the west. Immediately a 1957 Chevrolet swerved from behind Warren's car and hit Doug's government car head on. Warren estimated that the speed of the Chevrolet was at least 75 miles per hour.

The Chevrolet was hurled into the air and turned partially around, stopping in the westbound lane headed in a northwesterly direction. The government car was knocked off the road and up against an earthen bank.

The driver of the Chevrolet, Clift James, was seriously injured, and the passenger, Harry Owen, was killed instantly. Agent Denney was also killed instantly. Stratigos was seriously injured and pinned in the wreckage for almost an hour.

Every ATF agent in Georgia wanted to help in the investigation. It was my job to coordinate and put everything together to present to the U.S. Attorney for prosecution of James. He was in bad shape, but if he survived, I intended to have an airtight case of vehicular manslaughter against him. Area Supervisor John Guy came up the next day and helped take statements and gather evidence.

On Wednesday, along with what appeared to be every law enforcement officer in north Georgia, I attended Doug Denney's funeral in Gainesville. The church was full. More than a hundred officers had to listen to the service from outside. I don't remember much of what was said, but I can still see vividly Doug's casket draped with that big beautiful American flag he had fought for as a United States Marine and a U.S. Treasury Agent.

Doug left a wife and two fine children, as many law enforcement officers had. It was hard to see him go. I can still hear him calling me by the nickname "Charley Horse" after a cartoon character of the time. I still miss him.

I drove and John Guy sat in quiet meditation as we followed the hearse and a long line of cars toward Athens, where Doug was buried. All of a sudden, John seemed to remember something. He reached over and turned on the government radio. I was deep in my own thoughts when someone called John's badge number on the radio.

"585—585."

"Go ahead," John answered.

"Can you meet me at the usual place in about an hour?"

"Negative, I'll be tied up all day—I'll call you tonight," John replied.

"10-4," then silence.

My mind raced as I tried to figure out what the background noise was. In police work you learn to listen not only to what's being said on a telephone or radio, but also for anything else of significance. I had it! While listening to Koppe trailing the beeper that night, I had heard the same sounds in the background.

"That guy's in an airplane," I blurted out.

John looked sheepish for a minute, like a kid caught with his hand in the cookie jar. He said, "You're right. It's a fellow who's been helping me. He's about to work me to death. Would you like to help us?"

Ever since I was a kid in first grade drawing pictures of airplanes, I had loved anything to do with flying. "You bet," I said without hesitation, "but I've got to finish up this accident investigation as soon as I can."

"Okay, we'll work together, but this is a hush-hush thing about the airplane," said John. Now I knew how John was getting so much good information.

The James youngster died the following morning. Although Stratigos suffered from serious head, chest, hip and foot injuries, he recovered after weeks in the hospital and eventually was able to return to work.

John and I worked together the remainder of the week, interviewing witnesses and getting certified copies of Clift James' numerous traffic violations over the previous four years. This record began when he was 17 and continued until the fatal accident. In July of 1960, he was in an accident and received a citation. Two weeks later, he was given a warning ticket for speeding by state troopers. In November, 1960, he was arrested for speeding in Dawson County and pled guilty.

In May, 1961, he was arrested for speeding 75 miles an hour in Atlanta. In June of 1961 his license was suspended for the violation in 1960. In October of 1961, he was given a warning ticket for speeding by a state trooper in White County. In February, 1962, his driver's license was again suspended for two months. In June, 1962, he was arrested for driving under the influence. He pled guilty.

In March of 1963, he pled guilty and again had his license suspended for three years. During the March term of the Dawson County court, he was indicted for riot. This was still pending at the time of the fatal accident. In June, 1963, James had two separate cases made against him in Atlanta. The first was for improper turn and accident. The second was for leaving the scene of an accident and driving without a driver's license.

In August, 1963, his driver's license was again suspended for three years. In December, 1963, he was arrested for driving without a license and driving with a revoked license. This last arrest was less than a month before the fatal accident. He was a tragedy waiting to happen.

Lloyd Spray (named for a family member who was a whiskey tripper and championship stock car driver, killed in 1941 in an argument over a load of sugar), was racing Clift James at the time of the accident. He was never arrested for his connection with the accident.

What should have been done? How could this tragic accident have been avoided? Spray and James both passed a deputy sheriff at a high rate of speed in their home county where both were known by the deputy. What does that say about the local law enforcement at the time? Or the attitude of most of the people in Dawson County? By making local heroes of fast drivers and liquor haulers, did they condone this attitude of disrespect not only for traffic and liquor laws, but for all law?

I wrapped up all the loose ends and submitted my final report. With James' death, the case was closed.

* * *

A week and a half later, Wally Hay and I helped Bill Maine, Frank Frazier, and Frank Lane seize a huge distillery eight miles north of Dawsonville on Highway 19, in Lumpkin County. Maine, Frazier and Lane had raided the distillery early that morning. They arrested Duane "Skeeter" Fields, Jewell Mavis and Jewell Mavis, Jr.

The distillery was among the largest, most elaborate setups I had ever seen. Although it was similar to the still we had seized

222

north of Dahlonega where the lawyer intervened, it was larger and everything was new. It was in a new chicken house (150x75 feet), and was worked from behind a dwelling house. To look at the outside, you would think this was a legitimate business.

Inside were eighty-one 220-gallon barrel fermenters with a mash capacity of 18,000 gallons, and 534 gallons of moonshine. The still was operated full time, with the still hands living in the chicken house. It produced from 900 to 1,000 gallons of whiskey a day, every day of the week. The wrenches, burner, electrical wire and apparatus were all new. There was even a set of metal roller sections to use as conveyor belts for the huge numbers of jars and materials used in the production of the moonshine. From the location, size, type of equipment and the fact that Skeeter Fields was on it, I knew it was a J.R. operation. But how to prove it? It was frustrating.

I interviewed the defendants, to no avail. I helped destroy the distilling equipment, thinking, How does he do it—J.R.'s luck has got to run out sometime.

Regional Special Agents attend school in Atlanta

Regional supervisors and Special Agents—1960

Southeast regional supervisors and Special Agents—1964

Chapter XXVII
Two–Edged Sword

Every time the telephone rang, no matter where, I jumped with anticipation. This time it was the squad room phone and John Corbin's voice was serious.

"Charley, can you come up to my office?"

"Be right up." I walked up the long hallway that ran the length of the new Federal Building at Peachtree & Baker Streets wondering, What else can happen?

John closed the office door behind me and I really began to get worried. What had I done wrong? This had to be serious.

John got right down to business. "Charley, we've got a delicate situation to deal with. I want you to handle it."

I thought, Why do I always get the delicate cases?

John went on, "The U.S. Attorney just called. A government witness has apparently solicited a bribe from a defendant in one of our cases."

Regional special investigators worked jacketed liquor conspiracy cases 90% of the time, but when an ATF agent was assaulted or killed, a jacketed case was assigned. Attempted bribery also fell into this area.

The Internal Revenue Service had a group of agents in its inspection section, who performed the same duties as an Internal Affairs Division (IAD) of a large police department, investigating allegations of misconduct on the part of investigators in IRS, ATF and the Intelligence Division. Since there was no allegation here of misconduct on an agent's part, I got the case.

I left the federal building and headed over to the U.S. Attorney's office in the federal court house. I wondered what this was all about. ATF agents made so many federal cases, especially in Atlanta, they knew the U.S. Attorneys on a first-name basis. Charles Goodson and Bobby Milam were waiting anxiously when I arrived.

"What's up?" I asked.

Closing the door to the huge office, Bobby said, "As you probably know, John Elmer and Billy Word were to go on trial this afternoon for selling liquor to an ATF informer named Richard Ruff."

I thought, That's Harry Lauderdale's case—why didn't they call him? But I remained quiet as Milam continued.

"Billy Word's lawyer, Pierre Howard, came to my office with John Elmer. He said that the government's witness, Richard Ruff, had contacted Elmer and offered to slant his testimony to help Elmer and Word beat the government's case against them. He would do this for $800."

"That's hard to believe," I interrupted.

"I know," Bobby continued, "but we have to check it out." He called in Pierre Howard, John Elmer and Billy Word from an adjoining office. Elmer volunteered to telephone Ruff, with me listening on an extension, but no one answered. After Howard, Elmer and Word left for Howard's office, Goodson made things absolutely clear.

"We need an airtight case against Ruff. I've cleared it with your office for you to get all the help and equipment you need. This case needs to be made—and quickly. Elmer and Word are scheduled to go to trial at nine o'clock tomorrow morning."

Damn it, it's four in the afternoon and I'm supposed to make an involved jacketed obstruction of justice case by nine tomorrow morning. I was glad that John Guy had answered my radio call and joined me in this one. We had been working together writing the report of Doug's accident and had stayed in close contact. I knew John was the man I needed. He had the respect of every officer and attorney in the area. He had worked for years in Savannah and Atlanta. Although quiet and gentlemanly, he could be as firm and aggressive as anyone when the occasion arose.

So far, the situation had been like a Chinese fire drill. Elmer was unable to contact his lawyer, Bob Andrews. He called Word's lawyer, Pierre Howard, who verified the information by having Elmer call Ruff in his presence. Then Howard was unable to contact the U.S. Attorneys, who were out to lunch. Word showed up at court, while Ruff hid out. Now Guy and I were in the middle of it and it wasn't getting any less complicated.

After a brief discussion with the U.S. Attorneys as to how much evidence we would need to successfully prosecute Ruff—a lot—John and I went to the Healy Building in downtown Atlanta. Howard was one of the most respected and successful criminal lawyers in Atlanta and his office was representative of this fact. Nice! We arrived about four-thirty in the afternoon, having hashed out a rough plan of action on the way over.

John telephoned our district office. "Is Al Moreno still there?" he asked. A few moments wait, then, "Al, this is John Guy. We have a job for you. Can you get down to the Healy Building as soon as possible? I'll be waiting outside. Oh, by the way, keep that suit on that you wore to state court today. You need to look like a lawyer."

A questioning look came over Attorney Howard's face, but after I explained our plan, he seemed satisfied.

John left to meet Moreno. I began attaching my tape recorder to one of Howard's telephones. About that time, there was a knock on the door. Howard said, "That's Larry Cohran, an associate of mine in the law firm. Do you mind if he joins us?"

"Not at all." What else could I say? I noticed as he came in Cohran was carrying a nice briefcase with his name in small gold letters on the top.

Being reminded of a little sign Henry Gastley kept on his desk, "Trust everybody—but cut the cards!" I wondered what Cohran might have in his briefcase. About this time, Guy returned with Investigator Moreno. Al had been with ATF two years and was stationed in Augusta. He hadn't worked in the Atlanta area enough to be known and he looked like a lawyer. He was well-educated and well-dressed. When told we were planning to have him pose as a defense lawyer, he looked pleased. I still wasn't sure this was not just a set-up by Elmer to get our chief witness against him discredited in the eyes of the U.S. Attorney.

Although I had worked on numerous liquor cases in Atlanta since I first arrested Elmer in 1955, with the subsequent trial and the conviction being upheld by the Supreme Court, I had heard little of Elmer's participation in liquor activities. Each agent worked his own cases and undercover operations and kept them on a "need to know" basis.

But now, after nine years I was on Elmer's side if what he had told his lawyer proved to be true. I hated the thoughts of a paid government informant selling out to law violators. It was almost as bad as law enforcement officers taking bribes either not to enforce the law or to act as an accessory to a crime.

Upon meeting me again for the first time in several years, Elmer was friendly. He remembered vividly the first time we met, telling Howard, "This is one man who won't lie to get a conviction." Even though the compliment came from a man with felony convictions and a reputation for being a kingpin in bootlegging and lottery in Atlanta, I appreciated it.

With the recorder attached, and Attorney Howard and me listening in on two extensions, Elmer called Ruff. "After you called this morning, I've been trying to call you back all afternoon," Elmer began.

"I've been hiding from the U.S. Attorney all day," said Ruff.

Elmer explained to Ruff that Billy Word didn't understand how Ruff could help them beat their case and asked Ruff to talk to Word.

Word got on the telephone. Ruff said, "Look, I'm not the biggest chump in town. Why don't you and John come on over to my place and we can talk face to face. I don't like talking on the telephone."

Word continued the conversation, asking Ruff how much it would cost him and Elmer for the difference between Ruff's 1962 Pontiac and a 1964 Grand Prix. Ruff said, "Eight hundred dollars. I'm not asking for a fortune."

Word asked Ruff if he could bring his lawyer with him when he and Elmer came to Ruff's house.

"That'll be okay," Ruff answered, "but you've got to come here where I know nothing will go wrong." Then Ruff began hedging about the lawyer coming.

Word handed the phone back to Elmer. "Billy's afraid you're going to pull one on us. He doesn't know how you can help us."

"Look, man, you and Billy come on over here. I'll show you how to beat the case, but I'm not going to talk about it on the telephone."

Elmer told Ruff he would be there in 20 minutes.

I had heard enough. I was still not sure who made the first move, but after listening to Ruff on the phone, I knew he had larceny in his heart and was double-crossing the government. I looked back at Cohran's briefcase. "Could Al use your briefcase? It has your name on it and might just be the thing that convinces Ruff that Al is a lawyer."

Cohran handed the briefcase to me. I asked if he had anything important inside as I opened it up.

"Just some legal forms and a couple of files. Nothing that can't be replaced," he said. Someone suggested that we put a recorder in the briefcase or on Moreno. We quickly decided against this since Ruff had worked closely with some of the best ATF agents in the region and knew all the tricks of the trade—*almost* all.

Guy had secured ten $100 bills. We recorded the serial numbers and gave them to Elmer for the payoff money. With the briefcase and the three-piece suit, Moreno certainly looked the part of a prosperous attorney.

"Give us time to get in position to back you up in case we have any trouble," I told Al as John and I left. We had checked out the area of Ruff's apartment that afternoon and found a safe spot to hide our car with a view of the rear stairs leading up to the apartment.

We knew that Ruff would be super-cautious. The plan was for Elmer to make an excuse to leave the apartment after the payoff. When we saw Elmer come out, Guy and I would go in—fast.

At nine-thirty, Moreno, Word and Elmer arrived. As they walked up the back steps of the shabby apartment building, I was far more apprehensive than I would have been if I had been going in instead of Moreno. No one can ever anticipate what might happen in a case like this.

The three men entered Ruff's apartment. Moreno was introduced as Larry Cohran, an associate of Pierre Howard. Looking Moreno over, Ruff seemed particularly interested in the briefcase he was carrying.

Moreno took the offensive. "What kind of man do you think I am?" Moreno asked as he opened the briefcase and took out some papers, giving Ruff the opportunity to look into the briefcase.

Ruff was now on the defensive. "I trust you, I trust you," he stammered. Word was checking the adjoining room while this was going on.

"Billy's just a little nervous," Elmer said.

Ruff began talking to Moreno about the case against Word and Elmer. He said he could tell him how to get a verdict of acquittal the following day. Word asked Ruff, "How much?" several times, until Ruff finally said, "Eight hundred." With that, Elmer pulled out the ten $100 bills. He slowly counted off $800 and handed it to Ruff, who took the eight $100 bills and put them in his shirt pocket.

Now Ruff began in earnest to explain to Moreno how to question him about certain aspects of the case so Ruff could answer in vague ways and appear to be nervous and lying to the jury.

"I'll testify that entrapment was never discussed with me by any federal officers working on the case," he said. "That way, you can ask for a directed verdict of acquittal based on entrapment." (A legal defense—if it can be proven. One of the elements of entrapment is that you induce someone to do something he would not ordinarily do, either by trick or other illegal inducements.)

During the entire conversation, Ruff coached Moreno on how to conduct his defense. He showed Moreno the statement he had made for the government, and pointed out several areas that could be attacked with Ruff's assistance.

After 20 minutes, Moreno gave Elmer a signal.

"I've got to go—I live out in the country. See you later," Elmer told Ruff.

John and I were apprehensive, not knowing what was going on. Moreno's safety was uppermost in our minds. It was a relief when we saw Elmer come out the back door. John and I were inside in a flash. We found Moreno placing Ruff under arrest. Ruff was stunned.

I searched him and recovered the eight $100 bills from his shirt pocket. I found a straight razor in his pants pocket. On the bed in the next room was a loaded sawed-off shotgun and a loaded revolver was between the arm of the sofa and a cushion. Ruff was ready for trouble, but not this kind! He had been caught, like so many others, because of his own greed.

I felt a great deal of satisfaction as the steel doors of the Fulton County jail slammed on Richard Ruff. I only hoped that Harry Lauderdale had enough evidence against Elmer and Word to convict them without Ruff's testimony—but I didn't think so.

The case against Ruff had been made in less than 12 hours. We had enhanced ATF's image in the eyes of the U.S. Attorney by using ingenuity and resourcefulness to make a complicated case at a moment's notice.

Although it later resulted in Elmer and Word, two notorious criminals, going free it showed once again that the double-edged sword of justice cuts in both directions.

Chapter XXVIII
The Airplane Driver

Two days later, I was back in Lumpkin County with John Guy, checking a large distillery being moved in. Guy's unknown pilot had furnished this information also. I thought, This guy is uncanny. How does he do it? I didn't know it at the time, but this airplane driver was to have a profound effect on my life and career. John and I worked all weekend with Gainesville ATF investigators and returned to Atlanta on Monday.

The next day, we took Richard Ruff to a bond hearing before a U.S. Commissioner. We were on the way back to my office when the same voice I had heard the day of Doug's funeral came over the radio.

"Can you meet me at the usual place?" the voice asked John.

"I'll be there in 20 minutes," John answered. "Wanna go with me?" John asked me as he hung up the microphone.

"You bet!" Even though I had paperwork up to my ears in the Ruff case, I was ready and anxious. John headed north on the Northeast Expressway. In 15 minutes we were pulling into a parking space at the Peachtree-DeKalb Airport (PDK).

A tall, muscular man of 38 walked over to our car. "Charley, this is Jim Daniels. Jim, this is Charley." That was my introduction to a man who not only changed my life, but who also would make ATF a pioneer in the use of airplanes for surveillance of law violators nationwide.

As we stood talking in that parking lot, I wondered what Daniels did for a living and what he had to gain by giving his time and money (renting aircraft is not cheap) to locate illegal distilleries. In a word, it was adventure. Daniels loved the excitement of the chase. He would have made an excellent ATF agent. "I think I've got something good in north Georgia," Jim said. "We need to check it tonight."

"Okay, can you help us, Charley?" asked John.

I was way ahead of him. "Just tell me when and where."

I went home for a quick supper and met John and Daniels at nine-thirty.

"I'll drop you two off to check the suspected location," John said.

By the time we reached the area about six miles northeast of Dawsonville, it was ten-thirty. Most vehicles were off the road. As John dropped us out, he said, "I'll pick you up at midnight."

I didn't know how much experience Daniels had in the woods at night traveling without a light, but he appeared to know what he was doing. He quickly set off in the dark with me following. After half an hour of steady walking, Jim stopped. "I think it's just ahead," he whispered. I could see nothing. Then gradually, I made out a black line against the dark horizon. Any time you see straight outlines from the air or on the ground, it is some man-made object. That's the reason camouflage netting and paint schemes are all made up of irregular patterns. I could just make out the outline of a rectangular building covered with black tar paper.

"There's a dwelling house on the other side—we'll have to be careful." Jim had evidently done his homework. Now it was my turn to take the lead. I slowly eased up to the makeshift building and listened for any sound of activity inside. Still hands frequently lived in this type of structure. I didn't want to be surprised, especially with a civilian along. The night was deathly quiet, like most nights in rural areas. I found an opening in one wall and moved inside. Jim was right behind me.

I stood still for a time and listened again for any sounds from inside or outside. It was pitch black. I reached out and felt cold steel. It was a large vat. Moving cautiously, I made my way to the side of the enclosure nearest the residence. I looked through a small tear in the tar paper and could make out the outline of a dwelling house 75 yards from our location.

Jim and I turned our attention to the contents of the building. The illicit distillery was in the process of being set up. It was going to be a big one. We counted fifteen 500-gallon steel vat fermenters. I had seen enough for one night.

We walked back to our pick-up spot, talking quietly. I knew by now that this man had been briefed in great detail about liquor law violators, their methods and areas of operation. I also knew that if Guy trusted him with that much information, he was above reproach.

Recently I had initiated another undercover operation in north Georgia in an effort to obtain evidence against J.R., my adversary of long standing. The widow of a former major violator had contacted our office and agreed to assist in making large buys of moonshine, if the government would furnish her a place to live and pay rewards for any violators arrested due to her assistance.

Her name was Louise, but she was not the same Louise I had met previously. This one could pass for a businesswoman or school-teacher. She knew numerous liquor law violators in north Georgia. We rented a new mobile home and had it moved to a trailer park north of Marietta. Louise was to live there and it would be our base of operations. A regional special investigator stationed in Florida was assigned to work with Louise undercover. I will call him "Albert." He is still a good friend, but probably wouldn't be if I ever divulged his secret mission—his wife is very jealous. Albert and Louise had made some initial contacts and I was anticipating they would make their first buy the following week.

"Jim, do you think you could follow a car with your plane without being seen?" I asked in the darkness.

"He'll never see me," Jim answered confidently.

"Okay, we'll talk it over with John." On the way back to Atlanta, I cautiously broached the subject of the trailing job, worried that John might think I was trying to steal his informant. John was all for it. By the time I got home in the wee hours of the morning, my mind was spinning with all the possibilities that could be realized from this innovative surveillance technique. I hardly slept that night.

The next day, John contacted the Gainesville POD investi-gators and gave them the location of the distillery being moved in. They agreed to check it in a week. This would give the violators time to get completely set up. That weekend, James Stratigos called.

"Meet us at the office in Gainesville about six p.m." he said. He had checked the distillery and figured it would begin operation that night.

James and I dropped Bill Maine and Hugh Merrill out after dark, a mile from the distillery. At two o'clock Saturday morning, Bill called on the car radio. "It's in operation."

"We'll cover the area between the still house and the dwelling. Be ready to hit it at two-thirty," said James calmly. "It'll take us 15 minutes to get there." With that, Stratigos started the car.

I checked my flashlight and made sure I could get out of the car quickly. We knew that by now, Bill and Hugh would be moving in so close to the distillery that radio contact would be impossible. At two-thirty, we drove into the yard. James covered the house while I ran to the still house. Bill met me at the door.

Grinning, he said, "We've already caught them." I had mixed emotions. I always wanted to catch someone myself, yet I was glad no one got away.

The still was being operated for the first time and we had hurt the owner a great deal financially. There were more than a dozen 500-gallon steel fermenter vats of mash and almost 300 gallons of liquor. Omer Hodson and Harry Rider were arrested. We completed the destruction of the distillery and the whiskey at about eight that morning. Stratigos was curious as to how we located it on the first run, but like most of us, he was happy to get the information.

The next day, as I drove to meet Louise and Albert, I worked out my plan. Louise had said that her next contact with the violator was to be at a service station-country store six miles east of Dawsonville. I knew the location.

When I arrived at Louise's trailer, she had already called about the liquor. "They'll be at the service station at three o'clock this afternoon," she said.

I called Guy. "Jim and I will meet you at PDK Airport in 30 minutes," said John.

"I'll need the Buick for about 30 minutes," I told Albert and Louise, and crawled into the undercover car. I drove to PDK and met John and Jim. When I showed Jim the vehicle they would be using to pick up the liquor, he looked as happy as a kid in a candy store. John and I jumped into a Cessna 172 Jim had rented and we all left for Dawson County.

Jim was familiar with Dawson and Lumpkin counties and in no time we had located the service station meeting place. John and I decided that we would direct the operation from the ground to see if Jim could actually trail our undercover car. I told Jim the pre-arranged time of the meeting and we returned to Atlanta.

John and I were quiet as we drove back to meet Louise and Albert. Although we had high hopes that this type of surveillance would be successful, neither of us realized how profound an effect this buy would have on both our futures.

I was always apprehensive about the outcome of under-cover work. On more than one occasion, our agents had been assaulted and robbed. While working in the Chattanooga area, ATF investigator Jim Allred was lured into a remote mountainous area and robbed. Liquor law violators were not all innocent, good-natured victims of poverty, trying to feed their children.

In this instance, Jim contacted a known bootlegger in the Suck Creek area southwest of Chattanooga. After being told they were going after the liquor, Jim was led to a remote area. Before he knew what was happening, there was a .38-caliber revolver at his head. The violators took the $400 he had brought to pay for the whiskey and tied Jim hand and foot. One of the violators put a pistol to his head and said, "I think I'll just blow his brains out!"

Luckily for Jim, the other man began talking frantically. "We don't need to kill him! Don't do that! Let's go! We've got the money!" After some tense moments, they stripped Jim of his shoes and left him tied up.

One cannot imagine the terror Jim felt lying on that cold, rocky mountain path in the middle of the night with death so very close. Finally, he heard a car start up. When the sound faded away, he managed to free his hands and feet. Barefoot, Jim began the torturous trek back to civilization. After three hours, he finally reached a telephone and got help. He was in the hospital for two days with cut, swollen feet.

Both violators were identified by Jim and both were convicted of assaulting a federal officer. Their only defense was that they didn't know Allred was an officer. It was Jim's opinion that if they had discovered he was an officer, they would certainly have killed him.

These things worried me more when I was working as backup for the undercover man than when I was actually doing the work myself.

John and I arrived at Louise's trailer. I gave Albert $400 to make the buy of whiskey and we decided on a meeting place where they would give me the liquor after the buy. The airplane was not mentioned. If it worked, we would tell Albert later. Now the waiting began.

The meeting at the service station was to be at three o'clock. John and I had time for a barbecue sandwich at the Old Hickory House. Later, as we drove to Dawson County, John began to confide in me. "Jim Daniels is the one who has been furnishing me all the good information we've been working. In fact, he has found all the big outfits we've worked lately—he even found the Hill still where Gene Howell got hurt." John had really kept his secret and I appreciated his sharing it with me.

"How does he do it?" I asked.

"With time, patience and his eyeballs—and a plane," John replied. "We've got a meeting scheduled with the Chief of Enforcement and Bill Griffin, Chief of the Regional Specials, set for tomorrow to firm up our working relations with Jim Daniels. You want to be in on it?"

Although I was snowed under with cases, paperwork and other assignments, I jumped at the chance. In my wildest dreams, I could not imagine the doors that would be opened to me by this 1964 decision.

About four o'clock, the '59 Buick undercover car drove slowly into our meeting place on a back road of Dawson County. I could tell by the movement of the car and the smile on Albert's face that the car was loaded with whiskey.

"Did you get it?" I asked.

"A hundred and twenty gallons," said Albert, grinning. He and Louise got out of the Buick and into the car with Guy. I slid into the driver's side of the liquor car. John was to give me a few minutes to get ahead of him and then he would take Louise and Albert back to the trailer. We were to meet later at PDK Airport.

I was feeling great. We had made our first buy in this operation and I hoped it would lead to the elusive J.R. We were certainly in his area of operation. As I pulled into the parking lot at PDK, John and Daniels were standing next to a hangar talking. I parked some distance away and waited. They came over.

"How did it go?" I asked Daniels

"Fine. I think we've got something," he answered. "I followed your car to a farm in north Dawson County and saw them pull it into a barn behind the house. Fifteen minutes later, a different car left the house and drove about a mile in each direction from the house and then returned. The Buick came out of the barn and went back to the meeting place east of Dawsonville. What's in it?"

I pulled back the Army blanket and removed a half-gallon of moonshine, letting Daniels smell it. His face lit up. I knew then that even though he was not an officer, he was one of us and enjoyed helping catch the violator. After I left to take the whiskey to be processed for fingerprints and destroyed, Jim told Guy that I looked like "Boston Blackie" driving that liquor car. Jim became one of the best friends I ever had.

That night, Jim drew a detailed map of the location of the suspected farmhouse and barn. The next day, John put it in the hands of Gainesville ATF investigators who were assigned to work the territory. They immediately set up a surveillance of the area and three days later they arrested major violator Wilson Bright and several other defendants who were working in and around the moonshine stash house. They also seized a new Buick Riviera and a two-ton truck with 800 gallons of moonshine.

Although they were unable to trail the truck from the stash to the distillery, this was a good catch. It proved to me that you could indeed trail ground vehicles with aircraft without being detected.

The next day, Bill Griffin called me into his office. "Charley, keep this close to your vest. We're going to have to maintain close security in this operation for it to succeed. John Guy will handle most of the paperwork, which will be submitted directly to the

Regional Office. You and Wally Hay will continue to work your assigned cases. Can you handle that?"

"Yes, sir," I replied.

For 15 years, I worked under Griffin's supervision. He was always fair and honest. On numerous occasions he stuck his neck out for me and for others. He was much more than just an excellent ATF agent and supervisor. Although he rose to be Regional Director for Criminal Enforcement in the Southeast Region, Bill never lost his rapport with the agent in the woods or on the street. He never minced words or backed down from a fight. He jeopardized his own career for me and for others, sometimes for our sakes and sometimes to get the job done. I never had a better supervisor or friend.

This was one of those occasions. I.R.S. Headquarters in Washington would never approve ATF agents flying with anyone but contract pilots and they certainly would never approve the agents piloting aircraft. Griffin said, in his usual matter-of-fact tone, "Do what you need to do—just don't screw up!" That was enough, as far as I was concerned.

* * *

Daniels kept all three of us busy checking illicit distilleries and submitting huge amounts of paperwork these seizures and arrests entailed. During the next five-month period, Daniels located 76 illicit distilleries, having a mash capacity of 191,571 gallons. He was also responsible for the seizure of 5,167 gallons of moonshine and 38 vehicles. It was one of the most productive periods ever, both for ATF and for me. That was my new beginning.

Ever since I was six years old, I had a love of airplanes and the desire to fly. In the yearbook for Jonesboro High School, *Cardinal Echo 1944*, under "Our Future," a spoof on predictions for each member of the senior class, someone wrote, "At last Charles Harvey Weems has become a famous and popular pilot. He has the dangerous job of piloting the kiddies around in toy airplanes at Lakewood Amusement Park. His partner Johnny Orr assists him in keeping the planes in good condition, so there won't be a crack up." I was 16 at the time. Johnny was 17. Orr became a captain with Eastern Airlines, and 20 years after that prediction, I received my chance to learn to fly. Daniels made this dream come true.

The next day, I met Daniels and Guy at the airport and began a new learning experience. Jim had rented a Cessna 150, a small two-place trainer airplane with limited space. He was a big man at 6'1" and 190 pounds.

"Can Charley go with you?" John asked.

239

"Sure. Hop in," grinned Jim.

As we headed north towards Dawson County, Jim said, "You wanna fly it?" Eagerly I took the wheel and my instruction began. "One hand only on the wheel," Jim suggested. Like most first or second-time would-be pilots, I was gripping the wheel so tightly that I was truly a white knuckle flyer. Finally, I began to relax and Jim started identifying highways and locations I had seen from the ground a hundred times. They looked different from the air. Most people don't even recognize their own house on their first flight over it.

As Jim pointed out the homes of numerous moonshiners, I realized that he had been at this for some time and that he had been thoroughly briefed by Guy. He knew the area and a great deal about the M. O. of the violators. On subsequent flights, I learned that he was a captain with Eastern Airlines, flying Boeing 727's. Many times Jim would return to Atlanta after flying a 727 to New York, Chicago or Miami and go directly to Gunn Airfield, a small airstrip east of Atlanta. He would pick up a Cessna 150 and fly an additional four hours in north Georgia, observing activity in Dawson and Lumpkin counties. He became so proficient at this he discovered several large distilleries by watching activity late at night in remote areas. On his days off between flights for Eastern, he would rent a 150, and maintaining an altitude of 8,000 to 10,000 feet, would loiter high above a suspected area and watch for suspicious activity.

This paid off in a number of ways. Jim began to think like the moonshiners. With the experience and information Guy and I had accumulated over the years, we made a great team.

Wally Hay, with his knack for detail and intellectual approach, had submitted numerous requests and justifications for the use of aircraft. He continued to work toward getting approval for us to fly surveillance missions using ATF agents as pilots and observers. His tedious research and persistence finally paid off.

Daniels gave me training as we made more and more trips. The first week in April, with Jim's encouragement, I took my first formal lesson. The flight instructor could not believe this was my first time with an instructor. I explained that I had been flying some with a friend. We did a lot on that first flight and after only six hours of formal instruction, I soloed. Jim was there and he was as proud as I was. No one ever forgets his first solo flight.

From then on, I could log my flight time with Jim and in less than a year I qualified for both a private and a commercial pilot's license. This took what spare time I had, both flying and studying

240

for the written examinations. Dot certainly did not understand my desire to take on more time-consuming work, especially flying. She considered it more dangerous than my regular occupation. Although I did have a few close calls flying, I had far more dangerous moments raiding stills, chasing liquor cars at high speed and working undercover. The stress in my personal life during this time was constant, but I was so wrapped up in my job I didn't realize it until much later. The wives of ATF agents live with constant stress, perhaps more than the agents.

* * *

The pieces of the J.R. puzzle began to fall into place in April. Daniels called at noon and said he had something I needed to look at. Knowing Jim's reliability and usual understatement of his accomplishments, I knew he had something good. We met at Stone Mountain Airport outside Atlanta. I didn't ask questions.

Jim had a Cessna 150 ready to go and I hopped in. He headed directly north, explaining as he flew. "I've been watching a farm south of Dahlonega for the past several days. I want you to look at it."

I thought, Is that all?

As he climbed to 11,000 feet, Jim went on: "There's a large open field in back of this farm house and barn. I first noticed a tractor plowing around the edge of a field that borders a little creek. The next day, I noticed the tractor again, pulling a harrow around the same area. Two days later, I saw the tractor working the same field next to the creek. This made me suspicious.

"I studied the other side of the creek with binoculars and saw evidence of vehicle travel leading into a small wooded area. I came back late in the afternoon when the sun was low on the horizon and caught a reflection of light from the area. I think it's a big camouflaged distillery!"

By this time, we were over the farm. It was in J.R.'s territory all right and an ideal place for an illicit still. A long driveway ran about 900 yards off Highway 19, to the farmhouse and then past it to several outbuildings. The open field was behind the outbuildings and contained five or six acres. They could run electric power from the outbuildings underground to the wooded area across the creek. Using the farm tractor to cover truck tracks going to the still, they could operate without detection by driving in after dark and then disking out the sign the next day with the tractor.

"The only way we'll know is to walk in," I told Jim.

"I'm ready," he said. Then I made a big mistake. Knowing

that Guy was in federal court at Gainesville, I called on the radio. John answered. "Meet us at Gainesville 'Dry Dock' (our code for airport.) We'll be there in 15 minutes," I said.

John and Wally met us at the airport. We drove to a local greasy spoon restaurant for a hamburger. On the way, Jim and I brought John and Wally up to date on what we'd found.

"Let's check it tonight," I suggested.

We were still keeping Daniels' spy in the sky activity top secret, so John contacted Bob Scott, Gainesville Area Supervisor, to make sure we didn't interfere with anything the Gainesville agents were working on.

"We don't have anything going in that area. Call us if you need any help," said Scott.

Near midnight, John dropped Daniels and me out in a local schoolyard south of Dahlonega and a mile from the suspected stills. The Appalachian Mountains in north Georgia are wild and rough, especially at night. We had to pick our way carefully through the dense undergrowth. I was in my element. I could visualize how original American Indians must have slipped through the same area, moving to ambush the invading enemy, the white man.

In 1828, this region was known as the Cherokee Nation. That same year, gold was discovered near Dahlonega and the first major U.S. gold rush was on. Greedy men poured into the region, ignoring the Cherokee tribe's property rights. This led to the chain of events that put the Cherokees on the "Trail of Tears" in 1838. Eleven years later, many of these miners left to become forty-niners in the new gold rush in California. (From 1828 through 1933, over $310 million in gold was mined in north Georgia. The State Capitol dome in Atlanta is covered with Dahlonega gold.)

No one spoke. We walked quietly and after 20 minutes we came to the edge of a clearing. At night your vision plays tricks on you, so we got our bearings and crossed the creek. We were now on the side we wanted to check.

"It's up ahead," Daniels whispered. We began inching along the edge of the stream bank, placing our feet carefully in order to leave as little sign as possible.

Suddenly, the ground felt smooth under my feet. I knelt down and felt it with my hand. We were on the workway. We felt our way along and then it hit us—the odor of fermenting mash. We had something—but how big? We were in the still yard and surrounded by large aluminum vats and 220-gallon wood barrels filled with fermenting mash. Trying not to leave footprints or other sign, we carefully determined that it was a large steamer operation. It was covered with camouflage netting. Probably J.R.'s.

I was on top of the world as we left the area and returned to the schoolyard. Our walkie-talkie had been turned off since we first dropped out, but prior to this we had communicated car-to-car with Area Supervisors Scott and Guy. We heard other traffic on the radio from one of the state agents who worked the area, but we had gone to our "scrambled" mode on our radios and hoped he wouldn't know we were on to something nearby.

Despite the fact that the strong signal would indicate to anyone monitoring that we were nearby, we had to communicate in order to be picked up. As we were leaving the area, I heard more traffic on both ATF's frequency and the state frequency. Things like, "meet us at the usual place," and "we're close to that road where you got stuck."

This worried me to some extent, but I felt that we had time to return to Atlanta, get our surveillance equipment, and gather enough evidence from this distillery to connect J.R. in some way.

Scott agreed that we should handle the investigation until we were ready to make the seizure. In that way, none of the agents who regularly worked the territory would be seen in the area. He knew the importance of keeping information close to the vest.

John and I arrived in Atlanta again in the wee hours. After six hours of rest, we were back in the Regional Office securing camera equipment and getting gear together to spend several days in the woods. Since I had to attend federal court the next day, we planned to go back in that night.

The next morning, we headed to Gainesville with full field packs, cameras and binoculars. After court was adjourned, Hay and I planned to hit the woods with one of the Gainesville investigators and stay as long as possible gathering evidence on the operation. If we managed to make it for three days we would be lucky.

While I was sitting in the courtroom, one of the Gainesville investigators asked me to step outside. "The sheriff in Lumpkin County seized a large distillery south of Dahlonega last night," he said.

My heart sank.

It was common knowledge that one or two of the state revenue agents who worked north Georgia were not to be trusted. In most southern states in those days, the sheriffs and state agents were paid a relatively small salary. The sheriffs also operated on a fee system. State revenue agents were notorious for collecting copper radiators, fittings and other distillery paraphernalia to sell

243

as salvage. They retained the money and it was all legal.

Sheriffs and state agents also split the money from equipment sold by the sheriff—which was also legal. When federal ATF agents were in on the seizure, this was not allowed. We were required to destroy all distilling equipment and this often led to problems. On large illicit distillery seizures, tons of sugar, hundreds of gallons of fuel oil, expensive pumps, tools and other equipment were seized. Under federal law, they had to be destroyed. Some state agents and sheriffs wanted to haul in this loot. Although they wouldn't admit it, some sold it back to the liquor law violators. A few officers were even suspected of furnishing information to the violators.

I was naive enough to believe that people, especially law enforcement officers, were honest.

As soon as I was released from court, Hay, Scott and I made a beeline to Dahlonega. There, in back of the jail, we found two large stake-body trucks loaded with distillery equipment. As we examined the contents of the trucks, the sheriff approached with a sheepish grin on his face.

"Nice still, wasn't it?" he asked.

I was so infuriated, I just glared at him.

Scott, knowing that we could have big trouble in a short time, started talking to the sheriff and a state agent who worked that area.

During my career, I had had several confrontations with sheriffs and local officers of questionable reputation and I always had trouble controlling my temper. I never had that problem with moonshiners. I knew and they knew they were violating the law. When I was dealing with other law enforcement people, I expected them to be honest and forthright. I could understand a moonshiner violating the law to make money, but I could never understand a man sworn to uphold the law using his badge for personal gain. In my opinion, his crime was far worse than the moonshiner's.

The sheriff told Bob that he had received a call from the state agent with information about a big still in Lumpkin County. The state agent explained that he had received the information from a confidential informer and had then secured a state search warrant and notified the sheriff.

"Can I see the search warrant?" I asked.

The sheriff was apologetic, saying that he didn't have time to call in federal agents. Inside the jail, he produced a state search warrant. These warrants were state forms on which the officer merely filled in the blank spaces. They were perfectly legal if properly prepared. This one was illegal on the face of it and had been intentionally prepared to make it illegal in court, thereby giving the violator a legal defense against prosecution. The search warrant form required that the place to be searched be described in detail as required by the Constitution of the United States. The description on this warrant was so vague it could have been almost any farm on Highway 19 south of Dahlonega. Any lawyer just out of law school could get the warrant and all the evidence seized thrown out of court in five minutes. The sheriff knew this and so did the state agent.

It was obvious to me that the state officers had not discovered the location of the distillery merely by monitoring our radio traffic. They could surmise what area we were in, but could not have known the exact location without more information.

They had apparently gotten a call from someone close to the J.R. group that knew where the distillery was and that we had it located. J.R. then decided it would be better to have a state seizure made using an illegal warrant (to clear the man who lived on the farm), and then buy the equipment back through an intermediary at about one-fourth the original cost. In this way, everyone would come out better. The entire distillery would not be destroyed and the man living on the farm would not be arrested. Also, if the state officers were taking payoffs from J.R., this would give them extra loot. This was the only logical explanation for what had happened.

I made a copy of the state warrant and after marking some of the pumps and other equipment on the truck, left the courthouse.

As Bob, Wally and I drove back to Gainesville, we were each absorbed in our own thoughts. I think we were all wondering about the same thing—how did the state agents know where the still was? How did they know we were working on it? And most of all, how did they know we had already checked it and wouldn't be going back in until the following day? We had checked the distillery on Monday night, coming out at one o'clock Tuesday morning. We had spent Tuesday making plans and securing equipment to go back in on Wednesday night. On Tuesday at midnight, the state agents and the sheriff went in and seized the distillery. This was definitely not coincidence. Someone had to know that we had a big outfit located in the area, that it was probably J.R.'s because I was involved, and that we would not be watching the still on Tuesday night.

Six months before, while I was attending federal court in Gainesville, an ATF agent had approached me in strictest confidence. I have known and respected this agent for many years and have no reason to doubt his integrity or truthfulness. He is still a good friend. I will call him "Horace" to protect his anonymity.

Horace began by saying that he recently received information from sources he considered to be trustworthy and honest. "I'm telling you this for your use only. If you ever tell anyone I said this, I'll deny it!" I agreed, not knowing what a bombshell he was about to drop on me.

He said, "Charley, I've been holding this inside me for some time now. You've been working on J.R. for over a year. I know you've been close several times and had everything fall through on you. I think I know why." He hesitated. "I hate to say this, but I feel it's the truth and you should know what you're up against. We all know not to trust a couple of the state agents assigned to north Georgia. We work with them out of necessity on occasion and some of them are perfectly honest, but you know that."

What's he getting at? I thought.

"Charley, I'm beating around the bush because if you ever repeat this, my ass is mud. The guy I'm talking about is one of ours! He's connected with J.R. and maybe others."

"Who is it?" I asked, incredulous.

"You tell me." He continued, "Who's close friends with the suspected state agents? Who always has plenty of money and always wants more? Who is always in the area when something blows up on a J.R. investigation?"

Only one name came to my mind—"Spade!" I blurted out.

"That's the one! According to my information, he's tied in tight with J.R., and I'm confident the people who told me this are telling the truth."

I was dumbfounded. Although I had questioned Spade's integrity on a number of occasions, I had never thought he would sell himself to the other side. I had seen him take advantage of our agents when they were drinking and I didn't have much respect for him as an agent or a man, but I never thought he was a crooked turncoat.

This guy had been an agent much longer than I had and was a regional special investigator. He was a next-door neighbor and good friend of "Cutter," one of the top officials in ATF. To bring any sort of accusation against him would be throwing your career out the window. I saw why Horace had been so reluctant to tell anyone about this information.

But now, thinking back on the conversation with him, a lot of things began to click. Spade had been in the squad room while I was making preparations to return to the distillery in Lumpkin County. The state agent who received the so-called anonymous call was Spade's good friend. Spade apparently contacted J.R., and even if he didn't know the exact location of the still, told J.R. we were onto something in the area. After our radio traffic was heard in the area, J.R. decided to give up the still to the local officers rather than take the chance of having it seized and destroyed by federal agents. He was a cold-blooded businessman.

Looking back, I could remember all the times I had located vehicles belonging to the J.R. organization, only to have them never move again, or move when someone knew we were not observing them. The fact that J.R. never checked into the Howard Johnson Motel again after we found out about that—the disappearance of the roll of wire when we had tried to tap the telephone line—these and numerous other instances flashed through my mind. No wonder J.R. had never been caught. He had his own mole in ATF.

I felt sick, angry and frustrated. I knew it had to be true, but I could not confide in anyone.

Wally Hay broke into my thoughts. "What do you think happened?" he asked.

"I don't know—maybe they heard us on the radio and figured out where the still was—I just don't know." I was not about to mention my suspicions to anyone. I had no concrete proof and besides I had given my word not to repeat what I had been told. My stomach churned.

LUELLA

The next day, Frank Lane called and asked if I could get an airplane that afternoon. Bill Griffin had told me to use local contract pilots if needed. I called Executive Aviation and asked them to have a plane and pilot standing by.

Frank met me at PDK Airport at dusk, and we successfully trailed a suspected truck from a hideout in DeKalb County to a large distillery in Henry County. By the time we reached the Luella section of Henry, it was dark. The truck turned in at a farmhouse and the headlights went out. We continued circling overhead at about 10,000 feet and in a few minutes the taillights flashed in the woods behind the house. Then 30 minutes later, lights appeared in the edge of the woods as the truck left. We called Koppe and Sonny Strickland, who picked up the truck as it hit the city limits of Atlanta.

Sonny called back. "We got the truck and driver. He had over 300 gallons."

The following day, Lane and I flew back to the area and located the distillery. We made a map and turned it over to the agents who worked Henry County. They contacted Sheriff Hiram

Cook and Sheriff Bill Murray of Clayton County, two of the most honest, excellent law enforcement people I ever worked with. I could name many local and state officers who were in this category—only a few were not trustworthy, but one bad apple can spoil the barrel.

The seizures helped lift my spirits and I stayed so busy I didn't have time to dwell on J.R. Daniels was keeping Guy and Hay busy and I was getting all the outside flying assignments. I loved it.

Typical South Georgia steel-tank still

Chapter XXIX
In a Spin

My days often began with the telephone ringing, as it did early on the morning of April 29, 1964.

Jimmy Satterfield was on the phone.

"A truckload of whiskey just left the Anniston, Alabama area. It's headed toward Atlanta."

"Okay, we'll try to pick him up at the Georgia - Alabama line," I said. "Meet me at PDK."

I called Executive Aviation and a plane and pilot were waiting when Jimmy and I arrived. We took off at half past two that afternoon.

Heading out over U.S. Highway 78 to the Alabama line, we were advised by Alabama investigators that the truck was crossing into Georgia. They described the truck and we had no trouble picking it up visually.

"We've got him," Jimmy told them.

"Okay, he's all yours," they said, turning back into Alabama.

I looked at my watch. It was three-thirty. Following ground vehicles with an airplane requires concentration and continuous slow flight. It is demanding on both the pilot and the observer. Jimmy was in back on the pilot's side and I was up front in the four-place Cessna 172. This was a new experience for the pilot. As he attempted to keep the truck in sight by slow-flying and turning in tight circles, we suddenly fell into a spin. I hadn't been in a spin before, but was not unduly alarmed until I saw his reaction.

He had the control wheel pulled all the way back and turned hard right. We were spinning to the left. I didn't have much flying experience, but I knew the pilot had to first relax the back pressure and turn the wheel (ailerons) to a neutral position, and apply full opposite rudder to stop the spin. Then back pressure is applied to pull out of the dive. The pilot finally made all the right moves, but not before giving Jimmy and me a few more grey hairs.

Jimmy was not one to panic and we didn't say a word to the pilot. I think he was more frightened than we were. This was tame compared to some of the things Jimmy and I had experienced, but

I made up my mind then and there that if I was going to be killed in an airplane, I wanted to be flying it myself.

We continued trailing the truck and at sunset, we had passed through Atlanta and were nearing Athens.

"How much longer we gonna trail this guy?" the pilot asked.

"Till he sets down somewhere," I said.

"I can't fly with passengers after dark," said the pilot.

"Are you kidding?" asked Jimmy.

"No. I've got to get back to Atlanta. Our insurance won't cover us after dark."

Jimmy and I knew this was an excuse to quit, but we couldn't force him to continue.

John Guy and Wally Hay were monitoring our radio traffic and following on the ground. I called John and asked him to check at the Athens airport to see if anyone could fly us the rest of the way, wherever we were going. John called back and, as usual, had been able to do the impossible. An aircraft and pilot would be waiting for us at Athens. He and Wally would take our place as observers and we could pick up his car at the airport.

Our luck was holding. Just then the truck pulled into a truck stop for gas. We quickly ducked into the Athens airport and the swap was made just before dark. Fortunately, we were able to relocate the truck as it continued northeast. John and Wally were now with a Mr. Clark, an old-time flyer who didn't worry about darkness or anything else. He did a great job.

As we crossed over into South Carolina, Jimmy asked, "Where do you think he's going?"

"You've got me, Jimmy. I figured we'd have him in a hole by now. I thought he was headed to Atlanta, but now I've got no idea. We'll stay with him as long as we can and see what happens."

Satterfield and I were laying back a mile from the truck so that if he stopped, we would have time to stop before being seen. As we continued into South Carolina, John called and said they were beginning to have trouble seeing the vehicle due to low clouds and fog. He said the pilot had checked on the weather at Charlotte, North Carolina and that low ceilings and fog were reported. It was now well past midnight, and we were passing Fort Mill, South Carolina, south of Charlotte. We had to make a decision quickly.

"We're going to have to get gas in Charlotte—you need to get on the truck visually." Wally was obviously concerned—and rightly so.

"Stay with him for a few more minutes—I'll get help from the Charlotte office," I replied, and started looking for a telephone. Now

it was two-thirty, and we had been following the truck for 12 hou.
Doubts began to creep into my mind. Could we have gotten on tl
wrong truck in the beginning—could we have lost the original truck
and been trailing some innocent driver?

As I dialed the number of Nick Nicholson, ATF's top man in
North Carolina, I hoped this wasn't a wild goose chase. Nick
answered, wide awake. I had met him while working undercover in
North Carolina and knew him to be one of the best get the job done
men in ATF. I could hear Nick shuffling papers as I quickly
explained our situation.

"I'll have someone with you in 15 or 20 minutes. Anything
else?" Nick asked.

"Nope," and I was back in the car with Jimmy. As I pushed
the accelerator to the floor, Jimmy brought me up to date on the
location of the truck. It was now in the outskirts of Charlotte and
the plane was getting dangerously low on fuel. At that hour of the
morning, about the only thing on the road were trucks and not
many of them. I knew we had to make a visual sighting of the truck
soon, so I continued at break-neck speed, passing everything in
sight.

"Whoa—whoaaa!" Jimmy shouted.

I had almost passed the suspect truck in my frenzy to catch
up. I slammed on the brakes and whipped into a service station,
then pulled back out a safe distance behind.

"That was close," I sighed.

"We've got to land—now!" called Wally.

"Okay, we've got him," Jimmy replied. I could almost hear
a sigh of relief go up from the plane.

Just then the radio crackled. "Hey, Charley, do you need
any help?" Charlotte ATF Agent Stan Noel was already in the area.
He had apparently been monitoring our traffic and knew where we
were.

Quickly describing the truck to him, I explained that we
had followed it all the way from Alabama and that it was supposed
to be loaded with whiskey. The weather had really closed in by now
and we decided that if the truck continued on through Charlotte,
we would have to knock it off. We couldn't use the airplane any more
on this one.

After North Carolina agents Noel and Bill Vassar positively
identified the truck, Jimmy and I fell back and let them take over
the "eyeball."

"The guy driving the truck must be on pills—he's been
driving for at least 16 hours and shows no signs of stopping,"
Jimmy commented.

"Well, he's going to stop soon," I said emphatically.

"What do you want to do?" came the question from the Charlotte agents.

"It doesn't look like he's going to stop soon. If he's hauled moonshine this far to leave it in North Carolina, it would be like hauling coal to Newcastle. Go ahead and check him." (North Carolina and Georgia led the nation in the production of moonshine.)

Jimmy and I didn't participate in the seizure or arrest since we didn't want the driver to know we had followed him from Georgia.

We saw the truck being pulled over. We stopped some distance back and remained in our car. Stan and Bill played their part well. "We've got information that a truck like this is hauling raw materials to moonshiners in this area," they told the driver. While Bill kept a firm grip on the driver's belt, Stan opened the large back door of the van.

What a relief—half-gallon fruit jar cases were stacked to the ceiling. We found out later that the truck contained 2,210 gallons of moonshine. Needless to say, after they lodged the driver, Estil Graby, in jail, the Charlotte agents were eager to buy our breakfast. This was our first long trail job using aircraft, but it convinced me and several others, including Bill Griffin, that a new era in surveillance work was opening up.

ATF special agent/pilots would soon become a reality. In 1975, one of the longest air-to-ground surveillances occurred when ATF pilots trailed a huge load of illegal guns from Miami to Montreal, Canada, a distance of over 1,700 miles. It involved over 100 hours of slow flight through some of the most congested airspace in the world. This successful case was international in scope and proved beyond any doubt that the small beginning by John Guy and Jim Daniels resulted in ATF leading the way for other law enforcement agencies to follow. This is one instance where ATF was years ahead of the FBI in law enforcement techniques—and still is. We taught *them* how to do it.

John, Jimmy, Wally and I drove back to Atlanta. I don't think any of us realized how this pioneering of aerial surveillance would bring ATF one of its most effective tools in law enforcement during subsequent years.

ASSAULT

Two weeks later, I was just finishing a Saturday lunch at home with my wife and two boys. The telephone rang. Dot answered and with that "you've got to leave again" look in her eyes, she handed me the phone. The call was from the Clayton County police radio operator.

"Mr. Weems, Chief Howard Smith just called. There's been a shooting involving one of your agents."

"Where?" I asked.

The radio operator described the location, about a mile west of Ellenwood. I knew the area. As I went out the door, I told Dot, "I don't know when I'll be back." She'd heard that line many times before.

As I sped through roads that had been familiar to me since I was in high school, I worried about what could have happened. But I would soon know. Arriving in the area ten minutes after receiving the call, I saw Detective Lt. Bill Murray standing near a county police car on the side of the road. I parked on the shoulder of the road, grabbed my camera and notebook and joined him.

"Who got shot, Bill?" I asked.

Bill was his usual calm and matter-of-fact self. "Jimmy Satterfield had to shoot a still hand."

I was immediately relieved. "Was Jimmy hurt?"

"Yeah, the guy hit him in the face with a pint of whiskey and busted his nose and mouth pretty bad. "

There were two 400-gallon fermenter stills and more than 120 gallons of moonshine on the ground at the still site. Satterfield's mouth and nose were swollen and bleeding. The still pots were hot and steaming.

"There's the two we arrested at the still," commented Chief Smith, pointing to two black men leaning against a tree. "The other one's in the creek."

About 50 feet from the distillery, Eugene Ross was lying on the edge of the creek. I could tell he was still alive from his shallow breathing, but was mystified as to how, judging from the size of the split in the top of his head. About a third of his brain was protruding through a three-inch opening in the top of his skull. I made photographs of the man from every angle and then made pictures of the distillery, the still trail and other objects, including the broken bottle that smashed Satterfield's face.

I gathered up all the physical evidence, labeled it and asked a few preliminary questions of Chief Smith, Bill Murray and Bob Eckerd. Satterfield could hardly talk due to his mutilated face, but he remained at the scene.

The ambulance crew arrived. They had to walk several hundred yards through woods and fields to get their stretcher to the location.

They looked at the injured still hand, then decided to lower the stretcher down the creek bank and place him on it. Ross must have weighed 200 pounds. It took everyone present to get him out of the creek. He moaned a couple of times, but there was no other sign of consciousness. The last I saw of him was as the ambulance attendants and Clayton County officers struggled up the still path toward the public road. Ross was shot at three-thirty and died at nine at Grady Hospital in Atlanta.

After the wounded man was removed from the site, I turned my attention to getting preliminary statements from the other two still hands and the officers who participated in the raid.

Chief Smith had checked the still at one-thirty that afternoon. Hearing sounds of activity at the site, Howard had withdrawn and called ATF Agent Satterfield, who regularly worked this territory. Jimmy brought State Agent Bob Eckerd with him and they met Chief Smith and Lt. Murray. The officers parked their cars off Joy Lake Road and walked to the distillery area. When they were close enough to hear activity at the still, they separated. Satterfield and Eckerd were to come in on the still trail and make the initial move to the distillery. Smith and Murray covered the opposite side.

As Jimmy cautiously entered the still yard, he could see three black males working around the still. When one looked up and saw him, Jimmy exclaimed, "Federal officer—don't move!"

When Jimmy got within five feet of Ross, the moonshiner hurled a pint bottle filled with whiskey into Jimmy's face. The bottle shattered and so did Jimmy's teeth. It was a damaging blow.

As blood poured from the agent's mouth and nose, Ross fled down the creek. Jimmy followed, drawing his pistol. He fired a warning shot, again telling Ross to stop. Ross stopped suddenly, wheeled around and picked up a baseball-sized rock from the stream.

Jimmy fired again, this time hitting Ross in the top of his head. Ross dropped the rock and collapsed in the creek bed.

Satterfield fired in self-defense. A well-placed stone of this size can certainly kill a man. I knew that I had to tie up all the loose ends quickly. I got to a telephone and called John Corbin. He told me to continue with the case, taking all the time I needed.

"I'll assign someone to work with you if you need any help," John said.

"I'm sure I can get all the help I need locally from Chief Smith, but I'll keep you posted," I replied.

Two days later, I had taken statements from all the officers involved, plus statements from the other two still hands. Both said that Ross had talked them into working at the distillery and that it was his operation.

Ross had been in and out of trouble many times involving larceny and assault. One arrest was for assault with intent to kill. He was prone to violence, but this time he paid for it.

Satterfield paid a price, too. Due to the damage to his face and jaw, he lost most of his teeth. In the following months, he was cleared of any wrongdoing in the death of the moonshiner. He continued to be a top-notch agent for many more years.

Eckerd, the state agent involved in this case, later became an ATF agent. He was seriously injured in a shootout with a gun runner north of Chattanooga. The violator ran over Eckerd with an automobile and then, after wrecking the car, came out shooting at Bob and other ATF agents. He was armed with an automatic pistol and a .45-caliber Thompson machine gun. Eckerd and another agent killed him. Sometimes, officers have no choice.

These types of cases were not commonplace, but they did happen. Two ATF agents, Joe Cooper and Ralph Holt, were killed in Alabama in 1964 by a liquor shot-house operator who went berserk. He was also killed in the shootout. Many other agents were assaulted with knives and other weapons. Although most of the moonshiners with whom we dealt were not prone to violence, a great many were. Usually arrests where you expected trouble went smoothly, but it was the times when you least expected trouble that it occurred.

* * *

I was on my way to south Georgia one Sunday morning in June with Jim Daniels. John Guy and I had been given approval to use Daniels and the airplane in south Georgia "prospecting" for illicit distilleries in Emanuel, Bulloch, Truetlen and Candler counties. The previous week, John had secured detailed county maps and information from the local ATF agents about prime violator areas. Daniels and I flew until nine that night and then all the next day, checking locations and looking for sign of moonshine activity.

We located two large distilleries and left the area at sundown, arriving in Gainesville at seven o'clock. We made distillery investigations in Hall, Dawson and Lumpkin counties until two the next morning. These were long, hard days, but I was getting a lot of flight time and enjoying every minute of it.

The remainder of June was spent preparing case reports during the day and working with Daniels and Guy at night. We were really rolling now with the aircraft work and nearly every night we were walking out suspected distillery locations. John would drop

Jim and me out around midnight in the suspected area. Sometimes we would walk for hours through the dark, silent woods.

Some of the most apprehensive times of my career occurred when we checked around a house or outbuilding late at night, only to have the dogs catch our scent or see our movement and begin barking. On several occasions, we had to beat a hasty retreat when the farmer began shooting indiscriminately in our direction.

This was not at all unusual. People living in rural areas know the difference in the tone of a dog's bark and can tell if the dog is just barking to hear himself, or if there really is something in the farm yard. In the latter case, the resident usually shoots several times in the direction he thinks is suspicious and goes back to bed. He knows that if it is a fox after his chickens he has probably scared it away. This tactic succeeded in scaring me away several times!

The second week in July, Daniels and I trailed a large load of sugar into a remote area of Lumpkin County. After notifying Bob Scott and James Stratigos of the location, we continued our usual hectic schedule. There never seemed to be enough time to prepare reports and appear in court.

On Saturday morning, the ever-active telephone rang. "The only way we're going to have any time together with the boys is to get you away from that telephone," Dot said, as I picked up the receiver.

It was Area Supervisor Bob Scott.

"Charley, we just raided that big outfit you and John found last week. It could be J.R.'s."

"I'll be there within an hour—hold the prisoners there until I can talk to them."

With that, I left the home-cooked meal on the table. Dot handed me a sandwich she had quickly prepared, as she had so many times before, and I was out the door.

I picked up Wally Hay on the way and upon our arrival in Lumpkin County, we contacted Scott. It was indeed a big outfit, with thirty-six 220-gallon barrels, over 6,000 gallons of mash, and 300 gallons of moonshine. They had arrested three violators, J.M. Hood, E.T. Perry and B.L. Odom.

Wally and I began interrogating all three with little success. I had serious doubts as to their connection with J.R., but I thanked Bob and the other officers for the call. I appreciated the effort and interest these men exhibited in their work. We helped dynamite the distillery equipment and I got home at eight o'clock that night.

During April, May, June and July I was taking flying lessons on my own time, what little there was of it, and flying as much as I could with Daniels. At the end of July, I earned my Commercial Pilot Certificate. Another of my dreams had been fulfilled, but not without a lot of sweat and prayer. My family paid a huge price by my absence on birthdays, Christmas holidays and other important times.

We continued to secure aircraft and pilots from Executive Aviation at PDK Airport. But by now we had developed our aerial surveillance techniques to the point that we were needing aircraft on short notice and contract pilots were not always available.

Chief of Enforcement Griffin had followed our progress both with Daniels' and our own use of aircraft and was acutely aware of our needs. Knowing the cautious, skeptical approach I.R.S. Headquarters in Washington took to every innovation in ATF's operation, especially if it had the potential of being embarrassing to the outfit, I took an opportunity one day to talk to Griffin.

Most supervisors took the conservative approach to anything new—first of all making sure they were not laying themselves open to criticism and possibly harming their career; and secondly, they didn't want to make waves or rock the boat.

Later, when I was transferred to Washington, D.C., I met several supervisors of this bent. Luckily for me and for ATF, Griffin was a real man who would make his own decisions and he had the integrity and the guts to stand behind them.

I explained to Bill the problems we were experiencing and that I had a pilot's license and a great deal of flying time with Daniels. Bill knew of the tremendous work Daniels and Guy had accomplished during the past several months and the part I had played. I suggested setting up a contract with George Gunn, who owned a small airstrip south of Stone Mountain, to furnish aircraft for ATF's use on a full-time basis. George had furnished Daniels rental aircraft and I had taken my flight training at his airstrip. He trusted both Jim and me with his aircraft and I could get an airplane quickly any time, day or night.

Griffin leaned back in his big leather chair and looked sternly in my direction. I thought, I've said too much. He'll probably take me off the Jim Daniels project and I'll be back making cases the hard way.

Silence. Then Bill spoke with the matter-of-fact, no-nonsense tone he always used with no bureaucratic double talk.

"Charley, set it up—but for God's sake don't f— up!"

Enough said. I was out the door and on my way to the financial office to get a contract drawn up for the rental of aircraft. This was the official beginning of the most exciting, thrilling and educational experiences of my career. I became the first ATF special agent/pilot and I was just ending my first ten years with ATF. Dreams do come true.

Groundhog-type still where ATF Agent Satterfield was assaulted and a moonshiner shot. Clayton County, GA

Groundhog-type still where ATF Agent Satterfield was assaulted and a moonshiner shot. Clayton County, GA

ATF Agent Satterfield and the mortally wounded moonshiner.

Man Killed In Liquor Still Raid

A Negro man was shot and fatally wounded during a raid on a ground hog type liquor still in the Joy Lake area by federal, state and Clayton County officers Saturday, police said.

Charles H. Weems, a special investigator with the Alcohol & Tobacco Tax Division, U.S. Treasury Department, said the Negro, Eugene Moss, believed to be in his thirties, was shot when he attacked an agent with a bottle and a rock.

The agent, James H. Satterfield, required treatment at a private hospital for facial injuries received in the attack, Mr. Weems said.

Dectective Lt. Bill Murray of the Clayton County police force said the bottle which the Negro used in the attack was filled with liquor. He added that officers found some 110 to 115 gallons of illegal whisky.

Mr. Weems added that two other persons were arrested during the raid on charges of violating U.S. Internal Revenue laws.

The Negro man succumbed later at Grady Hospital of a bullet wound in the head.

261

Upright steam-boiler still hidden in a large chicken house in
Jackson County, Georgia being examined by an ATF Chemist

Chapter XXX
The Wild Card

A little before midnight on May 5, the ever-present telephone jangled again. I was sleeping so soundly it took me a minute to recognize the voice.

"Charley, this is Jim King. I just ran into something I don't know how to handle. Can you meet me at my house as soon as possible? It's got something to do with J.R."

"I'll be there in 30 minutes," I said, reaching for my pants.

"Something serious has happened. I don't know when I'll be back," I said as I kissed Dot goodbye.

Speeding through the dark night toward DeKalb County, a lot of thoughts passed through my mind, but none were even close to what I was about to hear from King. He was a close friend and an excellent agent, always cool under fire. He never panicked under any circumstance.

I pulled into Jim's driveway and could see a light on in the kitchen. He met me at the back door and we sat down to talk.

"I got a call from John Crunkelton (member of the vice squad in DeKalb County) about an hour ago."

John was a top-notch law enforcement officer and we had good working relations with the entire DeKalb County police department.

"He said he would pick me up in five minutes and explain on the way," Jim continued.

"John knew we had been working on J.R., and he had a description of J.R.'s midnight blue Pontiac, including the license number. The priest of a large church had been working late in his office when he noticed suspicious activity in the church parking lot. He called the DeKalb police. Lieutenant Davis responded to the priest's call and recognized the Pontiac with Dawson County plates as being a vehicle Crunkelton had asked him to watch for.

"The priest told him the driver of the Pontiac had met another vehicle in this lot almost every Tuesday night for the past several weeks and that the driver of the Pontiac always got into the other car. They would be gone for 15 to 30 minutes. The priest's curiosity was aroused and tonight after they left, he went out into the parking lot and looked into the Pontiac. The glove compartment was open and he could see several thousand dollars in various denominations of bills inside. This really aroused his suspicions and that's when he called the police.

"Lt. Davis immediately called Crunkelton, telling him what the priest had said. John told Davis to pull off of the Pontiac and he would be there as soon as he could. That's when he called me, saying he would pick me up in five minutes. I told him I'd be ready. I knew Crunkelton was all business and that if he said something needed to be done now, it needed to be done."

Neither King nor Crunkelton knew what to expect, but both thought that if they could see J.R. with some large-scale moonshine liquor dealer, perhaps that would help tie him up in a conspiracy case. They were in for a surprise. When they were within a block of the church, the police radio crackled: "John, a late-model Ford just drove into the church lot and circled the Pontiac. Now he's headed back out onto Briercliff Road. There's two men in the Ford—they might have spotted me." Lt. Davis' voice dropped a little with the last sentence.

"There he is!" Jim exclaimed, as he saw the Ford turning out of the church lot onto Briercliff toward Claremont Road.

"Okay, what do you want to do?" asked Crunkelton.

"We'll check their ass," said King.

Two blocks from the church, the Ford pulled into a large Baptist church parking lot. Crunkelton and King followed and as they stopped behind the Ford, King got a sick feeling in his stomach.

"That's one of our government cars," he said quietly.

By now, John was out of his car and as he approached the Ford, the driver got out and brushed past him, hurrying toward King. That's Spade and he's stepped in it this time, John thought. Looking into the government car, he saw J.R. sitting on the passenger side. What the hell's going on? John thought.

"Dammit, Spade, you know you're not supposed to be out here meeting major liquor law violators without notifying your supervisor and having a witness with you. I don't care whose informer he is. What kind of information has he given you?" Jim asked.

"I'll explain later," stammered Spade.

"Let's go. I've seen enough." King was upset as he and Crunkelton got back into the county car.

"I'll take care of this," Jim said.

"That S.O.B. is not right!" said John.

"I don't know how this will turn out, but it's got to be reported. Just keep it under your hat for now," said Jim.

Both men were silent. The implications of what had just happened were enormous. Not only could this seriously hurt one of our ATF agents, it could tarnish ATF's image. The bad apple in the barrel. It was hard to believe.

This clandestine meeting between Spade and one of the largest major violators of the liquor laws, plus the presence of several thousand dollars in cash, looked suspicious, to say the least.

Now, sitting in Jim's kitchen listening to what Jim had just witnessed, I was stunned. Things began to dawn on me. For three years I had been betrayed by a man who was on J.R.'s payroll and was keeping him advised of every move ATF made to shut down his illegal activities. Greed corrupted Spade.

King broke the silence. "This is a mess, Charley—you know how close Spade is to 'Cutter.' If we report this without any additional information, our asses will be mud."

"Our asses will be mud if we don't report it," I said. "Spade's crooked as a snake and taking payoffs from J.R. This is something that needs to be known above our grade level. I must make a telephone call. Could I use your phone—privately?" I asked.

Jim looked at me quizzically, but handed me the phone and left the room. I felt like a heel, but I had promised Horace some months before I would never divulge what he had told me about Spade. I desperately needed to use his information now that we had concrete evidence that Spade was crooked.

It was long-distance to north Georgia and I billed the call to my home telephone so that if Horace didn't agree to my using his information, no one else would ever know whom I called that night.

It was now about one-thirty. A sleepy voice answered on the other end.

"Horace, this is Charley Weems." After I was sure he was wide awake, I explained what had just happened, using the details supplied by King.

"Horace, Jim and I have got to report this. You know the shit is going to hit the fan when it's reported higher up. In order to make this allegation against Spade much stronger, I'm asking you to release me from my promise never to tell anyone what you told me. I know I'm putting you on the spot and you and Jim and I are going to be laying our asses on the line, but Spade is not right. I hope the incident tonight and your information will be enough to get something done."

There was a long silence. No one wants to get a fellow officer in trouble. Officers will lay their lives on the line and lie for their companions in some instances, but most officers I've known hate

265

a man who would bring disgrace to their organization by accepting bribe money.

Horace finally spoke. "Okay, if you need to use the information I have, go ahead."

I knew this was a hard decision for Horace to make. I also realized the trust he was putting in me and I appreciated it.

"How about being in your office in the morning in case John Corbin wants to talk to you. He's the one Jim and I have decided to report this to. It'll be up to him to make the next move. And thanks."

I went into the next room, where Jim was waiting. "Jim, it's not that I don't trust you—I made a promise I couldn't break without being released from it. You'll understand before the night is over."

"Let's call Corbin," Jim said.

We woke John up and explained that we had to talk to him immediately. "Come on over to my house," he said.

I felt better after talking to Horace, although I was still apprehensive about what we had to do. Corbin was waiting at the kitchen door. He had already made a pot of coffee. John is rather small in stature, but is a giant of a man when it comes to honesty and supervisory skills. I had grown to like and respect him as a person in the year he had been my supervisor. He was soft-spoken and having risen through the ranks, he knew the trials and tribulations of being a field agent.

We sat down at the kitchen table. Jim began to relate what had happened during the past five hours. I watched John's face as he began to realize the impact this would have on ATF's enforcement image. His serious countenance deepened as Jim told of the money, J.R. and Spade.

Spade was under John's immediate supervision as I was. John knew immediately that Spade had no legitimate reason to be consorting with the largest liquor-law violator in the country and that if for any reason he had to make contact with J.R., he should have cleared it with John first. It was never done otherwise. If some major law violator wanted to give information or contact an officer about anything, the officer always had to have a witness with him. An officer was laying himself wide open to suspicion if he didn't.

"I hope he has a good reason for doing this," was the only comment John made as Jim finished. "Anything else?" John asked.

"I've got something," I ventured. After what had happened, I had both men's undivided attention.

"A few months ago, one of our agents in north Georgia told me in strict confidence that Spade was not right."

"Say it plain, Charley," prompted John.

"Well, this ATF agent has information from reliable sources that Spade is close to J.R. The agent told me I should be aware of their association and advised me to be careful around Spade."

John was aware of the many times over the past two years I had been frustrated in my efforts to connect J.R. to illicit distilleries. He was also aware that J.R., despite his reputation for being involved in a large-scale whiskey business, had never been caught. Smarter people than I had worked on him in the past without success. Something or someone had to be wrong!

I continued, telling John and Jim that I didn't know the ATF agent's source for this information, but that I had the utmost confidence in his integrity and judgment.

"Who is he?" John asked.

I hesitated. I didn't want to get Horace involved if I could help it, but I felt he possibly could shed more light on the subject than he had told me.

Finally, I said, "Horace. I talked to him tonight, and he'll be in his office in the morning if you want to talk to him. He was hesitant about repeating this information, as Jim and I were, but we all felt that it had to be done."

"You did the right thing. Both of you be in the Regional Office in the morning. This will go all the way to the top in the Southeast Region and I only hope we can handle it in the region," John said quietly.

I knew what he was thinking. I.R.S.'s inspection unit operated much like the Internal Affairs Division of a large police department. These men were assigned out of headquarters in Washington and everyone dreaded seeing them come into the area. Although they are needed, most agents shunned them. Any suspicion of wrongdoing, especially taking bribes, was a prime case for the inspection service.

In a way, I hoped it didn't come to that. I wanted Spade to get what was coming to him, but on the other hand I didn't want to see ATF embarrassed by one of its agents being crooked. It would cast a dark shadow on the outfit that I had become so much a part of and loved so dearly.

I got home in time to grab an hour's sleep and was back in the office at eight o'clock. Corbin had warned us not to discuss this situation with anyone. Even now, three decades later, the few people left who know about it are hesitant to talk about it. I do so only because of the hundreds of ATF agents I worked with and helped to train, Spade was the only one I ever had reason to believe was not completely honest. The others were the hardest-working, most capable law enforcement officers in this country—bar none.

The detailed information Jim and I had given Corbin the night before was sufficient. We were not called in "on the carpet" to repeat what we knew. Horace was contacted, however, and satisfied top management that his information was correct. Along with the irrefutable evidence observed by King, this convinced the top supervisors that even though there was not enough concrete evidence to initiate an investigation, it would be better for ATF to transfer Spade to another region.

I never saw Spade again. He was transferred within the month to a large northern industrial city, about as far from Atlanta as possible.

Now I knew why most of the long, tedious hours of investigative work by many ATF agents had never resulted in the apprehension of J.R. It wasn't just good luck on his part—it was his sly, intelligent use of money. I guess he would call it a cost of doing business. I called it something else.

I had been given the J.R. Turner assignment on July 13, 1961. Now on July 23, 1964, I was closing out J.R.'s case without a recommendation for prosecution. I worked three years making seizures, accumulating evidence, taking statements and spending untold hours on stakeouts and intelligence gathering, and came up with only circumstantial evidence linking J.R. to any of the eight large distilleries I was certain he owned. We had located these distilleries through painstaking work and had cost the Turner organization great economic losses. We had hurt their illegal earnings, but the profits from large-scale moonshining were enormous.

With the increased workload brought on by my involvement in the air operation, Corbin suggested that I close the investigation. I did so with some reluctance, although I felt with the recent departure of Spade from the area, J.R. would slow down his operation for a while. At least, we could hope so. My first ten years with ATF came to a close and a new era was beginning for me.

I've always believed in the old saying, "For every door that closes to you, another one opens."

But that's another story.

EPILOGUE

In June of 1974, after 28 years of marriage, Charley Weems and his wife Dot divorced. The constant strain of the job and other pressures had changed his outlook and desire for the future. Both their sons, Joe and Charles, were married and on their own and Charley apparently wanted more freedom. There was no animosity on either side, and after several years Dot remarried and continues to live in the same general area where she and Charley grew up.

In January 1977, after serving as the first full time special agent/pilot for ATF and supervisor for regional air operations, Charley was transferred to ATF Headquarters, Washington, D. C. There he set up and supervised the Air Operations Section, placing pilots throughout the nation. After two years he had managed to initiate and coordinate a program which proved that aircraft could be used successfully as a surveillance tool in all areas of the country. ATF had pioneered this technique and demonstrated it to other agencies, including the FBI.

The J.R. Turner investigation was one of the biggest disappointments of his career—not because he was unable to make a case against J.R. but because ATF, due to of lack of sufficient evidence and in order to protect its image, transferred Agent Spade instead of prosecuting him. This has always "stuck in his craw." Not knowing every fact that was considered in making the decision, Charley is hesitant to criticize what was done to alleviate the situation, but feels that a crooked law enforcement officer is far worse than any moonshiner.

Charley retired in the fall of 1978 with 24 years service with ATF. He married Mary Linda Frye and took a job as a charter pilot for Raleigh-Durham Aviation in North Carolina. After two years of flying multi-engine and small jet aircraft, he bought a farm on top of a ridge about 16 miles north of Knoxville, Tennessee.

Charley and his wife "M.L." spent the next two years cutting trees, treating logs and building a log home from the ground up. The two of them laid every log and drove every nail in the house. This was a challenge they both enjoyed and they take pride in the finished product.

During 1985, '86 and '87 Charley worked as a contract investigator on a part-time basis for the Office of Personnel Management and Department of Energy, and then for the Inspector General's Office of TVA as a consultant. For the past two years, *A Breed Apart* has consumed a large portion of his time, along with aerial photography work in an airplane purchased in 1987. He flies out of a small airstrip on his farm. He keeps busy working with the building committee and teaching a Sunday School class at Cedar Ford Baptist Church in Luttrell, Tennessee.

Life continues to be exciting and challenging!

10/9/91

Congratulations Charlie, I understand your book on A.T.F. has gone to the publisher. IF your literary efforts paralell those of your career with the Agency, it should provide outstanding reading.

Knowing you as I have for all these years, I'm confidant the book with reflect the character & integrity of the author

Best wishes for another successful chapter in your long & colorful career —

Sincerely,

Bill Griffin

JOHN W. STOKES, JR.

ASSISTANT UNITED STATES ATTORNEY

402 OLD POST OFFICE BUILDING

ATLANTA, GEORGIA

September 26, 1961

Mr. Charles H. Weems, Jr.
6532 South Expressway
Jonesboro, Georgia

Dear Mr. Weems:

After seven and a half years in the United States Attorney's
office, I have recently submitted my resignation, effective
September 30, 1961. At that time I will become associated
in private practice with the law firm of Pittman, Kinney and
Pope, in Dalton, Georgia. While I would enjoy remaining in
my present position, the long range dictates of a legal career make it impossible for me to further delay the transi-
tion to private practice.

Before leaving I want to take the opportunity to tell you
how much I have valued and enjoyed our association during
these past years. The time I have spent in this office
has afforded me the finest associations and experiences
I have had in my life. The greatest share of credit for
this is due to the opportunity it provided me to work with
you and the many other fine federal and state officers in
this area.

For the future I will look forward to our continued friendship, and I know we will have opportunities to meet again.
If I can ever be of assistance in any way, please do not
hesitate to call on me.

Thanks again for having made this job so pleasant.

Sincerely,

John W. Stokes, Jr.

"I have really enjoyed *A Breed Apart*. You really stayed true to the events. It was good to see no embellishment – just "All The Facts.""
> A. Pearl Wilder, Atlanta, GA
> Retired "Miss ATF"

"I would like to tell you how much I enjoyed your book. It brought back fond memories of my childhood in vivid detail and gave me a better understanding of why things were the way they were. I thank you for that."
> Mike Powell, Jacksonville, AL
> Son of former ATF agent

"I read your book in one sitting and thoroughly enjoyed it. Your career was one to emulate and your devotion to the job a standard to strive for. I know that ATF is one of the best law enforcement agencies in the country, but unfortunately our story hasn't really been told."
> ATF Special Agent, Oakland, CA

"To say that I enjoyed *A Breed Apart* is putting it mildly. It is exciting, interesting and hard to stop reading."
> Janette Lamb, Jonesboro, GA
> Author's former schoolteacher

"I loved the book! It was extremely well written and brought back so many wonderful memories of the agents we all cared about and the violators whose names we knew as well as the names of our family members — I always said I would work for ATF for no salary at all I enjoyed it so."
> Frankie B. Hahn, Nashville, TN
> Retired ATF Office Supervisor

"When I got *A Breed Apart* I sat right down and read the whole thing non stop, and am now in the process of reading it again! I enjoyed every well written word and delighted in reading about some of the men I knew as a young boy."
> Russell P. Trickey, N. Canton, OH
> Son of former ATF agent

"Your book is outstanding! I'm glad you put down on paper the lives you guys lived."
> Jean Lane Slaughter, Marietta, GA

"I congratulate you for the outstanding job you did in writing *A Breed Apart*. Throughout all the years you and I worked together and have known each other, I recognized in you many good qualities which related to your character, commitment to the job, and ability as an agent. Well done!"
> John F. Corbin, Sylva, NC
> Retired Asst. Director (Criminal Enforcement) ATF

"Enjoyed the book. I knew many of the agents mentioned. Those were good times."
> Bruno Uptagrafft, Marysville, WA
> Retired Asst. Reg. Director ATF

"This is to congratulate you for your exceptionally good book. Reading your well written story was just like being there. I could see, hear and smell some of the men described — what a pleasure."
> Ed Hughes, Gainesville, GA
> Retired Special Agent in Charge, ATF

"I spent many happy hours reading *A Breed Apart*. The characters came very much alive to me. Revenue officers are born, not made. They truly are a breed apart."
> Pat Hadley Davis, N. Wilkesboro, NC
> Author

"I've just finished reading *A Breed Apart*. For those present and past who never participated in the moonshine liquor program, it should be required reading. For most of us, it is a bitter-sweet trip down memory lane. A wonderful chronicle of the joys and sorrows we all experienced on Thunder Road."
> John F. Rice, St. Simons Island, GA
> Executive Director, ATF Association of Retirees